Social Institutions

OF THE

United States.

An Authorized Reprint from "The American Commonwealth."

BY

James Bryce,

AUTHOR OF "THE HOLY ROMAN EMPIRE," ETC.
M.P. FOR ABERDEEN.

NEW YORK:

CHAUTAUQUA PRESS,

C. L. S. C. DEPARTMENT,

150 FIFTH AVENUE.

1891.

SET UP AND ELECTROTYPED MARCH, 1891.
REPRINTED SEPTEMBER, OCTOBER, 1891.

𝔘niversity 𝔓ress:
JOHN WILSON AND SON, CAMBRIDGE, U.S.A.

CONTENTS.

INTRODUCTION.

SEVERAL gentlemen interested in the Chautauqua gathering, and in the literary enterprises associated with it, have expressed a wish that the concluding chapters of my book on the American Commonwealth should be separately reprinted in a cheap form, so as to bring them within the reach of Chautauquan students and others who may not have leisure or opportunity to read the whole treatise. In acceding to their request, I have also promised to write a few sentences by way of introduction, explaining the relation of the above-mentioned chapters to the rest of my book, and the aim with which they were composed.

He who undertakes to describe the political system of a nation or state has a comparatively definite task before him, because it is pretty well understood what the term "politics" means and includes. The field is doubtless a wide one, but with sufficient time and pains it may be covered. To deal with those institutions of a country, those aspects of national life and character, which lie outside politics, is far more difficult, because the field is so wide that no one man or book can hope to exhaust it. All industrial movements, all social movements, all religious movements, much of what is included under the terms Literature, Manners, Education, Science, Art, come within this field; and the business of selecting for treatment those which can be treated concisely and in obvious relation to one another is a problem which may well perplex a writer. It was, however, a problem I had to face, because the object of the "American Commonwealth" was to convey to European readers some knowledge, not only of the Constitution and government of the United States, but also of their intellectual, moral, and social phenomena. Thus it became necessary to pick out a certain number — a limited number, in order that the book might not grow too big — of topics to be dealt with, choosing those which were of most general interest and which seemed most illustrative of American thought and life in general. A word may be said on the plan followed in making this selection.

There are in every country certain institutions which display and reveal the character of the community that has built them up, and which at the same time react upon and play their part in moulding the character of that community. Such are the great learned professions ; and I have therefore described the legal profession in its two branches, — the Bar and the Judicial Bench. Such is the organization of the religious bodies ; and I have therefore sketched the position of the Churches and the Clergy. Such again is the organization of the higher forms of instruction ; and a chapter has therefore been devoted to the Universities. There are also certain questions relating to every people which an intelligent foreigner asks, and which an intelligent citizen is apt to reflect upon, because they touch the spirit and tendency, not only of institutions, but of a people itself. Such are, — to take a few instances out of many, — the influence of the form of government upon intellectual production, as well as upon taste ; the absence or presence of social equality ; the position accorded to women by law and by usage ; the relation of national literature and national manners to the influences of other countries ; the tone and sentiment of social life as compared to that of older and less progressive countries ; above all, the forecasts of change and development in new directions which a study of existing phenomena disposes an observer to form.

These are some of the matters dealt with in the chapters of my book which are here reprinted. Those chapters do not purport or attempt to cover the whole field. Many other chapters might have been added, dealing with other questions, among which I will mention, for the sake of illustration, the following : the Race Problem in the Southern States ; experiments in the law of divorce, and their results ; the influences of European immigration, particularly from Germany and Ireland ; the control of railroads and telegraphs by Federal or State legislation ; the labor organizations and the attitude of public opinion towards them ; questions relating to land ownership and land taxation ; the influence of American scenery and climate upon character ; the differences between American and European moral standards ; the position and prospects of art and the taste for art in the United States. With these, or some of these, I hope that I may be able to deal in a future edition of the book. Meantime the descriptions and discussions contained in the chapters here reprinted seem to have proved useful, not only to European readers, but to American readers also, by showing them how their institutions and mental habits strike observers from Europe, and by suggesting to them other questions similar to those here examined, through pondering on which they may the better comprehend the phenomena and tendencies of their country and their time.

No other state or nation in the modern world offers such ample materials for observation and study. Nowhere else do we find so vast an area occupied by an equally numerous and equally intelligent population. The elements of this population are diverse in their origin, but all, except a few of the most recent immigrants, speak the same language and are exposed to the same intellectual and moral influences. The laws and institutions under which they live are in outline the same over the immense stretch of forty-four States and four Territories, yet with differences in details sufficient to enable the results of these differences and of other varying conditions to be instructively compared. Nowhere else has such free scope been allowed to men to organize themselves according to their own will and pleasure, to start enterprises, to try social as well as economic experiments; nowhere, therefore, is the complex product of what inventive activity has accomplished so largely due to what may be called natural causes, so little traceable to the compulsive interference of governments and laws. Nowhere, moreover, do changes follow one another so swiftly. New regions are settled, new industries are founded, wealth springs up in new quarters or assumes new forms; men's minds are continually occupied with the new problems which the progress of the country brings to the front, as well as with those old faults of human nature and human society which the increasing sensitiveness to suffering and ardor for reform make us regard as more intolerable than our predecessors found them. There is thus spread out in America before the student, not only of political science and Nomology, — the science of laws and legislation, — but of social phenomena in general, a field of surpassing and daily increasing interest, a harvest in which the laborers are as yet but few, and which grows again as fast as it is reaped.

It is not, however, to the professed political philosopher only that these phenomena ought to appeal. The main object of the Chautauquan movement has been, as I understand, to give to multitudes who have not the time to spend on a regular university course of instruction, and most of whom have passed the time of life when such a course can be taken, the means and opportunity of gaining an insight into scientific methods of study, and of receiving a stimulus, not only to intellectual exertion in general, but to habits of mental exactitude and dispassionately thoughtful inquiry. Such means and opportunities are specially useful in America, where the stress of life and keenness of business competition

leave little time for meditation.   In America there is much to
make men apt to think only of the Present, and forget that
it is the outcome of the Past.   But one of the best uses of
that study of the Past which the Chautauquan lecture and
reading courses inculcate is to enable those who have entered
into their spirit to apply the same methods of study to the
Present.   One may concisely describe the true temper of the
historian by saying that he ought to treat of the Past as if it
were the Present, and the Present as if it were the Past.   So
the man who trains himself to look on the phenomena of the
world he moves in as matter for calm inquiry and reflection,
will not only have an inexhaustible source of pleasure opened
to him, but will become a better citizen, less the victim of
political or ecclesiastical prejudice, more inclined to search
for the truth of things, to test evidence, and to base his
opinions upon it.   The discussions which this little volume
contains are not intended to enforce positive conclusions, and
will sufficiently serve their purpose if they aid any readers
to cultivate this spirit of unprejudiced inquiry, rouse their
interest in the world of contemporary America as a subject
for study and reflection, suggesting to them new questions or
new points of view.   I am grateful for the kindness with
which my book, whose deficiencies, as is natural, its author
knows better than any one else, has been received in America ;
and I therefore desire all the more that the method which I
have sought to apply to what may be called contemporary
history, — the most interesting and difficult kind of history, —
may commend itself to the younger generation of American
readers, and be found helpful by them.

January 19, 1891.

NOTE. — In this reprint the author has made a few small changes to
modify statements as to which he felt some doubt, and to bring other
statements up to date.

SOCIAL INSTITUTIONS.

CHAPTER I.

THE BAR.

AMONG the organized institutions of a country which, while not directly a part of the government, influence politics as well as society, the Bar has in England, Scotland, and France played a part only second to that played by the Church. Certainly no English institution is more curiously and distinctively English than this body, with its venerable traditions, its aristocratic sympathies, its strong, though now declining, corporate spirit, its affinity for certain forms of literature, its singular relation, half of dependence, half of condescension, to the solicitors, its friendly control over its official superiors, the judges. To see how such an institution has shaped itself and thriven in a new country is to secure an excellent means of estimating the ideas, conditions, and habits which affect and color the social system of that country, as well as to examine one of the chief among the secondary forces of public life. It is therefore not merely for the sake of satisfying the curiosity of English lawyers that I propose to sketch some of the salient features of the legal profession as it exists in the United States, and to show how it has developed apart from the restrictions imposed on it in England by ancient custom, and under the unchecked operation of the laws of demand and supply.

When England sent out her colonies, the Bar, like most of her other institutions, reappeared upon the new soil, and had gained, before the Revolution of 1776, a position similar to that it held at home, not owing to any deliberate purpose on the part of those who led and ruled the new communities (for the Puritan settlers at least held lawyers in slight esteem), but because the conditions of a progressive society required its existence. That disposition to simplify and popularize law, to make it less of a mystery and bring it more within the reach of an average citizen, which is strong in modern Europe, is of course still stronger in a colony, and naturally tended in America to lessen the corporate exclusiveness of the legal profession, and do away with the antiquated rules which had governed it in England. On the other hand, the increasing complexity of relations in modern society, and the development of many new arts and departments of applied science, bring into an always clearer light the importance of a division of labor, and, by attaching greater value to special knowledge and skill, tend to limit and define the activity of every profession. In spite, therefore, of the democratic aversion to exclusive organizations, the lawyers in America soon acquired professional habits and a corporate spirit similar to that of their brethren in England ; and some fifty years ago they had reached a power and social consideration relatively greater than the Bar has ever held on the eastern side of the Atlantic.

But the most characteristic peculiarity of the English system disappeared. In the United States, as in some parts of Europe and most British colonies, there is no distinction between barristers and attorneys. Every lawyer, or " counsel," is permitted to take every kind of business ; he may argue a cause in the Supreme Federal Court at Washington, or write six-and-eightpenny letters from a shopkeeper to an obstinate debtor. He may himself conduct all the proceedings in a cause, confer with the client, issue the writ, draw the declaration, get together the evidence, prepare the brief, and conduct the case when it comes on in court. He is employed, not like the English barrister, by another professional man, but by the client himself, who seeks him out and makes his bargain directly with him, just as in England people call in a physician or make their bargain with an architect. In spite, however, of this union of all a lawyer's functions in the same person, considerations of practical convenience have in many places established a division of labor similar to that existing in England. Where two or more lawyers are in partnership, it often happens that one member undertakes the court work and the duties of the advocate, while another or others transact the rest of the business, see the clients, conduct correspondence, hunt up evidence, prepare witnesses for examination, and manage the thousand little things for which a man goes to his attorney. The merits of the plan are obvious. It saves the senior member from drudgery and from being distracted by petty details; it introduces the juniors to business and enables them to profit by the experience and knowledge of the mature practitioner; it secures to the client the benefit of a closer attention to details than a leading counsel could be expected to give, — while yet the whole of his suit is managed in the same office, and the responsibility is not divided, as in England, between two independent personages. However, the custom of forming legal partnerships is one which prevails much more extensively in some parts of the Union than in others. In Boston and New York, for instance, it is common, and I think in the Western cities; in the towns of Connecticut and in Philadelphia, one is told that it is rather the exception. Even apart from the arrangement, which distributes the various kinds of business among the members of a firm, there is a certain tendency for work of a different character to fall into the hands of different men. A beginner is of course glad enough to be employed in any way, and takes willingly the smaller jobs; he will conduct a defence in a police-court, or manage the recovery of a tradesman's petty debt. I remember having been told by a very eminent counsel that when an old apple-woman applied to his son to have her market-license renewed, which for some reason had been withdrawn, he had insisted on the young man's taking up the case. As he rises, it becomes easier for him to select his business, and when he has attained real eminence he may confine himself entirely to the higher walks, arguing cases and giving opinions, but leaving most of the preparatory work and all the communications with the client to be done by the juniors who are retained along with him. He is, in fact, with the important difference that he is liable for any negligence, very much in the position of an English Queen's counsel, and his services are sought, not only by the client, but by another counsel, or firm of counsel who have an important suit in hand to which they feel themselves unequal. He may however be, and often is, retained directly by the client; and in that case he is allowed to retain a junior to aid him, or to desire the client to do so, naming the man he wishes for, — a thing which the etiquette of the English bar is supposed to forbid. In every great city there are several practitioners of this kind, — men who only undertake the weightiest business at the largest fees; and even in the minor towns court practice is in the hands of a comparatively small group. In one New England city, for instance, whose population is about fifty thousand, there are, I was told, some sixty or seventy practising lawyers, of whom not more than ten or twelve ever conduct a case in court, the remainder doing what Englishmen would call attorney's and conveyancer's work.

Whatever disadvantages this system of one undivided legal profession has, it has one conspicuous merit, on which any one who is accustomed to watch the career of the swarm of young men who annually press into the Temple or Lincoln's Inn full of bright hopes, may be pardoned for dwelling. It affords a far better prospect of speedy employment and an active professional life than the beginner who is not "strongly backed" can look forward to in England. Private friends can do much more to help a young man, since he gets business direct from the client instead of from a solicitor; he may pick up little bits of work which his prosperous seniors do not care to have, may thereby learn those details of practice of which in England a barrister often remains ignorant, may gain experience and confidence in his own powers, may teach himself how to speak and how to deal with men, may gradually form a connection among those for whom he has managed trifling matters, may commend himself to the good opinion of older lawyers, who will be glad to retain him as their junior when they have a brief to give away. So far he is better off than the young barrister in England. He is also, in another way, more favorably placed than the young English solicitor. He is not taught to rely in cases of legal difficulty upon the opinion of another person. He is not compelled to seek his acquaintances among the less-cultivated members of the profession, to the majority of whom law is not much of an art, and nothing of a science. He does not see the path of an honorable ambition, the opportunities of forensic oratory, the access to the judicial bench, irrevocably closed against him, but has the fullest freedom to choose whatever line his talents fit him for. Every English lawyer's experience, as it furnishes him with cases where a man was obliged to remain an attorney who would have shone as a counsel, so also suggests cases of persons who were believed, and with reason believed, by their friends to possess the highest forensic abilities, but literally never had the chance of displaying them, and languished on in obscurity, while others in every way inferior to them became, by mere dint of practice, fitter for ultimate success. Quite otherwise in America. There, according to the universal witness of laymen and lawyers, no man who is worth his salt, no man who combines fair talents with reasonable industry, fails to earn a competence and to have, within the first six or seven years of his career, an opportunity of showing whether he has in him the makings of something great. This is not due, as might be supposed, merely to the greater opportunities which everybody has in a new country, and which make America the working-man's paradise, for in the Eastern States at least the professions are nearly as crowded as they are in England. It is owing to the greater variety of practice which lies open to a young man, and to the fact that his patrons are the general public, and not, as in England, a limited class who have their own friends and connections to push. Certain it is that American lawyers profess themselves unable to understand how it can happen that deserving men remain briefless for the best years of their life, and are at the last obliged to quit the profession in disgust. In fact it seems to require an effort of politeness on their part to believe that such a state of things can exist as that with which England and Scotland have grown so familiar as to deem it natural and legitimate. A further result of the more free and open character of the profession may be seen in the absence of many of those rules of etiquette which are, in theory at least, observed by the English lawyer. It is not thought undignified, except in the great cities of the Eastern States, for a counsel to advertise himself in the newspapers. He is allowed to make whatever bargain he pleases with his client; he may do work for nothing, or may stipulate for a commission on the result of the suit, or a share in whatever the verdict produces, — a practice which is open to grave objections, and which in the opinion of more than one eminent American lawyer has produced a good deal of the mischief which caused it to be seventeen centuries ago prohibited at Rome. However, in some cities the sentiment of the Bar seems to be opposed to the practice, and in some States there are rules limiting it. A counsel can, except in New Jersey (a State curiously conservative in some points), bring an action for the recovery of his fees, and, *pari ratione*, can be sued for negligence in the conduct of a cause.

A lawyer can readily gain admission to practise in any Federal Court, and may by courtesy practise in the courts of every State. But each State has its own Bar, — that is to say, there is no general or national organization of the legal profession, the laws regulating which are State laws, differing in each of the thirty-eight commonwealths. In no State does there exist any body resembling the English Inns of Court, with the right of admitting to the practice of public advocacy and of exercising a disciplinary jurisdiction, and in very few have any professional associations, resembling the English Incorporated Law Society, obtained statutory recognition. Usually the State law vests in the courts the duty of admitting persons as attorneys, and of excluding them if guilty of any serious offence. But the oversight of the judges is necessarily so lax that in many States and cities voluntary bar associations have been formed, with the view of exercising a sort of censorship over the profession. Such associations can blackball bad candidates for admission, and expel offenders against professional honor; and they are said to accomplish some good in this way. More rarely they institute proceedings to have black sheep removed from practice. Being virtually an open profession, like stockbroking or engineering, the profession has less of a distinctive character and corporate feeling than the barristers of England or France have, and, I think, rather less than the solicitors of England have. Neither wig, bands, gown, cap, nor any other professional costume is worn; and this circumstance, trivial as it may seem, no doubt contributes to weaken the sentiment of professional privilege and dignity, and to obscure the distinction between the advocate as an advocate, not deemed to be pledging himself to the truth of any fact or the soundness of any argument, but simply presenting his client's case as it has been presented to him, and the advocate in his individual capacity.

In most States the courts impose some sort of examination on persons seeking to be admitted to practice, often delegating the duty of questioning the candidate to two or three counsel named for the purpose. Candidates are sometimes required to have read for a certain period in a lawyer's office; but this condition is easily evaded, and the examination, nowhere strict, is often little better than a form or a farce. Notwithstanding this laxity, the level of legal attainment is in some cities as high or higher than among either the barristers or the solicitors of London. This is due to the extraordinary excellence of many of the law-schools. I do not know if there is anything in which America has advanced more beyond the mother-country than in the provision she makes for legal education.* Twenty-five years ago, when there was nothing that could be called a scientific school of law in England, the Inns of Court having practically ceased to teach law, and the universities having allowed their two or three old chairs to fall into neglect, and provided scarce any new ones, many American universities possessed well-equipped law departments, giving a highly efficient instruction. Even now, when England has bestirred herself to make a more adequate provision for the professional training of both barristers and solicitors, this provision seems insignificant beside that which we find in the United States, where, not to speak of minor institutions, all the leading universities possess law-schools, in each of which every branch of Anglo-American law — that is, common law and equity as modified by Federal and State constitutions and statutes — is taught by a strong staff of able men, sometimes including the most eminent law-

---

* Modern England seems to stand alone in her comparative neglect of the theoretic study of law as a preparation for legal practice. Other countries, from Germany at the one end of the scale of civilization, to the Mohammedan East, at the other end, exact three, four, five, or even more years spent in this study before the aspirant begins his practical work.

yers of the State.* Here at least the principle of demand and supply works to perfection. No one is obliged to attend these courses in order to obtain admission to practice, and the examinations are generally too lax to require elaborate preparation ; but the instruction is found so valuable, so helpful for professional success, that young men throng the lecture-halls, willingly spending two or three years in the scientific study of the law which they might have spent in the chambers of a practising lawyer as pupils or as junior partners. The indirect results of this theoretic study in maintaining a philosophical interest in the law among the higher class of practitioners, and a higher sense of the dignity of their profession, are doubly valuable in that absence of corporate organizations on which I have already commented.†

In what may be called habits of legal thought, their way of regarding legal questions, their attitude towards changes in the form or substance of the law, American practitioners, while closely resembling their English brethren, seem on the whole more conservative. Such law reforms as have been effected in England during the last thirty years have mostly come from the profession itself. They have been carried through Par-

* This instruction is in nearly all the law-schools confined to Anglo-American law, omitting theoretic jurisprudence (that is, the science of law in general), Roman law, — except, of course, in Louisiana, where the Civil Law is the basis of the code, — and international law. Where the latter subjects are taught, which rarely happens, they are usually included in the historical curriculum. In some law-schools much educational value is attributed to the moot courts, in which the students are set to argue cases, — a method much in vogue in England two centuries ago.

† Some of the best American law-books — as, for instance, that admirable series which has made Justice Story famous — have been produced as lectures given to students. Story was professor at Harvard while judge of the Supreme Court, and used to travel to and from Washington to give his lectures. A few years ago there were several men in large practice who used to teach in the law-schools out of public spirit and from their love of the subject, rather than in respect of the comparatively small payment they received.

liament by attorneys-general or lord-chancellors, usually with
the tacit approval of the Bar and the solicitors. The masses
and their leaders have seldom ventured to lay profane fingers
on the law, either in despair of understanding it, or because
they saw nearer and more important work to be done. Hence
the profession has in England been seldom roused to oppose
projects of change, and its division into two branches, with
interests sometimes divergent, weakens its political influence.
In the United States, although the legislatures are largely
composed of lawyers, many of these have little practice, little
knowledge, comparatively little professional feeling. Hence
there is usually a latent and sometimes an open hostility
between the better kind of lawyers and the impulses of the
masses, seeking, probably at the instigation of some lawyer
of a demagogic turn, to carry through legal changes. The
defensive attitude which the upper part of the profession is
thus led to assume fosters those conservative instincts which
a system of case-law engenders, and which are further stimulated by the habit of constantly recurring to a fundamental
instrument, the Federal Constitution. Thus one finds the
same dislike to theory, the same attachment to old forms, the
same unwillingness to be committed to any broad principle,
which distinguished the orthodox type of English lawyers
sixty years ago. Prejudices survive on the shores of the
Mississippi which Bentham assailed seventy years ago when
those shores were inhabited by Indians and beavers; and in
Chicago, a place which living men remember as a lonely
swamp, special demurrers, replications *de injuria*, and various
elaborate formalities of pleading which were swept away by
the English Common Law Procedure Acts of 1850 and 1852,
flourish and abound to this day.

Is the American lawyer more like an English barrister or
an English solicitor? This depends on the position he holds.
The leading counsel of a city recall the former class, the
average practitioners of the smaller places and rural districts

the latter. But as every American lawyer has the right of advocacy in the highest courts, and is accustomed to advise clients himself, instead of sending a case for opinion to a counsel of eminence, the level of legal knowledge — that is to say, knowledge of the principles and substance of the law, and not merely of the rules of practice — is somewhat higher than among English solicitors, while the familiarity with details of practice is more certain to be found than among English barristers. Neither an average barrister nor an average solicitor is so likely to have a good working, all-round knowledge of the whole field of common law, equity, admiralty law, probate law, patent law, as an average American city practitioner, nor to be so smart and quick in applying his knowledge. On the other hand, it must be admitted that England possesses more men eminent as draftsmen, though perhaps fewer eminent in patent cases, and that much American business, especially in State courts, is done in a way which English critics might call lax and slovenly.

I have already observed that both in Congress and in most of the State legislatures the lawyers outnumber the persons belonging to other walks of life. Nevertheless, they have not that hold on politics now which they had in the first and second generations of the Republic. Politics have, in falling so completely into the hands of party organizations, become more distinctly a separate profession, and an engrossing profession, which a man occupied with his clients cannot follow. Thus among the leading lawyers, the men who win wealth and honor by advocacy, comparatively few enter a legislative body or become candidates for public office. Their influence is still great when any question arises on which the profession, or the more respectable part of it, stand together. Many bad measures have been defeated in State legislatures by the action of the Bar, many bad judicial appointments averted. Their influence strengthens the respect of the people for the Constitution, and is felt by the judges when they are called to deal

with constitutional questions. But taking a general survey
of the facts of to-day, as compared with those of sixty
years ago, it is clear that the Bar counts for less as a guiding
and restraining power, tempering the crudity or haste of
democracy by its attachment to rule and precedent, than it
did then.

A similar decline, due partly to this diminished political
authority, may be observed in its social position. In a country
where there is no titled class, no landed class, no military
class, the chief distinction which popular sentiment can lay
hold of as raising one set of persons above another, is the
character of their occupation, the degree of culture it implies,
the extent to which it gives them an honorable prominence.
Such distinctions carried great weight in the early days of the
Republic, when society was smaller and simpler than it has
now become. But of late years not only has the practice of
public speaking ceased to be, as it once was, almost their
monopoly, not only has the direction of politics slipped in
great measure from their hands, but the growth of huge mercantile fortunes and of a financial class has, as in France and
England, lowered the relative importance and dignity of the
Bar. An individual merchant holds perhaps no better place
compared with an average individual lawyer than he did forty
years ago; but the millionnaire is a much more frequent and
potent personage than he was then, and outshines everybody
in the country. Now and then a brilliant orator or writer
achieves fame of a different and higher kind; but in the main
it is the glory of successful commerce which in America and
Europe now draws wondering eyes. Wealth, it is true, is by
no means out of the reach of the leading lawyers; yet still
not such wealth as may be and constantly is amassed by con-
tractors, railway-men, financial speculators, hotel proprietors,
newspaper owners, and retail storekeepers. The incomes of
the first counsel in cities like New York are probably as large
as those of the great English leaders. I have heard firms

mentioned as dividing a sum of $250,000 (£50,000) a year, of which the senior member may probably have $100,000. It is, however, only in two or three of the greatest cities that such incomes can be made, and possibly not more than fifteen counsel in the whole country make by their profession more than $50,000 a year. Next after wealth, education may be taken to be the element or quality on which social standing in a purely democratic country depends. In this respect the Bar ranks high. Most lawyers have had a college training, and are, by the necessity of their employment, persons of some mental cultivation; in the older towns they, with the leading clergy, form the intellectual *élite* of the place, and maintain worthily the literary traditions of the Roman, French, English, and Scottish bars. But education is so much more diffused than formerly, and cheap literature so much more abundant, that they do not stand so high above the multitude as they once did. It may, however, still be said that the law is the profession which an active youth of intellectual tastes naturally takes to, that a large proportion of the highest talent of the country may be found in its ranks, and that almost all the first statesmen of the present and the last generation have belonged to it, though many soon resigned its practice. It is also one of the links which best serves to bind the United States to England. The interest of the higher class of American lawyers in the English law, Bar, and judges is wonderfully fresh and keen. An English barrister, if properly authenticated, is welcomed as a brother of the art, and finds the law reports of his own country as sedulously read and as acutely criticised as he would in the Temple.*

---

* American lawyers remark that the English Law Reports have become less useful since the number of decisions upon the construction of statutes has so greatly increased. They complain of the extreme difficulty of keeping abreast of the vast multitude of cases reported in their own country, from the courts of forty-four States as well as from Federal courts.

I have left to the last the question which a stranger finds it most difficult to answer. The legal profession has in every country, apart from its relation to politics, very important functions to discharge in connection with the administration of justice. Its members are the confidential advisers of private persons, and the depositaries of their secrets. They have it in their power to promote or to restrain vexatious litigation, to become accomplices in chicane, or to check the abuse of legal rights in cases where morality may require men to abstain from exacting all that the letter of the law allows. They can exercise a powerful influence upon the magistracy by shaming an unjust judge, or by misusing the ascendency which they may happen to possess over a weak judge or a judge who has something to hope for from them. Does the profession in the United States rise to the height of these functions, and in maintaining its own tone, help to maintain the tone of the community, especially of the mercantile community, which, under the pressure of competition, seldom observes a higher moral standard than that which the law exacts? So far as my limited opportunities for observation enable me to answer this question, I should answer it by saying that the profession, taken as a whole, seems to stand on a level with the profession, also taken as a whole, in England. But I am bound to add that some judicious American observers hold that the last thirty years have witnessed a certain decadence in the Bar of the greater cities. They say that the growth of enormously rich and powerful corporations, willing to pay vast sums for questionable services, has seduced the virtue of some counsel whose eminence makes their example important, and that in a few States the degradation of the Bench has led to secret understandings between judges and counsel for the perversion of justice. Whether these alarms be well founded I cannot tell. It is only in a few places that the conditions which give rise to them exist.

As the question of fusing the two branches of the legal profession into one body has been of late much canvassed in England, a few words may be expected as to the light which American experience throws upon it.

There are two sets of persons in England who complain of the present arrangements, — a section of the solicitors, who are debarred from the exercise of advocacy, and therefore from the great prizes of the profession; and a section of the junior Bar, whose members, depending entirely on the patronage of the solicitors, find themselves, if they happen to have no private connections among that branch of the profession, unable to get employment, since a code of etiquette forbids them to undertake certain sorts of work, or to do work except on a fixed scale of fees, or to take court work directly from a client, or to form partnerships with other counsel. An attempt has been made to enlist the general public in favor of a change by the argument that law would be cheapened by allowing the attorney to argue and carry through the courts a cause which he has prepared for trial; but so far the general public has not responded.

There are three points of view from which the merits or demerits of a change may be regarded. These are the interests respectively of the profession, of the client, and of the community at large.

As far as the advantage of the individual members of the profession is concerned, the example of the United States seems to show that the balance of advantage is in favor of uniting barristers and attorneys in one body. The attorney would have a wider field, greater opportunities of distinguishing himself, and the legitimate satisfaction of seeing his cause through all its stages. The junior barrister would find it easier to get on, even as an advocate; and if he discovered that advocacy was not his line, could subside into the perhaps not less profitable or agreeable function of a solicitor. The senior barrister, or leader, might suffer, for his attention would be more distracted by calls of different kinds.

The gain to the client is still clearer ; and even those (very few) American counsel who say that for their own sake they would prefer the English plan, admit that the litigant is more expeditiously and effectively served where he has but one person to look to and deal with throughout. It does not suit him, say the Americans, to be lathered in one shop and shaved in another. He likes to go to his lawyer, tell him the facts, get an off-hand opinion, if the case be a simple one (as it is nine times out of ten), and issue his writ with some confidence ; whereas under the English system he might either have to wait till a regular case for the opinion of counsel was drawn, sent to a barrister, and returned, written on, after some days, or else take the risk of bringing an action which turned out to be ill-founded. It may also be believed that a case is, on the whole, better dealt with when it is kept in one office from first to last, and managed by one person, or by partners who are in constant communication. Mistakes and oversights are less likely to occur, since the advocate knows the facts better, and has almost invariably seen and questioned the witnesses before he comes into court. It may indeed be said that an advocate does his work with more ease of conscience, and perhaps more *sang-froid*, when he knows nothing but his instructions, But American practitioners are all clear that they are able to serve their clients better than they could if the responsibility were divided between the man who prepares the case, and the man who argues or addresses the jury. Indeed, I have often heard them say that they could not understand how English counsel, who rarely see the witnesses beforehand, were able to conduct witness causes satisfactorily.

If, however, we go on to ask what is the result to the whole community of having no distinction between the small body of advocates and the large body of attorneys, approval will be more hesitating. Society is interested in the maintenance of a high tone among those who have that influence on the administration of justice and the standard of commercial morality which has been already adverted to. It is easier to maintain such a tone in a small body, which can be kept under a comparatively strict control and cultivate a warm professional feeling, than in a large body, many of whose members are practically just as much men of business as lawyers. And it may well be thought that the conscience or honor of a member of either branch of the profession is exposed to less strain where the two branches are kept distinct. The counsel is under less temptation to win his cause by doubtful means, since he is removed from the client by the interposition of the attorney, and therefore less personally identified with the client's success. He probably has not that intimate knowledge of the client's affairs which he must have if he had prepared the whole case, and is therefore less likely to be drawn into speculating — to take an obvious instance — in the shares of a client company, or otherwise playing a double and disloyal game. Similarly it may be thought that the attorney also is less tempted than if he appeared himself in court, and were not obliged, in carrying out the schemes of a fraudulent client, to call in the aid of another practitioner amenable to a strict professional discipline. Where the advocate is also the attorney, he may be more apt when he sees the witnesses, to lead them, perhaps unconsciously, to stretch their recollection ; and it is harder to check the practice of paying for legal services by a share of the proceeds of the action.

Looking at the question as a whole, I doubt whether the result of a study of the American arrangements is calculated to commend them for imitation, or to induce England to allow her historic Bar to be swallowed up and vanish in the more numerous branch of the profession. Those arrangements, however, suggest some useful minor changes in the present English rules. The passage from each branch to the other might be made easier; barristers might be permitted to form open (as they now sometimes do covert) partnerships among themselves; the education of students of both branches might be conducted together in the professional law-schools as well as in the universities.

CHAPTER II.

THE BENCH.

So much has already been said regarding the constitution and jurisdiction of the various courts, Federal and State, that what remains to be stated regarding the Judicial Bench need refer only to its personal and social side. What is the social standing of the judges, the average standard of their learning and capacity, their integrity and fidelity in the discharge of functions whose gravity seems to increase with the growth of wealth?

The English reader who wishes to understand the American judiciary ought to begin by realizing the fact that his conception of a judge is purely English, not applicable to any other country. For some centuries Englishmen have associated the ideas of power, dignity, and intellectual eminence with the judicial office; a tradition, shorter no doubt, but still of respectable length, has made them regard it as incorruptible. The judges are among the greatest permanent officials of the State. They have earned their place by success, more or less brilliant, but almost always considerable, in the struggles of the Bar; they are removable by the Crown only upon an address of both Houses of Parliament; they enjoy large incomes and great social respect. Some of them sit in the House of Lords; some are members of the Privy Council. When they traverse the country on their circuits they are received by the high sheriff of each county with the ceremonious pomp of the Middle Ages, and followed hither and thither by admir-

ing crowds.   The criticisms of an outspoken press rarely as-
sail their ability, hardly ever their fairness.   Even the Bar,
which watches them daily, which knows all their ins and outs
(to use an American phrase) both before and after their elevation, treats them with more respect than is commonly shown
by the clergy to the bishops.   Thus the English form their
conception of the judge as a personage necessarily and naturally dignified and upright; and having formed it, they carry
it abroad with them like their notions of land tenure and
other insular conceptions, and are astonished when they find
that it does not hold in other countries.   It is a fine and fruitful conception, and one which one might desire to see accepted everywhere, though it has been secured at the cost of
compelling litigants to carry to London much business which
in other countries would have been dealt with in local courts.
But it is peculiar to England; the British judge is as abnormal as the British Constitution, and owes his character to a
not less curious and complex combination of conditions.   In
most parts of the Continent the judge even of the superior
courts does not hold a very high social position.   He is not
chosen from the ranks of the Bar, and has not that community of feeling with it which England has found so valuable.
Its leaders outshine him in France; the famous professors of
law often exert a greater authority in Germany.   His independence, and even purity, have been at times by no means
above suspicion.   In no part of Europe do his wishes and
opinions carry the same weight, or does he command the
same deference as in England.   The English ought not, therefore, to be surprised at finding him in America different from
what they expect, for it is not so much his inferiority there
that is exceptional as his excellence in England.

In America the nine Federal judges of the Supreme Court
retain much of the dignity which surrounds the English Supreme Court of Judicature.   They are almost the only officials
who are appointed for life, and their functions are of the

utmost importance to the smooth working of the Constitution.
Accordingly, great public interest is felt in the choice of a
judge, and the post is an object of ambition. Though now
and then an eminent lawyer may decline it because he is already making by practice five times as much as the salary it
carries, still there has been no difficulty in finding first-rate
men to fill the court. The minor Federal judges are usually
persons of ability and experience. They are inadequately
paid, but the life-tenure makes the place desired and secures
respect for it.

Of the State judges it is hard to speak generally, because
there are great differences between State and State. In six
or seven commonwealths, of which Massachusetts is the best
example among Eastern and Michigan among Western States,
they stand high; that is to say, the post will attract a prosperous barrister, though he will lose in income, or a law professor, though he must sacrifice his leisure. But in some
States it is otherwise. A place on the bench of the superior
courts carries little honor, and commands but slight social
consideration. It is lower than that of an English county
court judge or stipendiary magistrate, or of a Scotch sheriff-
substitute. It raises no presumption that its holder is able
or cultivated, or trusted by his fellow-citizens. He may be
all of these, but if so, it is in respect of his personal merits
that he will be valued, not for his official position. Often he
stands below the leading members of the State or city bar in
all these points, and does not move in the best society.*
Hence a leading counsel seldom accepts the post, and men
often resign a judgeship, or when their term of office expires

---

* A prominent New Yorker once said to me, speaking of one of the
chief judges of the city, "I don't think him such a bad fellow; he has
always been very friendly to me, and would give me a midnight injunction, or do anything else for me at a moment's notice. And he's not an
ill-natured man. But of course he's the last person I should dream of
asking to my house." Things are better in New York to-day.

do not seek re-election, but return to practice at the bar.* Hence, too, a judge is not expected to set an example of conformity to the conventional standards of decorum. No one is surprised to see him in low company, or to hear, in the ruder parts of the South and West, that he took part in a shooting affray. He is as welcome to be " a child of nature and of freedom " as any private citizen.

The European reader may think that these facts not only betoken but tend to perpetuate a low standard of learning and capacity among the State judges, and from this low standard he will go on to conclude that justice must be badly administered, and will ask with surprise why an intelligent and practical people allow this very important part of their public work to be ill discharged. I shrink from making positive statements on so large a matter as the administration of justice over a vast country, whose States differ in many respects. But so far as I could ascertain, civil justice is better administered than might be expected from the character which the Bench bears in most of the States. In the Federal courts and in the superior courts of the six or seven States just mentioned it is equal to the justice dispensed in the superior courts of England, France, and Germany. In the remainder it is inferior, that is to say, civil trials, whether the issue be of law or of fact, more frequently give an unsatisfactory result ; the opinions delivered by the judges are wanting in scientific accuracy, and the law becomes loose and uncertain. This inferiority is more or less marked according to the general tone of the State, the better States taking more pains to secure respectable men. That it is everywhere less marked than à priori reasonings would have suggested, may be ascribed partly to the way shrewd juries have of rendering substantially just verdicts ; partly to the ability of

---

* Most States are full of ex-judges practising at the bar, the title being continued as a matter of courtesy to the person who has formerly enjoyed it. For social purposes, once a judge, always a judge.

the Bar, whose arguments make up for a judge's want of learning by giving him the means of reaching a sound decision;
partly to that native acuteness of Americans which enables
them to handle any sort of practical work, roughly perhaps,
but well enough for the absolute needs of the case. The
injury to the quality of State law is mitigated by the fact
that abundance of good law is produced by the Federal courts,
by the highest courts of the best States, and by the judges of
England, whose reported decisions are frequently referred to.
Having constantly questioned those I met on the subject, I
have heard comparatively few complaints from commercial
men as to the inefficiency of State tribunals, and not many
even from the leading lawyers, though their interest in the
scientific character of law makes them severe critics of current legislation, and opponents of those schemes for codify-
ing the common law which have been dangled before the
multitude in several States. It is otherwise as regards criminal justice. It is accused of being slow, uncertain, and unduly lenient both to crimes of violence and to commercial
frauds. Yet the accusers charge the fault less on the judges
than on the soft-heartedness of juries and on the facilities
for escape which a cumbrous and highly technical procedure,
allowing numerous opportunities for interposing delays and
raising points of law, provides for prisoners.* Indulgence to
prisoners is now as marked as harshness to them was in

---

* Even judges suffer from this misplaced leniency. I heard of a case
which happened in Kentucky a few years ago. A decree of foreclosure
was pronounced by a respected judge against a defendant of good local
family connections. The judge could not do otherwise than pronounce it,
for there was practically no defence. As the judge was walking from the
court to the railway station the same afternoon the defendant, who was
waiting near the road, shot him dead. It was hard to avoid arresting and
trying a man guilty of so flagrant an offence, so arrested he was, tried,
and convicted; but on an allegation of lunacy being put forward, the Court
of Appeals ordered a new trial; he was acquitted on the ground of in-
sanity, under instructions based on the opinion of an appellate court, and
presently allowed to escape into Ohio from the asylum to which he had

England before the days of Bentham and Romilly. The legislatures must bear the blame of this procedure, though stronger men on the Bench would more often overrule trivial points of law and expedite convictions.

The causes which have lowered the quality of the State judges have been referred to in previous chapters. Shortly stated they are : the smallness of the salaries paid, the limited tenure of office, often for seven years only, and the method of appointment, nominally by popular election, practically by the agency of party wirepullers. The first two causes have prevented the ablest lawyers, the last often prevents the most honorable men, from seeking the post. All are the result of democratic theory, of the belief in equality and popular sovereignty, pushed to extremes. And this theory has aggravated the mischief in withdrawing from the judge, when it has appointed him, those external badges of dignity which, childish as they may appear to the philosopher, have power over the imagination of the mass of mankind, and are not without a useful reflex influence on the person whom they surround, raising his sense of his position, and reminding him of its responsibilities. No American magistrate, except the judges of the Supreme Court when sitting at Washington, and the judges of the New York Court of Appeals at Albany, wears any robe of office or other distinctive dress, or has any attendant to escort him,* or is in any respect treated differently from an ordinary citizen. Popular sentiment tolerates nothing that seems to elevate a man above his fellows, even when his dignity is really the dignity of the people who have

been consigned. There was, I was told, a good deal of sympathy for him.

Cheisly of Dalry, the father of the famous Lady Grange, got into trouble in Scotland early in last century for shooting a judge who had decided against him, but was not so indulgently dealt with.

* Save that in the rural counties of Massachusets, and possibly of some other New England States, the sheriff, as in England, escorts the judges to and from the court-house.

put him where he is. I remember in New York eighteen years ago to have been taken into one of the courts. An ill-omened looking man, flashily dressed and rude in demeanor, was sitting behind a table, two men in front were addressing him; the rest of the room was given up to disorder. Had one not been told that he was a judge of the highest court of the city, one might have taken him for a criminal. His jurisdiction was unlimited in amount, and though an appeal lay from him to the Court of Appeals of the State, his power of issuing injunctions put all the property in the district at his mercy. This was what democratic theory had brought New York to; for the change which that State made in 1846 was a perfectly wanton change. No practical object was to be gained by it. There had been an excellent Bench, adorned not long before, as it happened, by one of the greatest judges of modern times, the illustrious Chancellor Kent. But the Convention of 1846 thought that the power of the people was insufficiently recognized while judges were named by the Governor and Council and held office for life, so theory was obeyed. The Convention in its circular address announced, in proposing the election of judges for five years by the voters of the district, that " the happiness of the people of this State will henceforth, under God, be in their own hands." But the quest of a more perfect freedom and equality, on which the Convention started the people, gave them in twenty-five years Judge Barnard instead of Chancellor Kent.

The limited attainments of the Bench in many States, and its conspicuous inferiority to the counsel who practise before it, are, however, less serious evils than the corruption with which it is often charged. Nothing has done so much to discredit American institutions in Europe as the belief that the fountains of justice are there generally polluted; nor is there any point on which a writer treating of the United States would more desire to be able to set forth incontrovertible facts. Unluckily, this is just what, from the nature of the

case, cannot be done as regards some parts of the country.
There is no doubt as to the purity of most States, but as
to others it is extremely hard to test the rumors that are
current. I give such results as many questions in many
districts enable me to reach.

The Federal judges are above suspicion. I do not know
that any member of the Supreme Court or any Circuit judge
has been ever accused of corruption; nor have the allega-
tions occasionally made by partisans against some of the
Southern District Federal judges been seriously pressed.

The State judges have been and are deemed honest and
impartial in nearly all the Northern and most of the Southern
and Western States. In a few of these States, such as Massachusetts, Pennsylvania, and Michigan, the Bench has within
the present generation included men who would do credit to
any court in any country. Even in other States an eminent
man is occasionally found, as in England there are some
County Court judges who are sounder lawyers and abler men
than some of the persons whom political favor has of late
years been unhappily permitted to raise to the bench of the
High Court.

In a few States, perhaps six or seven in all, suspicions have
at one time or another within the last twenty years attached
to one or more of the superior judges. Sometimes these suspicions may have been ill-founded.* But though I know of
only one case in which they have been substantiated, there

---

* A recent Western instance shows how suspicions may arise. A person living in the capital of the State used his intimacy with the superior
judges, most of whom were in the habit of occasionally dining with him,
to lead litigants to believe that his influence with the Bench would procure for them favorable decisions. Considerable sums were accordingly
given him to secure his good word. When the litigant obtained the decision he desired, the money given was retained. When the case went
against him, the confidant of the Bench was delicately scrupulous in hand-
ing it back, saying that as his influence had failed to prevail, he could not
possibly think of keeping the money. Everything was done in the most

can be little doubt that in several instances improprieties have been committed. The judge may not have taken a bribe, but he has perverted justice at the instance of some person or persons who either gave him a consideration or exercised an undue influence over him. It would not follow that in such instances the whole Bench was tainted; indeed, I have never heard of a State in which more than two or three judges were the objects of distrust at the same time.[*]

In one State, viz. New York, in 1869–71, there were flagrant scandals which led to the disappearance of three justices of the superior courts who had unquestionably both sold and denied justice. The Tweed Ring, when masters of New York city and engaged in plundering its treasury, found it convenient to have in the seat of justice accomplices who might check inquiry into their misdeeds. This the system of popular elections for very short terms enabled them to do; and men were accordingly placed on the bench whom one might rather have expected to see in the dock, — bar-room loafers, broken-down Tombs[†] attorneys, needy adventurers whose want of character made them absolutely dependent on their patrons. Being elected for eight years only, these fellows were obliged to purchase re-election by constant subservience to the party managers. They did not regard social censure, for they were already excluded from decent society; impeach-

secret and confidential way, and it was not till after the death of this judicious dinner-giver that it was discovered that he had never spoken to the judges about law-suits at all, and that they had lain under a groundless suspicion of sharing the gains their friend had made.

[*] For instance, there is a Western State in which, a year or two ago, there was one, but only one, of the superior judges whose integrity was doubted. So little secret was made of the matter that when a very distinguished English lawyer visited the city, and was taken to see the courts sitting, the newspapers announced the fact next day as follows: —

"Lord X. in the city;
He has seen Judge Y."

[†] The Tombs is the name of the city prison of New York, round which lawyers of the lowest class hover in the hope of picking up defences.

ment had no terrors for them, since the State legislature, as well as the executive machinery of the city, was in the hands of their masters. It would have been vain to expect such people, without fear of God or man before their eyes, to resist the temptations which capitalists and powerful companies could offer.

To what precise point of infamy they descended I cannot attempt, among so many discordant stories and rumors, to determine. It is, however, beyond a doubt that they made orders in defiance of the plainest rules of practice; issued in rum-shops injunctions which they had not even read over; appointed notorious vagabonds receivers of valuable property; * turned over important cases to a friend of their own stamp, and gave whatever decision he suggested. There were members of the Bar who could obtain from these magistrates whatever order or decree they chose to ask for. A leading lawyer and man of high character said to me in 1870 : " When a client brings me a suit which is before —— [naming a judge], I feel myself bound to tell him that though I will take it if he pleases, he had much better give it to So-and-So [naming a lawyer], for we all know that he owns that judge." A system of client robbery had sprung up by which each judge enriched the knot of disreputable lawyers who surrounded him; he referred cases to them, granted them monstrous allowances in the name of costs, gave them receiverships with a large per-

---

* " In the minds of certain New York judges," said a well-known writer at that time, " the old-fashioned distinction between a receiver of property in a Court of Equity and a receiver of stolen goods at common law may be said to have been lost." The abuses of judicial authority were mostly perpetrated in the exercise of equitable jurisdiction, — which is no doubt the most delicate part of a judge's work, not only because there is no jury, but because the effect of an injunction may be irremediable, whereas a decision on the main question may be reversed on appeal. In Scotland some of the local courts have a jurisdiction unlimited in amount; but no action can be taken on an interdict issued by such a court if an appeal is made with due promptness to the Court of Session.

centage, and so forth; they in turn either at the time sharing
the booty with him, or undertaking to do the same for him
when he should have descended to the Bar and they have
climbed to the Bench. Nor is there any doubt that criminals
who had any claim on their party often managed to elude
punishment. The police, it was said, would not arrest such
an offender if they could help it; the district-attorney would
avoid prosecuting; the court officials, if public opinion had
forced the attorney to act, would try to pack the jury; the
judge, if the jury seemed honest, would do his best to procure
an acquittal; and if, in spite of police, attorney, officials, and
judge, the criminal was convicted and sentenced, he might
still hope that the influence of his party would procure a par-
don from the governor of the State, or enable him in some
other way to slip out of the grasp of justice. For governor,
judge, attorney, officials, and police were all of them party
nominees; and if a man cannot count on being helped by his
party at a pinch, who will be faithful to his party?

Although these malpractices diverted a good deal of business from the courts to private arbitration, the damage to the
regular course of civil justice was much less than might have
been expected. The guilty judges were but three in number,
and there is no reason to think that even they decided unjustly
in an ordinary commercial suit between man and man, or took
direct money bribes from one of the parties to such a suit.
The better opinion seems to be that it was only where the influence of a political party or of some particular persons came
in that injustice was perpetrated; and the truth, I believe,
was spoken by another judge, an honest and worthy man,
who in talking to me at the time of the most unblushing of
these offenders, said, " Well, I don't much like —— ; he is
certainly a bad fellow, with very little delicacy of mind.
He'll give you an injunction without hearing what it's about,
but I don't think he takes money down from everybody." In
the instance which made most noise in Europe — that of the

Erie Railroad suits — there was no need to give bribes. The gang of thieves who had gained control of the line and were "watering" its stock were leagued with the political "ringsters" who ruled the city and nominated the judges; and nobody doubts that the monstrous decisions in these suits were obtained by the influence of the Tammany leaders over their judicial minions.

The fall of the Tammany Ring was swiftly followed by the impeachment or resignation of these judges, and no similar scandal has since disgraced the Empire State; though it must be confessed that many of the criminal courts of the city would be more worthily presided over if they were "taken out of politics." At present New York appoints her chief city judges for fourteen years and pays them a large salary; so she gets fairly good, if not first-rate, men. Unhappily the magnitude of this one judicial scandal, happening in the greatest city of the Union and the one which Europeans hear most of, has thrown over the integrity of the American Bench a shadow which does great injustice to it as a whole.

Although judicial purity has of late years come to be deemed an indispensable accompaniment of high civilization, it is one which has been realized in very few times and countries. Hesiod complained that the kings who heard the cause between himself and his brother received gifts to decide against him. Felix expected to get money for loosing Saint Paul. Among Orientals to this day an incorruptible magistrate is a rare exception.* In England a lord chancellor was removed for taking bribes as late as the time of George I. In Spain, Portugal, Russia, parts of the Austro-Hungarian monarchy, and, one is told, even in Italy, the judges, except perhaps those of the highest court, are not assumed by general opinion to be above suspicion. Many are trusted individually, but

---

* In Egypt, for instance, one is told that there may be here and there among the native judges a man who does not take bribes, but probably not more than two or three in the whole country.

the office is not deemed to guarantee the honor of its occupant.
Yet in all these countries the judges are appointed by the
government, and hold either for life or at its pleasure,* whereas in America suspicion has arisen only in States where popular election prevails ; that is to say, where the responsibility
for a bad appointment cannot be fixed on any one person.
The shortcomings of the Bench in these States do not, therefore, indicate unsoundness in the general tone either of the
people or of the profession from whom the offenders have been
taken, but are the natural result of a system which, so far
from taking precautions to place worthy persons on the seat
of justice, has left the choice of them in four cases out of five
to a secret combination of wirepullers. Thus we may note
with satisfaction that the present tendency is not only to make
judges more independent, by lengthening their term of office,
but to withdraw their appointment from popular vote and restore it to the governor, from whom, as a responsible officer,
the public may exact the utmost care in the selection of able
and upright men.

* There is the important difference between these countries and England that in all of them not only is little or no use made of the civil jury,
but public opinion is less active, and justice more localized ; *i. e.*, a smaller
proportion of important suits are brought before the supreme courts of
the capital. The centralization of English justice, costly to suitors, has
contributed to make law more pure as well as more scientific.

CHAPTER III.

RAILROADS.

No one will expect to find in a book like this a description of that prodigy of labor, wealth, and skill, the American railway system. Of its management, its finance, its commercial prospects, I do not attempt to speak. But railroads, and those who own and control them, occupy a place in the political and social life of the country which requires some passing words, for it is a place far more significant than similar enterprises have obtained in the Old World.

The United States are so much larger, and have a population so much more scattered, than any European State that they depend even more upon means of internal communication. It is these communications that hold the country together, and render it one for all social and political purposes as well as for commerce. They may indeed be said to have made the West, for it is along the lines of railway that the West has been settled; and population still follows the rails, stretching out to south and north of the great trunk lines wherever they send off a branch. The Americans are an eminently locomotive people. Were statistics on such a point attainable, they would probably show that the average man travels over thrice as many miles by steam in a year as the average Englishman, six times as many as the average Frenchman or German. The New Yorker thinks of a journey to Chicago (nine hundred miles) as a Londoner of a journey to Glasgow (four hundred miles); and a family at St. Louis will go for sea-bathing to Cape May, a journey of

thirty-five or forty hours, as readily as a Birmingham family
goes to Scarborough. The movements of goods traffic are
on a gigantic scale. The greatest branch of heavy freight
transportation in England, that of coal from the North and
West to London, is not to be compared to the weight of
cotton, grain, bacon, cattle, fruit, and ores which comes from
the inland regions to the Atlantic coast. This traffic does
not merely give to the trunk lines an enormous yearly turn-
over, it interests all classes, I might almost say all individuals, in railway operations, seeing that every branch of
industry and every profession, except divinity and medicine,
is more or less directly connected with the movements of
commerce, and prospers in proportion to its prosperity.
Consequently, railroads and their receipts, railroad directors
and their doings, occupy men's tongues and pens to a far
greater extent than in Europe.

Some of the great railway companies possess yet another
source of wealth and power. At the time when they were
formed, the enterprise of laying down rails in thinly-peopled
or perhaps quite uninhabited regions, in some instances over
deserts or across lofty mountains, seemed likely to prove so
unremunerative to the first shareholders, yet so beneficial
to the country at large, that Congress was induced to en-
courage the promoters by vast grants of unoccupied land,
the property of the United States, lying along the projected
line.* The grants were often improvident, and they gave
rise to endless lobbying and intrigue, first to secure them,
then to keep them from being declared forfeited in respect
of some breach of the conditions imposed by Congress on

---

* These grants usually consisted of alternate sections, in the earlier
cases of five to the mile along the line. The total grant made to the Union
Pacific Railway was 13,000,100 acres ; to the Kansas Pacific, 6,000,000 ;
to the Central Pacific, 12,100,100 ; to the Northern Pacific, 47,000,000 ; to
the Atlantic and Pacific, 42,000,000 · to the Southern Pacific, 9,520,000.
Enormous money subsidies, exceeding $60,000,000, were also granted by
Congress to the first transcontinental lines.

the company. However, the lines were made, colonists came, much of the lands has been sold to speculators as well as to individual settlers; but much still remains in the hands of two or three companies. These gifts made the railroads great landowners, gave them a local influence and divers local interests besides those arising from their proper business of carriers, and brought them into intimate and often perilously delicate relations with leading politicians.

No wonder, then, that the railroads, even those that held no land beyond that on which their rails ran, acquired immense power in the districts they traversed. In a new and thinly-peopled State the companies were by far the weathiest bodies, and able by their wealth to exert all sorts of influence. A city or a district of country might depend entirely upon them for its progress. If they ran a line into it or through it, emigrants followed, the value of fixed property rose, trade became brisk; if they passed it by, and bestowed transportation facilities on some other district, it saw itself outstripped, and began to languish. If a company owned a trunk line, it could, by raising or lowering the rates of freight on that line through which the products of the district or State passed towards the sea, stimulate or retard the prosperity of the agricultural population, or the miners, or the lumbermen. That is to say, the great companies held in their hands the fortunes of cities, of counties, even sometimes of States and Territories.* California was for many years practically at the mercy of the Central Pacific Railway, then her only road to the Mississippi valley and the Atlantic. Oregon and Washington were almost equally dependent upon the Oregon Railroad and Navigation Company,

---

* This was of course especially the case with the newer Western States; yet even in the older parts of the country any very large railway system had great power, for it might have a monopoly of communication; or if there were two lines, they might have agreed to "pool," as it is called, their traffic receipts and work in harmony.

and afterwards upon the Northern Pacific. What made the
position more singular was that although these railroads had
been built under statutes passed by the State they traversed
(or, in the case of Territories, wholly or partially under
Federal statutes), they were built with Eastern capital, and
were owned by a number, often a small number, of rich men
living in New York, Boston, or Philadelphia, unamenable
to local influences, and caring no more about the wishes and
feelings of the State whence their profits came than an
English bondholder cares about the feelings of Chili. Moreover, although the railroads held a fuller sway in the newer
States, they were sometimes potent political factors in the
older ones. In 1870 I often heard men say, " Camden and
Amboy [the Camden and Amboy Railroad] rules New Jersey." In New York the great New York Central Railroad,
in Pennsylvania the Pennsylvania Railroad, under its able
chief, exerted immense influence with the legislature, partly
by their wealth, partly by the opportunities of bestowing
favors on individuals and localities which they possessed,
including the gift of free passes, and possibly influence
exercised on the votes of their employees. Sometimes, at
least in Pennsylvania and New York, they even threw their
weight into the scale of a political party, giving it money as
well as votes. But more commonly they have confined themselves to securing their own interests, and obliged, or
threatened and used, the State leaders of both parties alike
for that purpose. The same sort of power was at one time
exerted over some of the cantons of Switzerland by the greater
Swiss railway companies ; though since the Constitution of
1874, it is said to have quite disappeared.*

In such circumstances conflicts between the railroads and
the State governments were inevitable. The companies might
succeed in " capturing " individual legislators or committees

* The Swiss railways are now under the control of the Federal
Government.

of either or both Houses, but they could not silence the discontented cities or counties, who complained of the way in which they were neglected, while some other city obtained better facilities, still less the farmers, who denounced the unduly high rates they were forced to pay for the carriage of their produce. Thus a duel began between the companies and the peoples of some of the States, which has gone on with varying fortune in the halls of the legislatures and in the courts of law. The farmers of the Northwest formed agricultural associations, called "Patrons of Husbandry," or popularly "Granges," and passed a number of laws imposing various restrictions on the railroads, and providing for the fixing of a maximum scale of charges. But although the railroad companies had been formed under, and derived their powers of taking land and making by-laws from, State statutes, these statutes had in some cases omitted to reserve the right to deal freely with the lines by subsequent legislation; and the companies therefore attempted to resist the Granger laws as being unconstitutional. They were defeated by two famous decisions of the Supreme Federal Court in 1876,* establishing the right of a State to impose restrictions on public undertakings in the nature of monopolies. But in other directions they had better luck. The Granger laws proved in many respects unworkable. The companies, alleging that they could not carry goods at a loss, refused to construct branches and other new lines, to the great disappointment of the people, and in various ways contrived to make the laws difficult of execution. Thus they procured (in most States) the repeal of the first set of Granger laws; and when further legislation was projected, secret engines of influence were made to play upon the legislatures, — influences which, since the first wave of popular impulse had now spent itself, often proved efficacious in averting further

* See *Munn* vs. *Illinois,* and *Peake* vs. *Chicago, Burlington, and Quincy Railroad,* 94 U. S. Reports.

restrictions or impeding the enforcement of those imposed.* Those who profited most by the strife were the less scrupu- lous among the legislators, who, if they did not receive some favor from a railroad, could levy blackmail upon it by bringing in a threatening bill.

The contest, however, was not confined to the several States ; it passed to Congress. Congress has no authority under the Constitution to deal with a railway lying entirely within one State, but is held entitled to legislate, under its power of regulating commerce between different States, for all lines (including connecting lines which are worked together as a through line) which traverse more than one State. And of course it has always had power over railways situate in the Territories. As the Federal courts decided a few years ago that no State could legislate against a railway lying partly outside its own limits, because this would trench on Federal competence, the need for Federal legislation, long pressed upon Congress, became urgent ; and after much debate an Act was passed, in 1887, establishing an Interstate Commerce Commission, with power to regulate railroad transportation and charges in many material respects. The companies had opposed it ; but after it had passed they discovered that it injured them less than they had feared, and in some points even has benefited them, — for having prohibited all dis- criminations and secret rebates, and required them to adhere to their published list of charges, it has given them a ready answer to demands for exceptional privileges.† On the other hand, it is over-stringent, and certainly needs to be amended in several points. Too little time has, however, yet elapsed

* The legislature of Iowa recently passed a statute giving the State Railway Commission full powers to fix charges ; and injunctions were ob- tained from the courts restraining the commission from imposing, as they were proceeding to do, rates so low as to be destructive of reasonable profits

† It has also attempted, though as yet with incomplete success, to put an end to the bestowal of free passes for passengers, — a form of preference which had assumed large proportions.

for the result of this momentous statute to be duly estimated. That the railroads had exercised autocratic and irresponsible power over some regions of the country, and had occasionally abused this power, especially by imposing discriminations in their freight-charges, is not to be denied.* They had become extremely unpopular, a constant theme for demagogic denunciations; and their success during some years in resisting public clamor by their secret control of legislatures, or even of the State commissioners appointed to deal with them, increased the irritation. All corporations are at present unpopular in America, and especially corporations possessed of monopolies. The agitation may possibly continue, — though the confidence felt in the commission has done something to allay it, — and attempts be made to carry still more stringent legislation. There is even a section of opinion which desires to see all railways, as well as telegraphs, in the hands of the nation, and that not merely for revenue purposes, but to make them serve more perfectly the public convenience. The objection which to most men seems decisive against any such arrangement is that it would throw a stupendous mass of patronage and power into the hands of the party for the time being holding office. Considering what a perennial spring of bitterness partisan patronage has been, and how liable to perversion under the best regulations patronage must always be, he would be a bold man who would toss hundreds of thousands of places, many of them important and highly paid, into the lap of a party minister. Economic gain, assuming that such gain could be secured, would be dearly bought by political danger.

Their strife with the State governments has not been enough to occupy the pugnacity of the companies, they must needs fight with one another; and their wars have been long and fierce, involving immense pecuniary interests, not

* I am informed by a high authority that the freight charges as well as passenger charges on American railways were, before 1887, generally lower than those in England and in western Europe generally.

only to the shareholders in the combatant lines, but also to the inhabitants of the districts which they served. Such conflicts have been most frequent between the trunk lines competing for the carriage of goods from the West to the Atlantic cities, and have been conducted not only by lowering charges so as to starve out the weaker line,* but by attacks upon its stocks in the great share-markets, by efforts to defeat its bills in the State legislatures, and by law-suits, with applications for injunctions, in the courts. Sometimes, as in the famous case of the struggle of the Atchison, Topeka, and Santa Fé Railway with the Denver and Rio Grande for the possession of the great cañon of the Arkansas River,† the easiest route into an important group of Rocky Mountain valleys, the navvies of the two companies fought with shovels and pickaxes on the spot, while their counsel were fighting in the law-courts sixteen hundred miles away. A well-established company has sometimes to apprehend a peculiarly annoying form of attack at the hands of audacious adventurers, who construct a competing line (and perhaps nearly parallel) where the traffic is only sufficient to enable the existing one to pay a dividend on the capital it has expended,‡ aiming, not at the creation of a profitable undertaking, but at levying blackmail on one which exists, and obtaining an opportunity of manipulating bonds and stocks for their own benefit. In such a case the railway company in possession has its choice between two courses : it may allow the new enterprise to go on, then lower its own rates, and so destroy all possibility of profits ; or it may buy up the rival line, perhaps at a heavy

* In one of these contests, one railway having lowered its rates for cattle to a figure below paying point, the manager of the other promptly bought up all the cattle he could find at the inland terminus, and sent them to the coast by the enemy's line, — a costly lesson to the latter.

† This so called "Royal Gorge" of the Arkansas is one of the most striking pieces of scenery on the North American continent, not unlike the grandest part of the famous Dariel Pass in the Caucasus.

‡ This is commonly called "nickel-plating"

price. Sometimes it tries the first course long enough to beat down the already small prospects of the new line, and then buys it. But this involves a hideous waste of the money spent in construction ; and those who ultimately suffer are probably not the " pirates " who have built the new line, but persons on whom the bond and stock holders, who were in the plot, have " unloaded " their interests. This is a form of raid upon property which evidently ought to be prevented by a greater care on the part of State legislatures in refusing to pass special Acts for unnecessary railroads, or in so modifying their general statutes as to prevent a group of promoters from using for purposes of blackmail the powers of taking land and constructing railroads which such statutes confer.

This atmosphere of strife has had something to do with the feature of railway management which a European finds most remarkable ; I mean its autocratic character. Nearly all the great lines are controlled and managed either by a small knot of persons or by a single man. Sometimes one man, or a knot of three or four capitalists acting as one man, holds an actual majority of the shares, and then he can of course do exactly what he pleases. Sometimes the interest of the ruling man (or knot) comes so near to being a controlling interest that he may safely assume that no majority can be brought against him, the tendencies of many shareholders being to support " the administration " in all its policy. This accumulation of voting power in a few hands seems to be due partly to the fact that the shares of new lines do not, in the first instance, get scattered through the general public, as in England, but are commonly allotted in masses to a few persons, often as a sort of bonus upon their subscribing for the bonds of the company.* In the

* " It is an extraordinary fact," says Mr. Hitchcock, " that the power of eminent domain, which the State itself confessedly ought never to use save on grounds of public necessity, should be at the command of irresponsible individuals for purposes of private gain, not only without any guar-

United States, shares do not usually represent a cash subscription, the practice being to construct a railway with
the proceeds of the bonds and to regard the shares as the
materials for future profit, — things which may, if the line be
of a speculative character, be run up in price and sold off by
the promoters ; or, if it be likely to prosper, be held by them
for the purpose of controlling as well as gaining profits from
the undertaking.* It is partly also to be ascribed to the
splendid boldness with which financial operations are conducted in America, where the leaders of Wall Street do not
hesitate to buy up enormous masses of shares or stock for
the purpose of some *coup*. Having once got into a single
hand, or a few hands, these stock masses stay there, and
give their possessors the control of the line. But the power
of the railways, and the position they hold towards local
governments, State legislatures, and one another, have also

antee that the public interest will be promoted thereby, but when it is
perfectly well known that it may be and has been deliberately availed of
for merely speculative purposes. The facility with which, under loosely
drawn railroad laws, purely speculative railroad charters can be obtained,
has contributed not a little to develop the law of receiverships. In Missouri there is nothing to prevent any five men, whose combined capital
would not enable them to build five miles of track on a level prairie,
from forming a railroad corporation with power to construct a road five
hundred miles long, and to condemn private property for that purpose,
for a line whose construction no public interest demands, and from which
no experienced man could expect dividends to accrue." — *Address to the
American Bar Association*, 1887.

    * The great Central Pacific Railway was constructed by four men, two
of whom were when they began storekeepers in a small way in San Francisco, and none of whom could be called capitalists. Their united funds
when they began in 1860 were only $120,000 (£24,000). They went on
issuing bonds and building the line bit by bit as the bonds put them in
funds, retaining the control of the company through the shares. This
Central Pacific Company ultimately built the Southern Pacific and numerous branches, and became by far the greatest power in the West, owning
nearly all the railways in California and Nevada. When one of the four
died in 1878, his estate was worth $30,000,000 (£6,000,000).

a great deal to do with the phenomenon. War is the natural
state of an American railway towards all other authorities
and its own fellows, just as war was the natural state of
cities towards one another in the ancient world. And as an
army in the field must be commanded by one general, so must
this latest militant product of an eminently peaceful civilization. The president of a great railroad needs gifts for
strategical combinations scarcely inferior to those, if not of
a great general, yet of a great war minister,— a Chatham or
a Carnot. If his line extends into a new country, he must
be quick to seize the best routes, — the best physically,
because they will be cheaper to operate ; the best in agricultural or mineral resources, because they will offer a greater
prospect of traffic. He must so throw out his branches as
not only to occupy promising tracts, but keep his competing
enemies at a distance ; he must annex small lines when he
sees a good chance, damaging them first, so as to get them
cheaper ; he must make a close alliance with at least one
other great line, which completes his communications with
the East or with the farther West, and be prepared to join
this ally in a conflict with some threatening competitor. He
must know the governors and watch the legislatures of the
States or Territories through which his line runs ; must have
adroit agents at the State capitals, well supplied with the
sinews of war, ready to " see " leading legislators and to
defeat any legislative attacks that may be made by black-
mailers or the tools of rival presidents. And all the while
he must not only keep his eye upon the markets of New
York, prepared for the onslaught which may be made upon
his own stock by some other railroad or by speculators desiring to make a profit as " bears," and maintaining friendly
relations with the capitalists whose help he will need when
he brings out a new loan, but must supervise the whole
administrative system of the railroad, — its stations, permanent way, locomotives, rolling-stock, engineering shops,

freight and passenger rates; perhaps also the sale of its land grants and their defence against the cabals of Washington. No talents of the practical order can be too high for such a position as this; and even the highest talents would fail to fill it properly except with a free hand. Concentration of power and an almost uncontrolled discretion are needed; and in America whatever commercial success needs is sure to be yielded. Hence, when a group of capitalists own a railway, they commit its management to a very small committee among themselves, or even to a single man; and when the shares are more widely distributed, the shareholders, recognizing the necessary conditions of prosperity, not to say of survival in the struggle for existence, leave themselves in the hands of the president, who has little to fear except from the shares being quietly bought up by some syndicate of enemies seeking to dethrone him.

Of these great railway chieftains, some have come to the top gradually, by the display in subordinate posts of brilliant administrative gifts. Some have begun as financiers, and have sprung into the presidential saddle at a bound, by forming a combination which has captured the railway by buying up its stock. Occasionally a great capitalist will seize a railroad only for the sake of manipulating its stock, clearing a profit, and throwing it away. But more frequently, when a really important line has passed into the hands of a man or group, it is held fast, and developed into a higher efficiency by means of the capital they command.

These railway kings are among the greatest men, perhaps I may say are the greatest men, in America. They have wealth, else they could not hold the position. They have fame, for every one has heard of their achievements; every newspaper chronicles their movements. They have power, more power — that is, more opportunity of making their personal will prevail — than perhaps any one in political life, except the President and the Speaker, who after all hold theirs only for four years and two years, while the railroad monarch may keep his for life. When the master of one of the greatest Western lines travels towards the Pacific on his palace car, his journey is like a royal progress. Governors of States and Territories bow before him; legislatures receive him in solemn session; cities and towns seek to propitiate him, — for has he not the means of making or marring a city's fortunes? Although the railroad companies are unpopular, and although this autocratic sway from a distance contributes to their unpopularity, I do not think that the ruling magnates are themselves generally disliked. On the contrary, they receive that tribute of admiration which the American gladly pays to whoever has done best what every one desires to do. Probably no career draws to it or unfolds and develops so much of the characteristic ability of the nation; and I doubt whether any congressional legislation will greatly reduce the commanding positions which these potentates hold as the masters of enterprises whose wealth, geographical extension, and influence upon the growth of the country and the fortunes of individuals, find no parallel in the Old World.

It may be thought that some of the phenomena I have described belong to an era of colonization, and that when the West has been filled up and all the arterial railways made, — when, in fact, the United States have become even as England or France, — the power of railroads and their presidents will decline. No doubt there will be less room for certain bold ventures and feats of constructive strategy; and as the network of railways grows closer, States and districts may come to depend less upon one particular company. At the same time it must be remembered that the more populous and wealthy the country, so much the larger the business of a trunk line, and the number of its branches and its employees; while the consolidation of small lines, or their absorption by large ones, is a process evidently destined to continue. It may therefore be conjectured that the railroad will long stand forth as a great and perplexing force in the economico-political life of the United States. It cannot be left to itself, — the most extreme advocate of *laissez faire* would not contend for that; for to leave it to itself would be to make it a tyrant. It cannot be absorbed and worked by the National Government, — only the most sanguine state socialist would propose to impose so terrible a strain on the virtue of American politicians, and so seriously to disturb the constitutional balance between the States and the Federal authority. Many experiments may be needed before the true mean course between these extremes is discovered. Meanwhile, the railroads illustrate two tendencies specially conspicuous in America, — the power of the principle of association, which makes commercial corporations, skilfully handled, formidable to individual men; and the way in which the principle of monarchy, banished from the field of government, creeps back again, and asserts its strength in the scarcely less momentous contests of industry and finance.

CHAPTER IV.

WALL STREET.

No invention of modern times, not even that of negotiable paper, has so changed the face of commerce and delighted lawyers with a variety of new and intricate problems as the creation of incorporated joint-stock companies. America, though she came latest into the field, has developed these on a grander scale and with a more refined skill than the countries of the Old World. Nowhere do trading corporations play so great a part in trade and industry; nowhere are so many huge undertakings in their hands; nowhere else has the method of controlling them become a political problem of the first magnitude. So vigorous, indeed, is the inventive genius of American commerce that, not satisfied with the new applications it has found for the principles of the joint-stock corporation, it has lately attempted a further development of the arts of combination by creating those anomalous giants called Trusts, — groups of individuals and corporations concerned in one branch of trade or manufacture, which are placed under the irresponsible management of a small knot of persons, who, through their command of all the main producing or distributing agencies, intend and expect to dominate the market, force manufacturers or dealers to submit, and hold the consumer at their mercy.*

* The question, what is the legal status (if any) of these Trusts, — a creation of the last few years, — has recently been actively discussed by American jurists, and some judicial decisions lately rendered have tended to restrict their action. The dangerous extent of the power they have begun to exert is generally recognized.

Here, however, I am concerned with the amazing expansion of joint-stock companies in America only as the cause of the not less amazing activity in buying and selling shares which the people display. This is almost the first thing that strikes a European visitor ; and the longer he remains, the more deeply is he impressed by it as something to which his own country, be it England, France, or Germany, furnishes no parallel. In Europe, speculation in bonds, shares, and stocks is confined to a section of the commercial world, with a few stragglers from other walks of business, or from the professions, who flutter near the flame and burn their wings. Ordinary steady-going people, even people in business, know little or nothing about the matter, and seldom think of reading the share lists. When they have savings to invest, they do as they are bidden by their banker or stockbroker, if indeed they have a stock-broker, and do not get their banker to engage one.* In the United States a much larger part of the population, including professional men as well as business men, seem conversant with the subject ; and there are times when the whole community, not merely city people, but also storekeepers in country towns, even farmers, even domestic servants, interest themselves actively in share speculations. At such times they watch the fluctuations of price in the stocks of the great railroads, telegraph companies (or rather the Telegraph Company, since there is practically but one), and other leading undertakings ; they discuss the prospects of a rise or fall, and the probable policy of the great operators ; they buy and sell bonds or stocks on a scale not always commensurate with their own means.† In the great cities the number of persons

* There are, of course, simple folk in England who take shares on the faith of prospectuses of new companies sent to them ; but the fact that it pays to send such prospectuses is the best proof of the general ignorance, in such matters, of laymen (including the clergy) and women in that country.

† In some of the country towns there are small offices, commonly called " bucket shops," to which farmers and tradesmen resort to effect their

exclusively devoted to this occupation is very large, and
naturally so, because, while the undertakings lie all over a
vast extent of country, the capital which owns them is mostly
situate in the cities, and, indeed, six sevenths of it (so far as
it is held in America) in four or five of the greatest Eastern
cities. It is chiefly in railroads that these Easterns speculate.
But in the Far West mines are an even more exciting and
pervasive interest. In San Francisco every one gambles in
mining stocks, even the nursemaids and the Chinese. The
share lists showing the oscillations of prices are hung up outside the newspaper offices, and fixed on posts in the streets,
and are changed every hour or two during the day. In the
silver districts of Colorado and New Mexico the same kind
of thing goes on.* It is naturally in such spots that the fire
burns hottest. But go where you will in the Union, except,
to be sure, in the more stagnant and impecunious parts of
the South, you feel bonds, stocks, and shares in the atmosphere all round you. *Te veniente die*, — they begin the day
with the newspaper at breakfast; they end it with the chat
over the nocturnal cigar.†

This eager interest centres itself in New York; for finance,
more perhaps than any other kind of business, draws to few

purchases and sales in the great stock markets of New York. Not a few
ruin themselves. Some States have endeavored to extinguish them by
penal legislation.

* In a mining town in Colorado the landlady of an inn in which I
stayed for a night pressed me to bring out in London a company to work
a mining claim which she had acquired, offering me what is called an
"option." I inquired how much money it would take to begin to work the
claim and get out the ore. "Less than thirty thousand dollars" (£6,000).
(The carbonates are in that part of Colorado very near the surface.) "And
what is to be the capital of your company?" "Five millions of dollars"
(£1,000,000)!

† Of course I am speaking of the ordinary man you meet in travelling,
who is a sample of the ordinary citizen. In polite society one's enter-
tainer would no more bring up such a subject, unless you draw him on to
do so, than he would think of talking politics.

points, and New York, which has as little claim to be the
social or intellectual as to be the political capital of the country, is emphatically its financial capital. And as the centre
of America is New York, so the centre of New York is Wall
Street. This famous thoroughfare is hardly a quarter of a
mile long, — a little longer than Lombard Street in London. It
contains the Sub-Treasury of the United States and the Stock
Exchange. In it and the four or five streets that adjoin or
open into it are situated the Produce and Cotton Exchanges,
the offices of the great railways, and the places of business of
the financiers and stockbrokers, together representing an accumulation of capital and intellect comparable to the capital and
intellect of London, and destined before many years to surpass
every similar spot in either hemisphere.* Wall Street is the
great nerve-centre of all American business; for finance and
transportation, the two determining powers in business, have
here their headquarters. It is also the financial barometer
of the country, which every man engaged in large affairs must
constantly consult, and whose only fault is that it is too
sensitive to slight and transient variations of pressure.

The share market of New York, or rather of the whole
Union, in "the Street," as it is fondly named, is the most
remarkable sight in the country after Niagara and the Yellowstone Geysers. It is not unlike those geysers in the violence
of its explosions, and in the rapid rise and equally rapid sub-
sidence of its active paroxysms. And as the sparkling column of the geyser is girt about and often half concealed by
volumes of steam, so are the rise and fall of stocks mostly surrounded by mists and clouds of rumor, some purposely created,
some self-generated in the atmosphere of excitement, curiosity, credulity, and suspicion which the denizens of Wall
Street breathe. Opinions change from moment to moment;
hope and fear are equally vehement and equally irrational;

* The balances settled in the New York Clearing House each day are
two thirds of all the clearings in the United States.

men are constant only in inconstancy, superstitious because
they are sceptical, distrustful of patent probabilities, and
therefore ready to trust their own fancies or some unfathered
tale. As the eagerness and passion of New York leave European stock markets far behind, — for what the Paris and London exchanges are at rare moments Wall Street is for weeks,
or perhaps, with a few intermissions, for months together, —
so the operations of Wall Street are vaster, more boldly conceived, executed with a steadier precision, than those of European speculators. It is not only their bearing on the prosperity of railroads or other great undertakings that is eagerly
watched all over the country, but also their personal and dra-
matic aspects. The various careers and characters of the leading operators are familiar to every one who reads a newspaper ; his schemes and exploits are followed as Europe followed
the fortunes of Prince Alexander of Battenberg or General
Boulanger. A great " corner," for instance, is one of the
exciting events of the year, not merely to those concerned
with the stock or species of produce in which it is attempted,
but to the public at large.

How far is this state of things transitory, due to temporary
causes arising out of the swift material development of the
United States? During the Civil War the creation of a
paper currency, which rapidly depreciated, produced a wild
speculation in gold, lasting for several years, whose slightest
fluctuations were followed with keen interest, because in
indicating the value of the paper currency they indicated
the credit of the nation and the view taken by the financial
community of the prospects of the war. The re-establishment
of peace brought with it a burst of industrial activity,
specially directed to the making of new railroads and general
opening up of the West. Thus the eyes that had been accustomed to watch Wall Street did not cease to watch it,
for these new enterprises involved many fortunes, had drawn
much capital from small investors, and were really of great

consequence — the transcontinental railways most of all — to the welfare of the country. It is some time since the work of railway construction began to slacken, as it slackened in England a generation ago, although from time to time there is a revival. Mines are less profitable since the great fall in silver; the price of United States bonds fluctuates hardly (if at all) more than Consols do in England. The last four or five years have been comparatively quiet. Yet even when transactions are fewer, the interest of the public in the stock markets does not greatly diminish. Trade and manufactures cover the whole horizon of American life far more than they do anywhere in Europe. They — I include agriculture, because it has been, in America, commercialized, and become really a branch of trade — are the main concern of the country, to which all others are subordinate. So large a part of the whole capital employed is in the hands of joint-stock companies; * so easy a method do these companies furnish by which the smallest investor may take part in commercial ventures and increase his " pile ; " so general is the diffusion of information (of course often incorrect) regarding their state and prospects ; so vehement and pervading is the passion for wealth ; so seductive are the examples of a few men who have realized stupendous fortunes by clever or merely lucky hits when there came a sharp rise or fall in the stock market ; so vast, and therefore so impressive to the imagination, is the scale on which these oscillations take place,† — that the

* The wealth of corporations has been estimated by high authorities at one fourth of the total value of all property in the United States. I find that in the State of Illinois alone (population in 1880, 3,077,000) there were formed during the year 1886, under the general law, 1714 incorporated companies, with an aggregate capital stock (authorized) of $819,101,110. Of these 632 were manufacturing companies, 104 mining companies, 41 railroad companies.

† The great rebound of trade in 1879–83 trebled within those years the value of many railroad bonds and stocks, and raised at a still more rapid rate the value of lands in many parts of the West.

universal attention given to stocks and shares, and the tendency to speculation among the non-financial classes which reveals itself from time to time, seem amply accounted for by permanent causes, and therefore likely to prove normal. Even admitting that neither such stimulations as were present during the war period, nor those that belonged to the era of inflated prosperity which followed, are likely to recur, it must be observed that habits formed under transitory conditions do not always pass away with those conditions, but may become a permanent and, so to speak, hereditary element in national life.

So far as politics are concerned, I do not know that Wall Street does any harm. There is hardly any speculation in foreign securities, because capital finds ample employment in domestic undertakings; and the United States are so little likely to be involved in foreign complications that neither the action of European powers nor that of the Federal Government bears directly enough upon the stock markets to bring politics into stocks, or stocks into politics.* Hence one source of evil which poisons public life in Europe, and is believed to have proved specially pernicious in France, — the influence of financial speculators or holders of foreign bonds upon the foreign policy of a government, — is wholly absent. An American Secretary of State, supposing him base enough to use his official knowledge for stock-jobbing operations, would have little advantage over the meanest broker in Wall Street.† Even as regards domestic politics,

* Of course the prospects of war or peace in Europe do sensibly affect the American produce markets, and therefore the railroads, and indeed all great commercial undertakings. But these prospects are as much outside the province of the American statesman as the drought which affects the coming crop, or the blizzard that stops the earnings of a railway.

† The Secretary of the Treasury, by his control of the public debt, has no doubt means of affecting the markets; but I have never heard any charge of improper conduct in such matters on the part of any one connected with the Treasury Department.

the division of power between Congress and the State legislatures reduces the power of the former over industrial undertakings, and leaves comparatively few occasions on which the action of the Federal Government tends to affect the market for most kinds of stocks, though of course changes in the public debt and in the currency affect by sympathy every part of the machinery of commerce. The shares of railroad companies owning land grants were, and to some slight extent still are, depressed and raised by the greater or slighter prospects of legislative interference; but it may be expected that this point of contact between speculators and politicians, which, like the meeting-point of currents in the sea, is marked by a good deal of rough and turbid water, will soon cease to exist as the remaining railroad lands get sold or are declared forfeited.

The more serious question remains: How does Wall Street tell on the character of the people? They are naturally inclined to be speculative. The pursuit of wealth is nowhere so eager as in America, the opportunities for acquiring it are nowhere so numerous. Nowhere is one equally impressed by the progress which the science and arts of gain — I do not mean the arts that add to the world's wealth, but those by which individuals appropriate an exceptionally large share of it — make from year to year. The materials with which the investor or the speculator has to work may receive no sensible addition; but the constant application of thousands of keen intellects, spurred by sharp desire, evolves new combinations out of these old materials, devises new methods and contrivances apt for a bold and skilful hand, — just as electricians go on perfecting the machinery of the telegraph, just as the accumulated labors of scholars present us with always more trustworthy texts of the classical writers, and more precise rules of Greek and Latin syntax. Under these new methods of business, speculation, though it seems to become more of a science, does not become less speculative.

People seem to buy and sell on even slighter indications than in Paris or London. The processes of " bulling" and " bearing" are more constant and more skilfully applied; the whole theory and practice of " margins" has been more completely worked out. However, it is of less consequence for our present purpose to dwell on the proficiency of the professional operator than to note the prevalence of the habit of speculation : it is not intensity so much as extension that affects an estimate of the people at large.

Except in the great horse-breeding State of Kentucky, in New York, and perhaps in Chicago, which is more and more coming to reproduce and rival the characteristics of New York, Americans bet less upon horse-races than the English do. Horse-races are, indeed, far less common, though there is a good deal of fuss made about trotting-matches. However, much money changes hands, especially in Eastern cities, over yacht-races, and plenty everywhere over elections.* The purchase and sale of " produce futures " — i. e., of cotton, wheat, maize, bacon, lard, and other staples not yet in existence, but to be delivered at some distant day — has reached an enormous development.† There is, even in the Eastern cities, where the value of land might be thought to have become stable, a real-estate market in which land and houses are dealt in as matter for pure speculation, with no intention of holding except for a rise within the next few hours or days ; while in the new West the price of lands, especially near cities, undergoes fluctuations greater than those of the most unstable stocks in the London market. It can hardly be doubted that the pre-existing tendency to encounter risks and " back one's opinion," inborn in the Americans, and fostered by the

---

* The mischief has been thought sufficient to be specially checked by the constitutions or statutes of some States.

† It is stated that the Cotton Exchange sells in each year five times the value of the cotton crop, and that in 1887 the Petroleum Exchange sold fifty times the amount of that year's yield.

circumstances of their country, is further stimulated by the existence of so vast a number of joint-stock enterprises, and by the facilities they offer to the smallest capitalists. Similar facilities exist in the Old World; but few of the inhabitants of the Old World have yet learned how to use and abuse them. The Americans, quick at everything, have learned long ago. The habit of speculation is now a part of their character, and it increases that constitutional excitability and high nervous tension of which they are proud.

Some may think that when the country fills up and settles down, and finds itself altogether under conditions more nearly resembling those of the Old World, these peculiarities will fade away. I doubt it. They seem to have already passed into the national fibre.

CHAPTER V.

THE UNIVERSITIES.

AMONG the universities of America there is none which has sprung up of itself like Bologna or Paris or El Azhar or Oxford, none founded by an Emperor like Prague, or by a Pope like Glasgow. All have been the creatures of private munificence or denominational zeal or State action. Their history is short indeed compared with that of the universities of Europe; yet it is full of interest, for it shows a steady growth, it records many experiments, it gives valuable data for comparing the educational results of diverse systems.

When the first English colonists went to America, the large and liberal mediæval conception of a university, as a place where graduates might teach freely and students live freely, was waxing feeble in Oxford and Cambridge. The instruction was given chiefly by the colleges, which had already become, what they long continued, organisms so strong as collectively to eclipse the university they had been meant to aid. Accordingly, when places of superior instruction began to grow up in the colonies, it was on the model, not of an English university, but of an English college, that they were created. The glory of founding the first place of learning in the English parts of America belongs to a Puritan minister and graduate of Cambridge, John Harvard of Emmanuel College,*

---

* Emmanuel was a college then much frequented by the Puritans: Of the English graduates who emigrated to New England between 1620 and 1647, nearly one hundred in number, three fourths came from the University of Cambridge.

who, dying in 1638, eighteen years after the landing of the Pilgrim Fathers, gave half his property for the establishment of a college in the town of Cambridge, three miles from Boston, which, originally organized on the plan of Emmanuel College, and at once taken under the protection of the infant commonwealth of Massachusets, has now grown into the most famous university on the North American continent.*

The second foundation was due to the Colonial Assembly of Virginia. So early as 1619, twelve years after the first settlement at Jamestown, the Virginia Company in England voted ten thousand acres of land in the colony for the establishment of a seminary of learning, and a site was in 1624 actually set apart, on an island in the Susquehanna River, for the " Foundinge and Maintenance of a University and such schools in Virginia as shall there be erected, and shall be called Academia Virginiensis et Oxoniensis." This scheme was never carried out. But in 1693 the Virginians obtained a grant of land and money from the home government for the erection of a college, which received the name of the College of William and Mary.† The third foundation was Yale

* In 1636 the General Court of the colony of Massachusetts Bay agreed "to give Four Hundred Pounds towards a school or college, whereof Two Hundred Pounds shall be paid the next year, and Two Hundred Pounds when the work is finished, and the next Court to appoint where and what building." In 1637 the General Court appointed a Commission of twelve "to take order for a college at Newtoun." The name Newtoun was presently changed to Cambridge. John Harvard's bequest being worth more than twice the £400 voted, the name of Harvard College was given to the institution ; and in 1642 a statute was passed for the ordering of the same.

† The Virginians had worked at this project for more than thirty years before they got their charter and grant. " When William and Mary had agreed to allow £2000 out of the quit-rents of Virginia towards building the college, the Rev. Mr. Blair went to Seymour, the Attorney-General, with the royal command to issue a charter. Seymour demurred. The country

College, established in Connecticut (first at Saybrook, then at New Haven) in 1700 ; the fourth Princeton, in New Jersey, in 1746. None of these received the title of university : Harvard is called a " school or colledge ; " Yale used the name " collegiate school " for seventeen years. " We on purpose gave your academy as low a name as we could, that it might the better stand the wind and weather," was the reason assigned. Other academies or colleges in New England and the Middle States followed : such as that which is now the University of Pennsylvania, in 1749 ; King's, now Columbia, College, in New York, in 1754 ; and Rhode Island College (now Brown University), in 1764 ; and the habit of .granting degrees grew up naturally and almost imperceptibly. A new departure is marked after the Revolution by the establishment, at the instance of Jefferson, of the University of Virginia, on lines bearing more resemblance to the universities of the European continent than to the then educationally narrow and socially domestic colleges of England.

At present most of the American universities are referable to one of two types, which may be described as the older and the newer, or the Private and the Public type. By the Old, or Private, type I denote a college on the model of a college in Oxford or Cambridge, with a head called the president, and a number of teachers, now generally called professors ; a body of governors or trustees, in whom the property and general control of the institution are vested ; a prescribed course of instruction, which all students are expected to fol-

---

was then engaged in war, and could ill afford to plant a college in Virginia. Mr. Blair urged that the institution was to prepare young men to become ministers of the gospel. ' Virginians,' he said, ' had souls to be saved as well as their English countrymen.' ' Souls !' said Seymour, ' Damn your souls ! Make tobacco ! ' " — *The College of William and Mary*, by Dr. H. B. Adams, published by the U. S Bureau of Education in 1887. This oldest of Southern colleges was destroyed in the Civil War (1862), and has never been restored.

low; buildings, usually called dormitories, provided for the lodging of the students; and a more or less strict, but always pretty effective, discipline enforced by the teaching staff. Such a college is usually of private foundation, and is almost always connected with some religious denomination.

Under the term New, or Public, type I include universities established, endowed, and governed by a State, usually through a body of persons called regents. In such a university there commonly exists considerable freedom of choice among various courses of study. The students, or at least the majority of them, reside where they please in the city, and are subject to very little discipline. There are seldom or never denominational affiliations, and the instruction is often gratuitous.

There are, however, institutions which it is hard to refer to one or other type. Some of these began as private foundations, with a collegiate and quasi-domestic character, but have now developed into true universities, generally resembling those of Germany or Scotland. Harvard in Massachusetts and Yale in Connecticut are instances. Others have been founded by private persons, but as fully equipped universities, and wholly undenominational. Cornell at Ithaca in western New York is an instance; Johns Hopkins in Baltimore is another of a different order. Some have been founded by public authority, yet have been practically left to be controlled by a body of self-renewing trustees. Columbia College in New York city is an instance. Still, if we were to run through a list of the universities and colleges in the United States, we should find that the great majority were either strictly private foundations governed by trustees, or wholly public foundations governed by the State. That is to say, the two familiar English types, — namely, the University, which, though a public institution, is yet little interfered with by the State, which is deemed to be composed of its graduates and students, and whose self-government consists in its being governed by the graduates; and the College, which is a private corporation, consisting of a head, fellows, and scholars, and governed by the head and fellows, — neither of them appear in modern America. On the other hand, the American university of the Public type differs from the universities of Germany in being placed under a State Board, not under a Minister. Neither in Germany nor in Scotland do we find anything corresponding to the American university or college of the Private type, for in neither of these countries is a university governed by a body of self-renewing trustees.*

It is impossible within the limits of a chapter to do more than state a few of the more salient characteristics of the American universities. I shall endeavor to present these characteristics in the fewest possible words, and for the sake of clearness shall group what I have to say under separate heads.

Statistics. — The report for 1885–86 of the United States Education Bureau gives the total number of institutions granting degrees and professing to give an instruction, higher than that of schools, in the liberal arts, at 345, with 4,670 professors and 67,623 students; namely, 25,393 preparatory, 14,426 classical, 4,872 scientific.† Many of these institutions have also professional departments for theology, law, or medicine. But these figures are confessedly imperfect, because some institutions omit to send returns, and cannot be compelled to do so, the Federal Government having no authority in the matter. The number of degree-giving bodies, teachers, and students is therefore somewhat larger than is

---

* The Scotch universities (since the Act of 1858), under their University Courts, and the Victoria University in Manchester present, however, a certain resemblance to the American system, inasmuch as the governing body is in these institutions not the teaching body.

† Institutions for women only are not included in this list.

here stated, but how much larger it is not easy to ascertain. Besides these there are returned, —

Schools of science		90	with	974	teachers	10,532	students.
"	theology	142	"	803	"	6,344	"
"	law	49	"	283	"	3,054	"
"	medicine *	175	"	2,829	"	16,407	"

(including dentistry and pharmacy.)

The number of degrees conferred is returned as being, in classical and scientific colleges 7,185, and in professional schools 3,296, besides 475 honorary degrees.

General Character of the Universities and Colleges. — Out of this enormous total of degree-granting bodies very few answer to the modern conception of a university. If we define a university as a place where teaching of a high order, teaching which puts a man abreast of the fullest and most exact knowledge of the time, is given in a range of subjects covering all the great departments of intellectual life, not more than twelve, and possibly only eight or nine, of the American institutions would fall within the definition. Of these nearly all are to be found in the Atlantic States. Next below them come some thirty or forty foundations which are scarcely entitled to the name of university, — some because their range of instruction is still limited to the traditional literary and scientific course such as it stood thirty years ago ; others because, while professing to teach a great variety of subjects, they teach them in an imperfect way, having neither a sufficiently large staff of highly trained professors, nor an adequate provision of laboratories, libraries, and other external appliances. The older New England colleges are good types of the former group. Their instruction is sound and thorough as far as it goes, well calculated to fit a man for the professions of law or divinity ; but it omits many branches of learning and

* Of these 175, 13 institutions (with 212 teachers and 1103 students) are homœopathic.

science which have grown to importance within the last fifty years. There are also some Western colleges which deserve to be placed in the same category. Most of the Western State universities belong to the other group of this second-class, — that of institutions which aim at covering more ground than they are as yet able to cover. They have an ambitious programme, but neither the state of preparation of their students nor the strength of the teaching staff enables them to do justice to the promise which the programme holds out. They are true universities rather in aspiration than in fact.

Below these again there is a third and much larger class of colleges, let us say three hundred, which are for most intents and purposes schools. They differ from the *gymnasia* of Germany, the *lycées* of France, the grammar-schools of England and high-schools of Scotland, not only in the fact that they give degrees to those who have satisfactorily passed through their prescribed course or courses, but in permitting greater personal freedom to the students than boys would be allowed in those countries. They are universities or colleges as respects some of their arrangements, but schools in respect of the educational results attained. These three hundred may be further divided into two sub-classes, distinguished from one another partly by their revenues, partly by the character of the population they serve, partly by the personal gifts of the president, as the head of the establishment is usually called, and of the teachers. Some seventy or eighty, though comparatively small, are strong by the zeal and capacity of their teachers, and while not attempting to teach everything, teach the subjects which they do undertake with increasing thoroughness. The remainder would do better to renounce the privilege of granting degrees, and be content to do school work according to school methods. The West and South are covered with these small colleges. In Illinois I find 25 named in the Report of the United States Education Bureau, in Tennessee 18, in Kentucky 12. In Ohio more than 33 are returned, — and the number is probably larger, — none of which deserves to be called a university. The most fully equipped would seem to be the State University at Columbus, with a faculty of 26 teachers ; but of its students 141 are in the preparatory department, only 34 in the classical, and 29 in the scientific branch of the collegiate department. Oberlin, Wooster, and Marietta (all denominational) have larger totals of students, and are probably quite as efficient ; but in these colleges also the majority of students are to be found in the Preparatory Department.

Revenues. — Nearly all, if not all, of the degree-granting bodies are endowed, the great majority by private founders, but a good many also by grants of land made by the State in which they stand, partly out of lands set apart for educational purposes by the Federal government. In most cases the lands have been sold and the proceeds invested. Many of the State universities of the West receive a grant from the State treasury, voted annually or biennially by the legislature. The greater universities are constantly being enriched by the gifts of private individuals, often their own graduates ; but the complaint is heard that these gifts are too frequently appropriated to some specific purpose, instead of being added to the general funds of the university. Harvard, Yale, Columbia, Cornell, and Johns Hopkins are now all of them wealthy foundations, and the stream of munificence swells daily.* Before long there will be universities in America with resources far surpassing those of any Scottish university, and approaching the collective income of the university and all the colleges in Oxford or in Cambridge. In some States the real property and funds of universities are exempt from taxation.

* Mr. Johns Hopkins gave £700,000 to the university he founded at Baltimore. Within the last five years a magnificent endowment has been given by Mr. Leland Stanford, Senator for California, to found a new university at Palo Alto in that State.

Government. — As already remarked, no American university or college is, so far as I know, governed either by its graduates alone, like Oxford and Cambridge, or by its teaching staff alone, like the Scotch universities before the Act of 1858. The State universities are usually controlled and managed by a board, generally called the regents, sometimes elected by the people of the State, sometimes appointed by the governor or the legislature. There are States with an enlightened population, or in which an able president has been able to guide and influence the regents or the legislature, in which this plan has worked excellently, securing liberal appropriations, and interesting the commonwealth in the welfare of the highest organ of its intellectual life. Such a State is Michigan. There are also States, such as California, in which the haste or unwisdom of the legislature seems for a time to have cramped the growth of the university.

All other universities and colleges are governed by boards of governors or trustees, sometimes allowed to renew themselves by co-optation, sometimes nominated by a religious denomination or other external authority.* The president of the institution is often, but not always, an *ex-officio* member of this board, to which the management of property and financial interests belongs, while internal discipline and educational arrangements are usually left to the academic staff. A visitor from Europe is struck by the prominence of the president in an American university or college, and the almost monarchical position which he sometimes occupies towards the professors as well as towards the students. Far more authority

---

* In Harvard the government is vested in a self-renewing body of seven persons, called the Corporation, or, technically, the President and Fellows of Harvard College, who have the charge of the property ; and in a Board of Overseers, appointed formerly by the legislature, now by the graduates, five each year, to serve for six years, with a general supervision of the educational system, educational details and discipline being left to the Faculty.

seems to be vested in him, far more to turn upon his individual talents and character, than in the universities of Europe. Neither the German pro-rector, nor the vice-chancellor in Oxford and Cambridge, nor the principal in a Scottish university, nor the provost of Trinity College in Dublin, nor the head in one of the colleges in Oxford or Cambridge, is anything like so important a personage in respect of his office, whatever influence his individual gifts may give him, as an American college president.* In this, as in not a few other respects, America is less republican than England.

Of late years there have been active movements to secure the representation of the graduates of each university or college upon its governing body ; and it now frequently happens that some of the trustees are elected by the alumni. Good results follow, because the alumni are disposed to elect men younger and more abreast of the times than most of the persons whom the existing trustees co-opt.

The Teaching Staff. — The Faculty, as it is usually called, varies in numbers and efficiency according to the popularity of the university or college and its financial resources. The largest staff mentioned in the tables of the United States Bureau of Education is that of Harvard, with 62 professors, instructors, and lecturers in its collegiate department (excluding theology, law, and medicine) ; while Yale has 46, Columbia 50, Princeton 39, the University of Michigan 47, Johns Hopkins 49. Cornell returns 74, but apparently not all of these are constantly occupied in teaching.

---

* The president of a college was formerly usually, and in denominational colleges almost invariably, a clergyman, and generally lectured on mental and moral philosophy. (When a layman was chosen at Harvard in 1828 the clergy thought it an encroachment.) He is to-day not so likely to be in orders. However, of the 33 Ohio colleges, 15 have clerical presidents. The greater universities of the East (except Yale, Princeton, and Brown) and the Western State universities are now usually ruled by laymen, sometimes by persons who have shown executive capacity in business or public office, but have never been engaged in teaching.

In the colleges of the West and Northwest the average number of teachers is ten in the collegiate, three in the preparatory department. It is larger in the State universities, but in some of the Southern and ruder Western States sinks to five or six, each of them taking two or three subjects. I remember to have met in the Far West a college president — I will call him Mr. Johnson — who gave me a long account of his young university, established by public authority, and receiving some small grant from the legislature. He was an active, sanguine man, and in dilating on his plans frequently referred to " the Faculty " as doing this or contemplating that. At last I asked of how many professors the Faculty at present consisted. " Well," he answered, " just at present the Faculty is below its full strength, but it will soon be more numerous." " And at present? " I inquired. " At present it consists of Mrs. Johnson and myself."

The salaries paid to professors seem small compared with the general wealth of the country and the cost of living. The highest known to me are those in Columbia College, a few of which exceed $5000 (£1000) a year. I doubt if any others reach this figure. Even in Harvard and Yale, Johns Hopkins and Cornell, most fall below $4000. Over the country generally I should guess that a president rarely receives $4000, often only $3000 or $2000, and the professors less in proportion. Under these conditions it may be found surprising that so many able men are to be found on the teaching staff of not a few colleges as well as universities, and that in the greater universities there are also many who have trained themselves by a long and expensive education in Europe for their work. The reason is to be found partly in the fondness for science and learning which has lately shown itself in America, and which makes men of intellectual tastes prefer a life of letters with poverty to success in business or at the Bar; partly, as regards the smaller Western colleges, to religious motives, these colleges being largely officered by the clergy of the denomination they belong to, especially by those who love study, or find their talents better suited to the class-room than to the pulpit.

The professors seem to be always among the social aristocracy of the city in which they live, though usually unable, from the smallness of their incomes, to enjoy social life as the corresponding class does in Scotland, or even in England. The position of president is often one of honor and influence; no university dignitaries in Great Britain are so well known to the public, or have their opinions quoted with so much respect, as the heads of the seven or eight leading universities of the United States.

The Students. — It is the glory of the American universities, as of those of Scotland and Germany, to be freely accessible to all classes of the people. In the Eastern States comparatively few are the sons of working-men, because parents can rarely bear the expense of a university course, or dispense with a boy's earnings after he reaches thirteen. But even in the East a good many come from straitened homes, receiving assistance from some richer neighbor or from charitable funds belonging to the college at which they may present themselves. In the West, where there is little distinction of classes, though great disparity of wealth, so many institutions exact a merely nominal fee, or are so ready to receive without charge a promising student, that the only difficulty in a young man's way is that of supporting himself during his college course; and this he frequently does by earning during one half the year what keeps him during the other half. Often he teaches school; nearly all the eminent men of the last forty years, including several Presidents of the United States, have taught school in some part of their earlier careers. Sometimes he works at a trade, as many a student has done in Scotland; and, as in Scotland, he is all the more respected by his classmates for it. The instruction which he gets in one of these Western colleges may not carry him very far, but it opens a door through which men of real power can pass into the professions, or even into the domain of learning and scientific research. In no country are the higher kinds of teaching more cheap or more accessible. There is a growing tendency for well-to-do parents to send their sons to one of the greater universities, irrespective of the profession they contemplate for him; that is to say, purely for the sake of general culture, or of the social advantages which a university course is thought to confer. The usual age at which students enter one of the leading universities of the East is, as in England, from eighteen to nineteen, and the usual age of graduation twenty-two to twenty-three,* the regular course covering four years. In the West many students come at a more advanced age, twenty-four or twenty-five, their early education having been neglected; so the average in Western colleges is higher than in the East. In Scotland boys of fourteen and men of twenty-four used to sit side by side in university class-rooms and compete on equal terms. The places of less note draw students from their immediate vicinity only; to those of importance boys are sent from all parts of the Union. The University of Michigan has been a sort of metropolitan university for the Northwestern States. Harvard and Yale, which used to draw only from the Atlantic States, now receive students from the West, and even from the shores of the Pacific. A student generally completes his four years' graduation course at the same institution; but there are some who leave a small college after one year to enter at a larger one. A man who has graduated in a college which has only an Arts or collegiate department will often, in case he designs himself for law or medicine, resort to the law or medical school of a larger university, or even, if he means to devote himself to science or philology, will pursue what is called a " post-graduate course " at some one of the greatest seats of learning. Thus it may happen, as in

---

* President Eliot gives it for Harvard at 22 years and 7 months.

Germany, that a man has studied at three or four universities in succession.

Buildings and External Aspect. — Few of the buildings in any college or university are more than a century old,* and among these there is none of an imposing character, or with marked architectural merit. Many of the newer ones are handsome and well arranged, but I have heard it remarked that too much money is now being spent, at least in the West, upon showy buildings, — possibly with the view of commanding attention. The ground plan is rarely or never that of a quadrangle, as in England and Scotland, not because it was desired to avoid monastic precedents, but because detached buildings are thought to be better adapted to the cold and snows of winter. At Harvard and Yale the brick dormitories (buildings in which the students live) and class-rooms are scattered over a large space of grass, planted with ancient elms, and have a very pleasing effect. But none of the universities frequented by men, unless it be the University of Wisconsin, has such an ample and agreeable pleasure-ground surrounding it as those possessed by the two oldest women's colleges, Vassar and Wellesley.

Time spent in Study. — Vacations are shorter than in England or Scotland. That of summer usually lasts from the middle of June to the middle of September, and there are generally ten days or more given at Christmas, and at least a week in April. Work begins earlier in the morning than in England, but seldom so early as in Germany. Very few students seem to work as hard as the men reading for high honors do at Cambridge in England.

Local Distribution of Universities and Colleges. — The number of degree-granting bodies seems to be larger in the Middle and Northwestern States than either in New England or in the South. In the tables of the Bureau of Education, I find

---

* I remember one in Yale of A. D. 1753, called South Middle, which was venerated as the oldest building there.

New York, Pennsylvania, Ohio, Illinois, Iowa, credited with 124, — more than one third of the total for the United States; but as many are small and indifferent, the mere number does not necessarily speak of an ample and solid provision of education. Indeed Ohio and Illinois, with a population of about seven millions, have not a single institution approaching the first rank. The thirteen Southern States (including Missouri, Maryland, and Delaware) stand in the tables as possessing 92; but no one of these, except the University of Virginia, attains the first rank, and the great majority are under-manned, and hampered by the imperfect preparation of the students whom they receive.* In this respect, and as regards education generally, the South, though advancing, is still far behind the other sections of the country. There are several colleges, all or nearly all of them denominational, established for colored people only.

System and Methods of Instruction. — Thirty years ago it would have been comparatively easy to describe these, for nearly all the universities and colleges prescribed a regular four years' curriculum to a student, chiefly consisting of classics and mathematics, with the elements of mental and moral philosophy, and leading up to a B. A. degree. A youth had little or no option what he would study, for everybody was expected to take certain classes in each year, and received his degree upon having satisfactorily performed what was in each class required of him.† The course was not unlike that of the Scottish universities: it began with Latin, Greek, and mathematics, and wound up with logic, mental and moral philosophy, and a tincture of physics. Instruction was mainly, indeed in the small colleges wholly, catechetical. Nowadays the simple uniformity of this traditional

* It is hoped that the recently founded Tulane University in New Orleans will eventually make its way to the front rank. It has an endowment of about $2,000,000 (£400,000).

† The University of Virginia was an exception, having received from the enlightened views of Jefferson an impulse towards greater freedom.

system has vanished in the greater universities of the Eastern
and Middle States, and in most of the State universities of
the West. There are still regular classes, a certain number
of which every student must attend; but he is allowed to
choose for himself between a variety of courses or curricula,
by following any one of which he may obtain a degree. The
freedom of choice is greater in some universities, less in
others: in some, choice is permitted from the first; in some
only after two years. In Harvard this freedom seems to
have reached its maximum. This so-called elective system
has been and is the subject of a warm controversy, which
has raged chiefly round the question whether Greek shall be
a compulsory subject. The change was introduced for the
sake of bringing scientific subjects into the curriculum and
enabling men to specialize in them and in matters like history
and Oriental or Romance philology, and was indeed a necessary concomitant to such a broadening of universities as may
enable them to keep pace with the swift development of new
branches of study and research during the last forty years.
It is defended both on this ground and as being more likely
than the old strictly limited courses to give every student
something which will interest him. It is opposed as tending
to bewilder him, to disperse and scatter his mind over a too
wide range of subjects, perhaps unconnected with one another,
to tempt him with the offer of an unchartered freedom which
he wants the experience to use wisely. Several of the leading
universities — Yale and Princeton, for example — and all or
nearly all the smaller colleges * have clung to the old system
of one or two prescribed degree courses, in which little variation is admitted.† An elective system is indeed possible

* The small colleges are the more unwilling to drop Greek as a compulsory subject because they think that by doing so they would lose the
anchor by which they hold to the higher culture, and confess themselves
to be no longer universities.

† Yale, under the administration of its lately appointed president, has
very recently begun to allow a greater range of choice.

only where the teaching staff is able to do justice to a wide range of subjects.

A parallel change has passed upon the methods of teaching. Lecturing, with few or no questions to the class interposed, is becoming the rule in the larger universities, those especially which adopt the elective system ; while what are called "recitations" — that is to say, catechetical methods resembling those of Scotland or of a college (not university) lecture in Oxford twenty-five years ago — remain the rule in the more conservative majority of institutions, and are practically universal in Western colleges. Some of the Eastern universities have recently established a system of informal instruction by the professor to a small group of students on the model of the German Seminar. Private "coaching," such as prevailed largely in Oxford, and still prevails in Cambridge, is almost unknown.

Requirements for Entrance. — All the better universities and colleges exact a minimum of knowledge from those who matriculate. Some do this by imposing an entrance examination. Others allow certain schools, of whose excellence they are satisfied, to issue leaving certificates, the production of which entitles the bearer to be admitted without examination. This plan is said to work well.* No State seems to have succeeded better than Michigan in establishing a judiciously regulated and systematized relation between the public schools and the State university.†

Degrees and Examinations. — It is only institutions which have been chartered by State authority that are deemed entitled to grant degrees. There are others which do so without

---

* At Harvard I was informed that about one third of the students came from the public (*i. e.* publicly supported) schools. The proportion is in most universities larger. There is a growing tendency in America, especially in the East, for boys of the richer class to be sent to private schools, and the number and excellence of such schools increases.

† See President Angell's Commemorative Address to the University of Michigan, June 30, 1887.

any such legal title; but as the value of a degree *per se* is slight, the mischief done by these interlopers can hardly be serious. B. A., M. A., D. D., and LL. D., the two latter usually for honorary purposes,* are the only degrees conferred in the great majority of colleges; but of late years the larger universities have, in creating new courses, created a variety of new degrees also.† Degrees are awarded by examination, but never, I think, as often in Europe, upon a single examination held after the course of study has been completed. The student as he goes through the various classes which make up his course is examined, sometimes at frequent intervals, sometimes at the end of each year, on the work done in the classes or on prescribed books; and the degree is ultimately awarded or refused on the combined result of all these tests. At no point in his career is he expected to submit to any one examination comparable, for the combined number and difficulty of the subjects in which he is questioned, to the final honor examinations at Oxford or Cambridge, even as now constituted, much less as they stood fifty years ago.

There is, indeed, no respect in which the American system is more contrasted with that of Oxford and Cambridge than the comparatively small part assigned to the award of honors. In England the Class list or Tripos has for many years past, ever since the universities awoke from their lethargy of last century, been the main motive power in stimulating undergraduates to exertion, and in stemming the current which runs

* Honorary degrees are in some institutions, and not usually those of the highest standing, conferred with a profuseness which reveals an exaggerated appreciation of inconspicuous merit.

† Mr. D. C. Gilman (president of Johns Hopkins University) mentions the following among the degree titles awarded in some institutions to women, the titles of Bachelor and Master being deemed inappropriate: Laureate of Science, Proficient in Music, Maid of Philosophy, Mistress of Polite Literature, Mistress of Music (*North American Review* for March, 1885).

so strongly towards amusement and athletic exercises. Examinations have governed teaching instead of being used to test it. In the United States, although most universities and colleges reward with some sort of honorable mention the students who have acquitted themselves conspicuously well, graduation honors are not a great object of ambition; they win little fame within the institution, they are scarcely noticed beyond its walls. In many universities there is not even the stimulus, which acts powerfully in Scotland, of class prizes, awarded by examination or by the votes of the students. It is only a few institutions that possess scholarships awarded by competition. American teachers seem to find the discipline of their regular class system sufficient to maintain a reasonable level of diligence among their students, being doubtless aided by the fact that in all but a very few universities the vast majority of the students come from simple homes, possess scanty means, and have their way in life to make. Diligence is the tradition of the American colleges, especially of those remote from the dissipating influences and social demands of large cities. Even the greater universities have never been, as the English universities avowedly were in last century, and to a great extent are still, primarily places for spending three or four pleasant years, only incidentally places of instruction. With some drawbacks, this feature of the American seminaries has two notable merits. One is that it escapes that separation which has grown up in Oxford and Cambridge between pass or poll men and honor men. Every student supposes himself to have come to college for the purpose of learning something. In all countries, even in Switzerland and Scotland, there is a percentage of idle men in places of study; but the idleness of an American student is due to something in his own character or circumstances, and does not, as in the case of the English " poll-man," rest on a theory in his own mind, probably shared by his parents, that he entered the university in order to enjoy himself and form useful social connections. The other merit is that the love of knowledge and truth is not, among the better minds, vulgarized by being made the slave of competition and of the passion for quick and conspicuous success. An American student is not induced by his university to think less of the intrinsic value of what he is learning than of how far it will pay in an examination; nor does he regard his ablest fellow-students as his rivals over a difficult course for high stakes, — rivals whose speed and strength he must constantly be comparing with his own. Americans who have studied in an English university after graduating in one of their own, have told me that nothing surprised them more in England than the incessant canvassing of one another's intellectual capabilities which went on among the undergraduates.* Probably less work is got out of the better American students than the examination system exacts from the same class of men in Oxford and Cambridge. Possibly the qualities of readiness and accuracy are not so thoroughly trained. Possibly it is a loss not to be compelled to carry for a few weeks a large mass of facts in one's mind, under the obligation of finding any one at a moment's notice. Those who direct the leading American universities recognize in these points the advantages of English practice. But they conceive that the corresponding disadvantages are much greater, and are in this matter more inclined to commiserate Oxford and Cambridge than to imitate them.

Nearly all American students do graduate; that is to say, as those who would be likely to fail drop off before the close of the fourth year, the proportion of plucks in the later examinations is small. As regards the worth of the degrees given, there is, of course, the greatest possible difference between those of the better and those of the lower institutions; nor is this difference merely one between the few great uni-

---

* If this be true of England, the evil is probably no smaller under the class prize system of Scotland.

versities and the mass of small colleges or Western State universities, for among the smaller colleges there are some which maintain as high a standard of thoroughness as the greatest. The degrees of the two hundred colleges to which I have referred as belonging to the lower group of the third class have no assignable value, except that of indicating that a youth has been made to work during four years at subjects above the elementary. Those of institutions belonging to the higher group and the two other classes represent, on an average, as much knowledge and mental discipline as the poll or pass degrees of Cambridge or Oxford, — possibly rather less than the pass degrees of the Scottish universities. Between the highest American degrees and the honor degrees of Oxford and Cambridge it is hard to make any comparison.

A degree is in the United States given only to those who have followed a prescribed course in the teaching institution which confers it. No American institution has so far departed from the old and true conception of a university, approved by both history and policy, as to become a mere examining board, awarding degrees to anybody who may present himself from any quarter. However, the evils of existing arrangements, under which places below the level of German *gymnasia* are permitted to grant academic titles, are deemed so serious by some educational reformers that it has been proposed to create in each State a single degree-conferring authority, to which the various institutions within the State should be, so to speak, tributary, sending up their students to its examinations, which would of course be kept at a higher level than most of the present independent bodies maintain. This is what physicians call a " heroic remedy ; " and with all respect to the high authorities who now advocate it, I hope they will reconsider the problem, and content themselves with methods of reform less likely to cramp the freedom of university teaching.

Notwithstanding these evils, and the vast distance between

the standard of a university like Johns Hopkins at the one end of the scale, and that of the colleges of Arkansas at the other, a degree, wherever obtained, seems to have a certain social value. " It is," said one of my informants, " a thing which you would mention regarding a young man for whom you were writing a letter of introduction." This does not mean very much, but it is better than nothing ; it would appear to give a man some sort of advantage in seeking for educational or literary work. In several States a man who can point to his degree obtains speedier entrance to the Bar, and some denominations endeavor to secure that their clergy shall have graduated.

Post-graduate Courses. — Several of the leading universities have lately instituted sets of lectures for students who have completed the regular four years' collegiate course and taken their B. A. or B. Sc., hoping in this way to provide for the special study of subjects for which room cannot be found in the regular course. Johns Hopkins University has devoted itself especially to this function. Its object was not so much to rival the existing universities as to discharge a function which many of them had not the means of undertaking, — that of providing the highest special instruction, not necessarily in every subject, but in subjects which it could secure the ablest professors to teach. It has already done much admirable work in this direction, and made good its claim to a place in the front rank of transatlantic seats of education. There are also many graduates who, desiring to devote themselves to some particular branch of science or learning, such as experimental physics, philology, or history, spend a semester or two at a German university. Extremely few come to Oxford or Cambridge. American professors, when asked why they send their men exclusively to Germany, considering that in England they would have the advantage of a more interesting social life, and of seeing how England is trying to deal with problems similar in many respects to their own, answer that the English universities make no provision for any students except those who wish to go through one of the regular degree courses, and are so much occupied in preparing men to pass examinations as to give, except in two or three branches, but little advanced teaching. There can be no doubt that if Oxford and Cambridge offered the advantages which Leipzig and Berlin do, the afflux to the two former of American graduates would soon be considerable.

Professional and Scientific Schools. — Besides the very large number of schools for all the practical arts, agriculture, engineering, mining, and so forth, as well as for the professions of theology, law, and medicine, statistics of which have been already given, some universities have established scientific schools, or agricultural schools, or theological, legal, and medical faculties. The theological faculties are usually denominational; but Harvard, which used to be practically Unitarian, has now an unsectarian Faculty, in which there are several learned divines belonging to Trinitarian denominations, and no difficulty seems to have arisen in working this arrangement. The law school is usually treated as a separate department, to which students may resort who have not graduated in the university. The course is usually of two, sometimes of three, years, and covers all the leading branches of common law, equity, crimes, civil and criminal procedure. Many of these schools are extremely efficient.

Research. — No special provision seems to have been made (except by the Johns Hopkins and Harvard fellowships) for the promotion of research as apart from the work of learning and teaching; but there has been some talk as to the desirability of founding fellowships or other endowments for this purpose, and the unceasing munificence of private benefactors may be expected to supply the necessary funds. There is now, especially in the greater universities, a good deal of specialization in teaching, so an increasing number of professors are able to occupy themselves with research.

Aids to Deserving Students. — Extremely few colleges have scholarships or bursaries open to competition, like those of the colleges in Oxford and Cambridge and of the Scottish universities; still fewer have fellowships. But in a large number there exist funds, generally placed at the disposal of the president or the Faculty, which are applicable for the benefit of industrious men who need help; and it is common to remit fees in the case of those whose circumstances warrant the indulgence. When, as occasionally happens, free places or grants out of these funds are awarded upon examination, it would be thought improper for any one to compete whose circumstances placed him above the need of pecuniary aid; when the selection is left to the college authorities, they are said to discharge it with honorable impartiality. Having often asked whether favoritism was complained of, I could never hear that it was. In some colleges there exists a loan fund, out of which money is advanced to the poor student, who afterwards repays it.* The denominations often give assistance to promising youths who intend to enter the ministry. Says one of my most experienced informants: " In our country any young fellow of ability and energy can get education without paying for it." † The experiment tried at Cornell University in the way of providing remunerative labor for poor students who were at the same time to follow a course of instruction, seems to have had a very qualified success, for the double effort is found to impose too severe a strain.

Social Life of the Students. — Those who feel that not only the keenest pleasure, but the most solid moral and intellect-

---

* President Garfield obtained his education at Williams College by the help of such a fund.

† Fees, in the West especially, are low; indeed many Western State universities require none. In the University of Michigan a student belonging to the State pays $10 on admission, and an annual fee of $20 (Literary Department), or $25 (other departments); students from without the State paying $25 (admission), $30 (Literary Department), $35 (other departments).

ual benefit of their university life lay in the friendships which they formed in that happy spring-time, will ask how in this respect America compares with England. Oxford and Cambridge, with their historic colleges maintaining a corporate life from century to century, bringing the teachers into easy and friendly relations with the taught, forming between the members of each society a close and almost family tie which is not incompatible with loyalty to the great corporation for whose sake all the minor corporations exist, have succeeded in producing a more polished, graceful, and I think also intellectually stimulative, type of student life than either Germany, with its somewhat boyish frolics of duelling and compotations, or Scotland, where the youth has few facilities for social intercourse with his classmates, and none with his professor. The American universities occupy an intermediate position between those of England and those of Germany or Scotland. Formerly all or nearly all the students were lodged in buildings called dormitories, — which, however, were not merely sleeping places, but contained sitting-rooms jointly tenanted by two or more students, — and meals were taken in common. This is still the practice in the smaller colleges, and remains firmly rooted in Yale, Harvard, and Princeton. In the new State universities, and in nearly all universities planted in large cities, the great bulk of the students board with private families, or (more rarely) live in lodgings or hotels ; and an increasing number have begun to do so even in places which, like Harvard and Brown University (Rhode Island) and Cornell, have some dormitories. The dormitory plan works well in comparatively small establishments, especially when, as is the case with the smaller denominational colleges, they are almost like large families, and are permeated by a religious spirit. But in the larger universities the tendency is now towards letting the students reside where they please. The maintenance of discipline gives less trouble ; the poorer student is less inclined to imitate or envy the luxurious habits of the rich. The chief breaches of order which the authorities have to deal with arise in dormitories from the practice of " hazing ; " that is, playing practical jokes, especially upon freshmen. In an American college the students are classed by years, those of the first year being called freshmen, of the second year sophomores, of the third year juniors, of the fourth year seniors. The bond between the members of each " class " (that is, the entrants of the same year) is a pretty close one, and they are apt to act together. Between sophomores and freshmen — for the seniors and juniors are supposed to have put away childish things — there is a smouldering jealousy which sometimes breaks out into a strife sufficiently acute, though there is seldom anything more than mischievously high spirits behind it, to give the president and Faculty trouble.* Otherwise the conduct of the students is generally good. Intoxication, gaming, or other vices are rare, those who come to work, as the vast majority do, being little prone to such faults ; one scarcely hears them mentioned as evils to be dealt with except in two or three of the universities situate in or near large cities, and resorted to by the sons of the rich. Of late years the passion for base-ball, foot-ball, rowing, and athletic exercises generally, has become very strong in the universities last mentioned, where fashionable youth congregates, and the student who excels in these seems to be as much a hero among his comrades as a member of the University Eight or Eleven is at Cambridge or Oxford.

The absence of colleges constituting social centres within a university has helped to develop in the American universities one of their most peculiar and interesting institutions, — I mean the Greek-letter societies. These are clubs or fraternities of students, denoted by two or three Greek letters, the

---

* Sophomores and freshmen have a whimsical habit of meeting one another in dense masses and trying which can push the other aside on the stairs or path. This is called " rushing." In some universities the admission of women as students has put an end to it.

initials of the secret fraternity motto.   Some of these fraternities exist in one college only, but the greater are established
in a good many universities and colleges, having in each what
is called a Chapter, and possessing in each a sort of club
house, with several meeting and reading rooms, and sometimes also with bedrooms for the members.   In some colleges
as many as a third or a half of the students belong to a fraternity, which is an institution recognized and patronized by
the authorities.   New members are admitted by the votes of
the Chapter ; and to obtain early admission to one of the
best is no small compliment.   They are, so far as I know,
always non-political, though political questions may be debated and political essays read at their meetings ; and one is
told that they allow no intoxicants to be kept in their buildings or used at the feasts they provide.   They are thus something between an English club and a German *Studenten
Corps*, but with the element of the literary or " mutual improvement " society thrown in.   They are deemed a valuable
part of the university system, not so much because they cultivate intellectual life as on account of their social influence.
It is an object of ambition to be elected a member ; it is a
point of honor for a member to maintain the credit of the
fraternity.   Former members, who are likely to include some
of the university professors, keep up their connection with
the fraternity, and often attend its chapters in the college, or
its general meetings.   Membership constitutes a bond between old members during their whole life, so that a member
on settling in some distant city would probably find there
persons who had belonged to his fraternity, and would be
admitted to their local gatherings.*   Besides these there exist

* There are, of course, other students' societies besides these Greek-
letter ones, and in some universities the Greek-letter societies have become
purely social rather than literary.   One of them is regarded with much
suspicion by the authorities.

In some places (as, for instance, in Rochester) the societies provide apart-
ments for nearly all the students, and thus supply the place of dormitories.

a few honorary societies into which students are elected in virtue of purely literary or scientific acquirements, as evidenced in the college examinations. The oldest and most famous is called the Φ B K, which is said to mean φιλοσοφία βίου κυβερνήτης, and exists in nearly all the leading universities in most of the States.

Religion. — I have already observed that many of the American universities, and probably a majority of the smaller colleges, are denominational. This term, however, does not mean what it would mean in Europe, or at least in England. It means that they have been founded by or in connection with a particular church, and that they remain to some extent associated with it or influenced by it. But except as regards the Roman Catholic institutions, there is seldom any exclusion of teachers, and never of students belonging to other churches, nor any attempt to give the instruction (except, of course, in the theological department, if there be one) a sectarian cast. Although it usually happens that students belonging to the church which influences the college are more numerous than those of any other church, students of other persuasions abound ; nor are efforts made to proselytize them. For instance, Harvard retains a certain flavor of Unitarianism, and has one or two Unitarian clergymen among the professors in its Theological Faculty ; Yale has always been Congregationalist, and has by its charter ten Congregationalist clergymen among its trustees, and it always has a Congregationalist clergyman as its president, as Brown University has a Baptist clergyman. Princeton is still more specifically Presbyterian, and the Episcopalians have several denominational colleges, in which the local bishop is one of the trustees.* But neither Harvard, Yale, Brown, nor Princeton now gives a preference as regards the choice

* Brown University, formerly called Rhode Island College (founded in 1764), is in the rather peculiar position of having by its regulation four denominations, Baptists, Congregationalists, Episcopalians, and Quakers,

of its professors to one denomination over another; all are resorted to alike by students belonging to any church, or to none.

In all the older universities, and in the vast majority of the more recent ones, there is a chapel in which religious services are regularly held, short prayers on the five week-days, and sometimes also a full service twice on Sundays. In most institutions every student, unless of course he has some conscientious objection, is expected to attend. The service seldom or never contains anything of a sectarian character, and arrangements are sometimes made for having it conducted by the clergy of various denominations in turn. Even among the professedly neutral new State universities, there are some which, like the University of Michigan, have daily prayers. There are of course persons who think that an unsectarian place of education cannot be a truly Christian place of education, and Cornell University in its early days had to face attacks directed against it on this score.* But the more prevalent view is that a university ought to be in a general sense religious without being sectarian.†

represented on its two governing bodies, — the trustees and the Fellows, — the Baptists having a majority.

* At Cornell University there exists a Sunday preachership endowed with a fund of $30,000 (£6,000), which is used to recompense the services of distinguished ministers of different denominations who preach in succession during twenty-one Sundays of the academic year. The founder was an Episcopalian, whose first idea was to have a chaplaincy limited to ministers of his denomination; but the trustees refused the endowment on such terms. The only students who absent themselves are Roman Catholics.

† This idea is exactly expressed in the regulations for the most recent great foundation, that of Mr. Leland Stanford in California. It is declared to be the duty of the trustees " to prohibit sectarian instruction, but to have taught in the university the immortality of the soul, the existence of an all-wise and benevolent Creator, and that obedience to his laws is the highest duty of man." The founders further declare, " While it is our desire that there shall be no sectarian teaching in this institution, it is very

The Provision of University Education for Women. — The efforts made and experiments tried in this matter furnish matter for a treatise. All I have space to mention is that these efforts have chiefly flowed in two channels. One is the admission of women to co-education with men in the same places of higher education. This has gone on for many years in some of the denominational colleges of the West, such as Oberlin and Antioch in Ohio. Both sexes have been taught in the same classes, meeting in the hours of recreation, but lodged in separate buildings. My informants all commended the plan, declaring that the effect on the manners and general tone of the students was excellent. The State universities founded of late years in the West are by law open to women as well as to men. The number of women attending is always smaller than that of men, yet in some institutions it is considerable ; as, for instance, at the University of Michigan at Ann Arbor there were, in 1885-86, 135 women and 461 men, while Antioch had 80 women and 114 men. Students live where they will, but are taught in the same classes, — generally, however, sitting on opposite sides of the class-room. The evidence given to me as to the working of this system in the Universities of California and Michigan, as well as in Cornell University, was favorable.

In the Eastern States the tendency has been to establish universities or colleges exclusively for women. There are persons even in the East who would prefer the scheme of co-education ; but the more general view is that the stricter etiquette and what is called the " more complex civilization " of the older States render this undesirable. Among these colleges the best known, and apparently the most complete

far from our thoughts to exclude divine service. We have provided that a suitable building be erected, wherein the professors of the various religious denominations shall from time to time be invited to deliver discourses not sectarian in character."

and efficient,* are Vassar, at Poughkeepsie, New York; Wellesley and Smith in Massachusetts; Bryn Mawr in Pennsylvania. I visited the two former, and was much impressed by the earnestness and zeal for learning by which both the professors and the students seemed to be inspired, as well as by the high level of the teaching given. They have happily escaped the temptation to which some similar institutions in England seem to yield, of making everything turn upon degree examinations. Harvard has established, in what is called its Annex, a sort of separate department for women, in which the university professors lecture. I have no adequate data for comparing the quality of the education given to women in America with that provided by women's colleges, and especially by Girton and Newnham, in England; but there can be no doubt that the eagerness to make full provision for women has been keener in the former country, and that a much larger number avail themselves of what has been provided.†

General Observations. — The European reader will by this time have perceived how hard it is to give such a general estimate of the educational and social worth of the higher teaching in the United States as one might give of the universities of Germany, England, or Scotland. In America the universi-

---

* In 1885-86 Wellesley had 520 students, with 75 professors and teachers (61 women and 14 men), and an income from its endowment of $23,000.

† The tables (for 1887) of the Bureau of Education mention 204 institutions for the superior instruction of women, and state that about two thirds of these are authorized by law to confer degrees. Nearly all of these, indeed all but four or five, are practically schools. The two thirds giving degrees " offer a curriculum closely resembling the ordinary college course; greater option, however, seems to be allowed than in the Arts colleges for men, and as a rule modern languages engage more attention than the classics. On the whole, the experience of these schools seems to indicate that identity of training for the two sexes is not as yet generally demanded in the United States." — *Report,* p. 440.

ties are not, as they are in those countries, a well-defined class
of institutions. Not only is the distance between the best
and the worst greater than that which in Germany separates
Leipzig from Rostock, or in England Cambridge from Dur-
ham, but the gradations from the best down to the worst are
so imperceptible that one can nowhere draw a line and say
that here the true university stops and the pretentious school
begins.* As has been observed already, a large number present the external seeming and organization — the skeleton
plan, so to speak — of a university with the actual performance of a rather raw school.

Moreover, the American universities and colleges are in a
state of transition. True, nearly everything in America is
changing, the apparently inflexible Constitution not excepted.
But the changes that are passing in the universities are only
to be paralleled by those that pass upon Western cities. The
number of small colleges, especially in the Mississippi and
Pacific States, is increasing. The character of the Eastern
universities is being constantly modified. The former multiply, because under the Federal system every State likes to
have its own universities numerous and its inhabitants independent of other States, even as respects education; while
the abundance of wealth, the desire of rich men to commemo-
rate themselves and to benefit their community, and the
rivalry of the churches, lead to the establishment of new
colleges where none are needed, and where money would be
better spent in improving those which exist. Individualism
and *laissez faire* have in this matter at least free scope, for a
State legislature is always ready to charter any number of

* Even in Europe it is curious to note how each country is apt to
think the universities of the other to be rather schools than universities.
The Germans call Oxford and Cambridge schools, because they have
hitherto given comparatively little professional and specialized teaching.
The English call the Scotch universities schools, because many of their
students enter at fifteen.

new degree-giving bodies.* Meanwhile the great institutions of
the Atlantic States continue to expand and develop, not merely
owing to the accretion of wealth to them from the liberality of
benefactors, but because they are in close touch with Europe,
resolved to bring their highest education up to the European
level, and to keep pace with the progress of science, filled with
that love of experiment and spirit of enterprise which are so
much stronger in America than anywhere else in the world.

Not the least interesting of the phenomena of to-day is the
struggle which goes on in the Middle and Western States between the greater, and especially the State, universities and
the small denominational colleges. The latter, which used to
have the field to themselves, are now afraid of being driven
off it by the growth of the former, and are redoubling their
exertions, not only to increase their own resources and students, but — at least in some States — to prevent the State
university from obtaining larger grants from the State treasury. They allege that the unsectarian character of the State
establishments, as well as the freedom allowed to their students, makes them less capable of giving a moral and religious training. But as the graduates of the State universities
become numerous in the legislatures and influential generally,
and as it is more and more clearly seen that the small colleges cannot, for want of funds, provide the various appliances
— libraries, museums, laboratories, and so forth — which universities need, the balance seems likely to incline in favor of
the State universities. It is probable that while these will
rise towards the level of their Eastern sisters, many of the
denominational colleges will subside into the position of places
of preparatory training.

* The New York legislature recently offered a charter to the Chautauqua
Assembly, — one of the most interesting institutions in America, standing
midway between a university and a religious assembly, and representing
both the religious spirit and the love of knowledge which characterize the
better part of the native American population. Some of its features recall
those of the European universities in the earlier part of the Middle Ages.

One praise which has often been given to the universities of Scotland may be given to those of America. While the German universities have been popular but not free, while the English universities have been free * but not popular, the American universities have been both free and popular. Although some have been managed on too narrow a basis, the number has been so great that the community have not suffered. They have been established so easily, they have so fully reflected the habits and conditions of the people, as to have been accessible to every stratum of the population. They show all the merits and all the faults of a development absolutely uncontrolled by government, and little controlled even by the law which binds endowments down to the purposes fixed by a founder,† because new foundations were constantly rising, and new endowments were accruing to the existing foundations. Accordingly, while a European observer is struck by their inequalities and by the crudeness of many among them, he is also struck by the life, the spirit, the sense of progress, which pervade them. In America itself educational reformers are apt to deplore the absence of control. They complain of the multiplication of degree-giving bodies, and consequent lowering of the worth of a degree. They point to the dissipation over more than thirty colleges, as in Ohio, of the funds and teaching power which might have produced one first-rate university. One strong institution in a State does more, they argue, to raise the standard of teaching and learning, and to civilize the region which it serves, than can be done by twenty weak ones.

* Free as regards self-government in matters of education, for they were tightly bound by theological restrictions till A. D 1871.

† The law of most American States has not yet recognized the necessity of providing proper methods for setting aside the dispositions made by founders when circumstances change or their regulations prove unsuitable. Endowments, if they continue to increase at their present rate, will become a very doubtful blessing unless this question is boldly dealt with.

The European observer, while he admits this, conceives that his American friends may not duly realize the services which these small colleges perform in the rural districts of the country. They get hold of a multitude of poor men, who might never resort to a distant place of education. They set learning in a visible form — plain, indeed, and humble, but dignified even in her humility — before the eyes of a rustic people, in whom the love of knowledge, naturally strong, might never break from the bud into the flower but for the care of some zealous gardener. They give the chance of rising in some intellectual walk of life to many a strong and earnest nature who might otherwise have remained an artisan or storekeeper, and perhaps failed in those avocations. They light up in many a country town what is at first only a farthing rushlight, but which, when the town swells to a city, or when endowments flow in, or when some able teacher is placed in charge, becomes a lamp of growing flame, which may finally throw its rays over the whole State in which it stands. In some of these smaller Western colleges one finds to-day men of great ability and great attainments, one finds students who are receiving an education quite as thorough, though not always as wide, as the best Eastern universities can give. I do not at all deny that the time for more concentration has come, and that restrictions on the power of granting degrees would be useful. But one who recalls the history of the West during the last fifty years, and bears in mind the tremendous rush of ability and energy towards a purely material development which has marked its people, will feel that this uncontrolled freedom of teaching, this multiplication of small institutions, have done for the country a work which a few State-regulated universities might have failed to do. The higher learning is in no danger. The great universities of the East, as well as one or two in the West, are already beginning to rival the ancient universities of Europe. They will soon have far greater

funds at their command with which to move towards the same
ideal as Germany sets before herself ; and they have already
what is better than funds, — an ardor and industry among the
teachers which equals that displayed fifty years ago in Germany by the foremost men of the generation which raised the
German schools to their glorious pre-eminence.

It may be thought that an observer familiar with two universities which are among the oldest and most famous in
Europe, and are beyond question the most externally sumptuous and beautiful, would be inclined to disparage the corresponding institutions of the United States, whose traditions
are comparatively short, and in whose outward aspect there
is little to attract the eye or touch the imagination. I have
not found it so. An Englishman who visits America can
never feel sure how far his judgment has been affected by the
warmth of the welcome he receives. But if I may venture to
state the impression which the American universities have
made upon me, I will say that while of all the institutions of
the country they are those of which the Americans speak
most modestly, they are those which seem to be at this moment making the swiftest progress, and to have the brightest
promise for the future. They are supplying exactly those
things which European critics have hitherto found lacking to
America ; and they are contributing to her political as well as
to her contemplative life elements of inestimable worth.

CHAPTER VI.

THE CHURCHES AND THE CLERGY.

IN examining the National Government and the State Governments, we have never once had occasion to advert to any ecclesiastical body or question, because with such matters government has in the United States absolutely nothing to do. Of all the differences between the Old World and the New, this is perhaps the most salient. Half the wars of Europe, half the internal troubles that have vexed European states, from the Monophysite controversies in the Roman Empire of the fifth century down to the Kulturkampf in the German Empire of the nineteenth, have arisen from theological differences, or from the rival claims of church and state. This whole vast chapter of debate and strife has remained unopened in the United States. There is no established church. All religious bodies are absolutely equal before the law, and unrecognized by the law, except as voluntary associations of private citizens.

The Federal Constitution contains the following prohibitions : —

" Art. VI. No religious test shall ever be required as a qualification to any office or public trust under the United States.

"Amendment I. Congress shall make no law respecting an establishment of religion or prohibiting the free exercise thereof."

No attempt has ever been made to alter or infringe upon these provisions. They affect the National Government only, placing no inhibition on the States, and leaving the whole subject to their uncontrolled discretion, though subject to the general guarantees against oppression.

Every State constitution contains provisions generally similar to the above. Most declare that every man may worship God according to his own conscience, or that the free enjoyment of all religious sentiments and forms of worship shall be held sacred ; * most also provide that no man shall be compelled to support or attend any church ; some forbid the creation of an established church, and many the showing of a preference to any particular sect ; while many provide that no money shall ever be drawn from the State treasury, or from the funds of any municipal body, to be applied for the benefit of any church or sectarian institution or denominational school. Twenty-seven constitutions forbid any religious test to be required as a qualification for office ; some declare that this principle extends to all civil rights ; some specify that religious belief is not to affect a man's competence as a witness. But in several States there still exist qualifications worth noting. Vermont and Delaware declare that every sect ought to maintain some form of religious worship, and Vermont adds that it ought to observe the Lord's Day. Six Southern States exclude from office any one who denies the existence of a Supreme Being. Besides these six, Pennsylvania and Tennessee pronounce a man ineligible for office who does not believe in God and in a future state of rewards and punishments. Maryland and Arkansas even make such a person incompetent as a juror or witness.† Religious free-

---

* Four States provide that this declaration is not to be taken to excuse breaches of the public peace ; many that it shall not excuse acts of licentiousness, or justify practices inconsistent with the peace and safety of the State ; and three, that no person shall disturb others in their religious worship.

† Full details on these points will be found in Mr. Stimson's valuable collection entitled " American Statute Law."

dom has been generally thought of in America in the form
of freedom and equality as between different sorts of Christians, or at any rate different sorts of theists ; persons opposed to religion altogether have till recently been extremely
few everywhere, and practically unknown in the South.
The neutrality of the state is therefore not theoretically
complete.*

In earlier days the States were very far from being neutral.
Those of New England, except Rhode Island, began with a
sort of Puritan theocracy, and excluded from some civil rights
persons who stood outside the religious community.   Con-
gregationalism was the ruling faith, and Roman Catholics,
Quakers, and Baptists were treated with great severity.   The
early constitutions of several States recognized what was virtually a State church, requiring each locality to provide for
and support the public worship of God.   It was not till 1818
that Connecticut in adopting her new constitution placed all
religious bodies on a level, and left the maintenance of
churches to the voluntary action of the faithful.   In Massachusetts a tax for the support of the Congregationalist
churches was imposed on all citizens not belonging to some
other incorporated religious body until 1811, and religious
equality was first fully recognized by a constitutional amendment of 1833.   In Virginia, North and South Carolina, and
Maryland, Protestant Episcopacy was the established form
of religion till the Revolution, when under the impulse of the
democratic spirit, and all the more heartily because the Anglican clergy were prone to Toryism (as attachment to the
British connection was called), and because, at least in Virginia, there had been some persecution of Nonconformists, all
religious distinctions were abolished, and special ecclesiastical
privileges withdrawn.   In Pennsylvania no church was ever

* Nevada has recently disfranchised all Mormons resident within
her bounds; but Mormonism is attacked not so much as a religion as in
respect of its social features and hierarchical character.

legally established. In New York, however, first the Dutch Reformed, and afterwards the Anglican Church, had in colonial days enjoyed a measure of state favor. What is remarkable is that in all these cases the disestablishment, if one may call it by that name, of the privileged church was accomplished with no great effort, and left very little rancor behind. In the South it seemed a natural outcome of the Revolution. In New England it came more gradually, as the necessary result of the political development of each commonwealth. The ecclesiastical arrangements of the States were not inwoven with the pecuniary interests of any wealthy or socially dominant class; and it was felt that equality and democratic doctrine generally were too palpably opposed to the maintenance of any privileges in religious matters to be defensible in argument. However, both in Connecticut and Massachusetts there was a political struggle over the process of disestablishment, and the Congregationalist ministers predicted evils from a change which they afterwards admitted to have turned out a blessing to their own churches. No voice has ever since been raised in favor of reverting — I will not say to a state establishment of religion — but even to any state endowment, or state regulation of ecclesiastical bodies. It is accepted as an axiom by all Americans that the civil power ought to be not only neutral and impartial as between different forms of faith, but ought to leave these matters entirely on one side, regarding them no more than it regards the artistic or literary pursuits of the citizens.* There seem to be no two opinions on this subject in the United States. Even the Protestant Episcopalian clergy, who are in many ways disposed to admire and envy their brethren in England, — even the Roman Catholic

* There is, however, and has for some time been, a movement, led I think by some Baptist and Methodist ministers, for obtaining the insertion of the name of God in the Federal Constitution. Those who desire this appear to hold that the instrument would be thereby in a manner sanctified, and a distinct national recognition of theism expressed.

bishops, whose creed justifies the enforcement of the true faith by the secular arm, — assure the European visitor that if state establishment were offered them they would decline it, preferring the freedom they enjoy to any advantages the state could confer. Every religious community can now organize itself in whatever way it pleases, lay down its own rules of faith and discipline, create and administer its own system of judicature, raise and apply its funds at its uncontrolled discretion. A church established by the state would not be able to do all these things, because it would also be controlled by the state, and it would be exposed to the envy and jealousy of other sects.

The only controversies that have arisen regarding State action in religious matters have turned upon the appropriation of public funds to charitable institutions managed by some particular denomination. Such appropriations are expressly prohibited in the constitutions of some States. But it may happen that the readiest way of promoting some benevolent public purpose is to make a grant of money to an institution already at work, and successfully serving that purpose. As this reason may sometimes be truly given, so it is also sometimes advanced where the real motive is to purchase the political support of the denomination to which the institution belongs, or at least of its clergy. In some States, and particularly in New York, State or city legislatures are often charged with giving money to Roman Catholic institutions for the sake of securing the Catholic vote.* In these cases, however, the money always purports to be voted, not for a religious, but for a philanthropic or educational purpose. No ecclesiastical body would be strong enough to obtain any grant to its general funds, or any special immunity for its ministers. The passion for equality in religious as

* In 1870 the Roman Catholic schools and charities of New York received more than $400,000 (£80,000); about $72,000 were then also given to other denominational institutions.

well as secular matters is everywhere in America far too strong to be braved, and nothing excites more general disapprobation than any attempt by an ecclesiastical organization to interfere in politics. The hostility to Mormonism is due not merely to the practice of polygamy, but also to the notion that the hierarchy of the Latter Day Saints constitutes a secret and tyrannical *imperium in imperio* opposed to the genius of democratic institutions.

The refusal of the civil power to protect or endow any form of religion is commonly represented in Europe as equivalent to a declaration of contemptuous indifference on the part of the state to the spiritual interests of its people. A state recognizing no church is called a godless state; the disestablishment of a church is described as an act of national impiety. Nothing can be farther from the American view, to an explanation of which it may be well to devote a few lines.

The abstention of the state from interference in matters of faith and worship may be advocated on two principles, which may be called the political and the religious. The former sets out from the principles of liberty and equality. It holds any attempt at compulsion by the civil power to be an infringement on liberty of thought, as well as on liberty of action, which could be justified only when a practice claiming to be religious is so obviously anti-social or immoral as to threaten the well-being of the community. Religious persecution, even in its milder forms, such as disqualifying the members of a particular sect for public office, is, it conceives, inconsistent with the conception of individual freedom, and the respect due to the primordial rights of the citizen, which modern thought has embraced. Even if state action stops short of the imposition of disabilities, and confines itself to favoring a particular church, whether by grants of money or by giving special immunities to its clergy, this is an infringement on equality, putting one man at a disadvantage com-

pared with others in respect of matters which are not fit
subjects for State cognizance.*

The second principle, embodying the more purely religious
view of the question, starts from the conception of the church
as a spiritual body existing for spiritual purposes, and moving along spiritual paths.   It is an assemblage of men who
are united by their devotion to an unseen Being, their memory
of a past divine life, their belief in the possibility of imitat-
ing that life so far as human frailty allows, their hopes for
an illimitable future.   Compulsion of any kind is contrary
to the nature of such a body, which lives by love and reverence, not by law.   It desires no State help, feeling that its
strength comes from above, and that its kingdom is not of
this world.   It does not seek for exclusive privileges, con-
ceiving that these would not only create bitterness between
itself and other religious bodies, but might attract persons
who did not really share its sentiments, while corrupting the
simplicity of those who are already its members.   Least of
all can it submit to be controlled by the state, for the state,
in such a world as the present, means persons, many or most
of whom are alien to its beliefs and cold to its emotions.
The conclusion follows that the church as a spiritual entity
will be happiest and strongest when it is left absolutely to
itself, not patronized by the civil power, not restrained by
law except when and in so far as it may attempt to quit its
proper sphere and intermeddle in secular affairs.

Of these two views it is the former much more than the
latter that has moved the American mind.   The latter would
doubtless be now generally accepted by religious people.
But when the question arose in a practical shape in the earlier
days of the Republic, arguments of the former, or political,

---

* The question of course follows : What are the matters fit for state
cognizance ?   But into this I do not enter, as I am not attempting to argue
these intricate questions, but merely to indicate the general aspect they
take in current discussion.

order were found amply sufficient to settle it, and no practical purpose has since then compelled men either to examine the spiritual basis of the church, or to inquire by the light of history how far state action has during fifteen centuries helped or marred her usefulness. There has, however, been another cause at work, — I mean the comparatively limited conception of the state itself which Americans have formed. The State is not to them, as to Germans or Frenchmen, and even to some English thinkers, an ideal moral power, charged with the duty of forming the characters and guiding the lives of its subjects. It is more like a commercial company, or perhaps a huge municipality created for the management of certain business in which all who reside within its bounds are interested, levying contributions and expending them on this business of common interest, but for the most part leaving the shareholders or burgesses to themselves. That an organization of this kind should trouble itself, otherwise than as matter of police, with the opinions or conduct of its members, would be as unnatural as for a railway company to inquire how many of the shareholders were total abstainers. Accordingly, it never occurs to the average American that there is any reason why state churches should exist, and he stands amazed at the warmth of European feeling on the matter.

Just because these questions have been long since disposed of, and excite no present passion, and perhaps also because the Americans are more practically easy-going than pedantically exact, the National Government and the State Governments do give to Christianity a species of recognition inconsistent with the view that civil government should be absolutely neutral in religious matters. Each House of Congress has a chaplain, and opens its proceedings each day with prayers. The President annually, after the end of harvest, issues a proclamation ordering a general thanksgiving, and occasionally appoints a day of fasting and humil-

iation. So prayers are offered in the State legislatures,*
and State governors issue proclamations for days of religious
observance. Congress in the crisis of the Civil War (July,
1863) requested the President to appoint a day for humilia-
tion and prayer. In the army and navy provision is made
for religious services, conducted by chaplains of various denominations, and no difficulty seems to have been found in
reconciling their respective claims. In most States there
exist laws punishing blasphemy or profane swearing by the
name of God (laws which, however, are in some places openly
transgressed, and in few or none enforced), laws restricting
or forbidding trade or labor on the Sabbath, as well as laws
protecting assemblages for religious purposes, such as camp-
meetings or religious processions, from being disturbed. The
Bible is read in the public State-supported schools, and
though controversies have arisen on this head, the practice is
evidently in accord with the general sentiment of the people.

The whole matter may, I think, be summed up by saying
that Christianity is in fact understood to be, though not the
legally established religion, yet the national religion.† So
far from thinking their commonwealth godless, the Americans
conceive that the religious character of a government consists
in nothing but the religious belief of the individual citizens,
and the conformity of their conduct to that belief. They
deem the general acceptance of Christianity to be one of the
main sources of their national prosperity, and their nation
a special object of the divine favor.

The legal position of a Christian church is in the United
States simply that of a voluntary association, or group of

* Though Michigan and Oregon forbid any appropriation of State
funds for religious services.

† It has often been said that Christianity is a part of the common law
of the States, as it has been said to be of the common law of England;
but on this point there have been discrepant judicial opinions, nor can it
be said to find any specific practical application. A discussion of it may
be found in Justice Story's opinion in the famous Girard will case

associations, corporate or unincorporate, under the ordinary law. There is no such thing as a special ecclesiastical law; all questions, not only of property, but of church discipline and jurisdiction, are, if brought before the courts of the land, dealt with as questions of contract; * and the court, where it is obliged to examine a question of theology, — as, for instance, whether a clergyman has advanced opinions inconsistent with any creed or formula to which he has bound himself; for it will prefer, if possible, to leave such matters to the proper ecclesiastical authority, — will treat the point as one of pure legal interpretation, neither assuming to itself theological knowledge, nor suffering considerations of policy to intervene.†

As a rule, every religious body can organize itself in any way it pleases. The State does not require its leave to be asked, but permits any form of church government, any ecclesiastical order, to be created and endowed, any method to be adopted of vesting church property, either simply in trustees, or in corporate bodies formed either under the general law of the State or under some special statute. Sometimes a limit is imposed on the amount of property or of real estate which an ecclesiastical corporation can hold; but, on the whole, it may be said that the civil power manifests no jealousy of the spiritual, but allows the latter a perfectly free field for expansion. Of course if any ecclesiastical authority were to become formidable either by its wealth or by its control over the members of its body, this easy tolerance would disappear; all I observe is that the difficulties often experienced, and still more often feared, in Europe from the growth of organizations exercising tremendous spiritual powers, have in America never proved serious. Religious

* Or otherwise, as questions of private civil law. Actions for damages are sometimes brought against ecclesiastical authorities by persons deeming themselves to have been improperly accused or disciplined or deprived of the enjoyment of property.

† The Emperor Aurelian decided in a like neutral spirit a question that had arisen between two Christian churches.

bodies are in so far the objects of special favor that their property is in most States exempt from taxation; * and this is reconciled to theory by the argument that they are serviceable as moral agencies, and diminish the expenses incurred in respect of police administration.   Two or three States impose restrictions on the creation of religious corporations, and one, Maryland, requires the sanction of the legislature to dispositions of property to religious uses.   But speaking generally, religious bodies are the objects of legislative favor.†

I pass on to say a few words as to the religious bodies of the country.‡   Their respective numbers are uncertain, for the attempt made to take a religious census in 1880 failed. According to the figures given by the denominations themselves in 1887, the statistics of the chief among them are as follows : —

	Ministers.	Members.
Methodists —		
Episcopal	14,075	1,990,377
Episcopal of the South . . .	4,434	1,056,058
Other Methodist bodies . . .	——	1,480,000
Baptists	19,377	2,732,570
Minor Baptist bodies	5,872	854,000
Presbyterians	5,654	696,827
Southern Presbyterian Church	1,116	150,398
Other Presbyterian bodies .	2,486	270,000
Lutherans	4,215	987,600
Congregationalists	4,090	436,379
Protestant Episcopalians . . .	3,919	432,323

* In his message of 1881 the Governor of Washington Territory recommends the legislature to exempt church property from taxation, not only on the ground that "churches and school-houses are the temples of education, and alike conduce to the cultivation of peace, happiness, and prosperity," but also because "churches enhance the value of contiguous property, which, were they abolished, would be of less value, and return less revenue."

† New Hampshire has lately taxed churches on the value of their real estate exceeding $10,000 (£2,000).

‡ An interesting and impartial summary view of the history of the chief denominations in the United States may be found in Dr. George P. Fisher's "History of the Christian Church," pp. 559–582.

No data seem to exist for forming an estimate of the number of the Roman Catholics, but it is no doubt very large, especially in the great cities, where so many of the European immigrants are to be found ; they state it themselves at upwards of six millions. Of the above-mentioned denominations, the Methodists and Baptists are numerous everywhere, but the Methodists especially numerous in the South, where they have been the chief evangelizers of the negroes. The Congregationalists are chiefly to be found in New England and such parts of the Western States as have been peopled from New England. The Presbyterians are strongest in the Middle States, New York, New Jersey, Pennsylvania, and in the South,* but are well represented over the West also. The Unitarians are very few outside New England and the regions settled from New England, but have exercised an influence far beyond that of their numbers, owing to the eminence of some of their divines, such as Channing, Emerson, and Theodore Parker, and to the fact that they include a large number of highly-cultivated men.† The Roman Catholics are, except in Maryland and Louisiana, nearly all either of Irish, or German, or French-Canadian extraction. Of late years many Southern negroes are said to have been brought within the Roman fold.

It need hardly be said that there exist no such social distinctions between different denominations as those of England. No clergyman, no layman, either looks down upon or looks up to any other clergyman or layman in respect of his worshipping God in another way. The Roman Catholic Church of course stands aloof from the Protestant Christians,

---

* The strength of Presbyterianism in the South is probably due in part to the immigration into those States of Ulstermen in the middle of last century, and of settlers from Holland at a still earlier date.

† The Unitarian ministers are returned at 459.

whom she considers schismatic; and although what is popularly called the doctrine of apostolic succession is less generally deemed vital by Protestant Episcopalians in America than it has come to be by them of late years in England, the clergy of that church do not admit to their pulpits pastors of other churches, though they sometimes appear in the pulpits of those churches. Such exchanges of pulpit are common among Presbyterians, Congregationalists, and other orthodox Protestant bodies. In many parts of the North and West the Protestant Episcopal Church has long been slightly more fashionable than its sister churches, and people who have no particular " religious preferences," but wish to stand well socially, will sometimes add themselves to it.* In the South, however, Presbyterianism (and in some places Methodism) is equally well regarded from a worldly point of view; while everywhere the strength of Methodists and Baptists and Roman Catholics resides in the masses of the people.†

Of late years proposals for union between some of the leading Protestant churches, and especially between the Presbyterians and Congregationalists and Lutherans, have been freely canvassed. They witness to a growing good feeling among the clergy, and a growing indifference to minor points of doctrine and church government. The vested interests of the existing clergy create some difficulties serious

* The proposal, which has been more than once made in the annual convention of the Protestant Episcopal Church, that it should call itself " The National Church of America," has been always rejected by the good sense of the majority, who perceive that an assumption of this kind would provoke much displeasure from other bodies of Christians.

† The Methodists and Baptists are said to make more use of social means in the work of evangelizing the masses, and to adapt themselves more perfectly to democratic ideas, than do the other Protestant bodies.

in small towns and country districts ; but it seems possible
that before many years more than one such union will be
carried through.

The social standing of the clergy of each denomination
corresponds pretty closely to the character of the denomination itself. As in Great Britain, comparatively few are the
sons of the wealthy, and few come from the working-classes.
The position of a minister of the Gospel always carries with it
some dignity ; that is to say, it gives a man a certain advantage in the society, whatever it may be, to which he naturally
belongs in respect of his family connections, his means, and
his education. In the great cities the leading ministers of the
chief denominations, including the Roman Catholic and Protestant Episcopal bishops, whether they be eminent as preachers
or as active philanthropists, or in respect of their learning,
are among the first citizens, and exercise an influence often
wider and more powerful than that of any layman. In cities
of the second order, the clergymen of these denominations,
supposing them (as is usually the case) to be men of good
breeding and personally acceptable, move in the best society
of the place. Similarly in country places the pastor is better
educated and more enlightened than the average members of
his flock, and becomes a leader in works of beneficence. The
level of education and learning is rising among the clergy
with the steady improvement of the universities. This advance is perhaps most marked among those denominations
which, like the Methodists and Baptists, have heretofore
lagged behind, because their adherents were mostly among
the poor. So far as I could learn, the incomes of the clergy
are also increasing. Some few in the great cities receive
$10,000 (£2000), or even more ; while in smaller cities the
average from all sources, including fees and gifts, among
Presbyterians, Congregationalists, Episcopalians, and Unitarians, is stated to be about $3000 (£600), and in rural dis-

tricts seldom to fall below $1000 (£200).* These figures, which, however, may be a little too high for some parts of the country, compare favorably with the incomes received by the clergy in England or Scotland, and are of course much above the salaries paid to priests in France or to Protestant pastors in Germany. Reckoning in the clergy of all denominations in Great Britain and in the United States, I think that, so far as it is possible to strike an average, both the pecuniary and the social position of the American clergy must be pronounced slightly better than that of the British.

Although the influence of the clergy is still great, it has changed its nature, yielding to the universal current which makes for equality. At the beginning of the century the New England ministers enjoyed a local authority not unlike that of the bishops in Western Europe in the sixth century, or of the Presbyterian ministers of Scotland in the seventeenth. They were, especially in country places, the leaders as well as instructors of their congregations, and were a power in politics scarcely less than in spiritual affairs.† That order of things has quite passed away. His profession and his education still secure respect for a clergyman, ‡ but he must not now interfere in politics ; he must not speak on any secular subject *ex cathedra;* his influence, whatever it may be, is no

---

* The incomes of Baptist and Methodist pastors are smaller, except in a few cities, because the congregations are poorer.

† In some States clergymen are still declared ineligible, by the constitution, as members of a State legislature. They do not seem to have in the early days sat in these bodies, and they very rarely sit in Congress ; but one finds them in conventions. Some of the best speeches in the Massachusetts Convention of 1788, which ratified the Federal Constitution, were made by ministers. In New England they were all, or nearly all, advocates of the Constitution, and passed into the Federalist party.

‡ The clergy are the objects of a good deal of favor in various small ways, — for instance, they often receive free passes on railroads ; and the recent Interstate Commerce Act of 1887, while endeavoring to check the system of granting free passes, which had been much abused, specially exempted clergymen from the prohibition it imposed.

longer official, but can only be that of a citizen distinguished
by his talents or character, whose office gives him no greater
advantage than that of an eminence where shining gifts may
be more widely visible.   Now and then this rule of abstention
from politics is broken through.   Mr. Henry Ward Beecher
took the field as a Mugwump in the presidential campaign of
1884, and was deemed the more courageous in doing so because the congregation of Plymouth Church were mostly
" straight-out " Republicans.   A powerful demonstration of
clergymen was organized in the same year on behalf of Mr.
Blaine.   The Roman Catholic bishops are sometimes accused
of lending secret aid to the political party which will procure
subventions for their schools and charities, and do no doubt,
as indeed their doctrines require, press warmly the claims of
denominational education.   But otherwise they also abstain
from politics.   Such action as is constantly taken in England
by ministers of the Established Church on the one side of
politics, by Nonconformist ministers on the other, would in
America excite disapproval.   It is only on platforms or in
conventions where some moral cause is to be advocated, such
as Abolitionism was thirty years ago or temperance is now,
that clergymen can with impunity appear.

Considering that the absence of State interference in matters of religion is one of the most striking differences between
all the European countries on the one hand, and the United
States on the other, the European reader may naturally expect some further remarks on the practical results of this
divergence.   "There are," he will say, "two evil consequences with which the European defenders of established
churches seek to terrify us when disestablishment and dis-
endowment are mentioned, — one, that the authority and influence of religion will wane if state recognition is withdrawn ;
the other, that the incomes of the clergy and their social status
will sink, that they will in fact become plebeians, and that the
centres of light which now exist in every country parish will

be extinguished.   There are also two benefits which the advocates of the ' free church in a free state' promise us, — one, that social jealousies and bitternesses between different sects will melt away; and the other, that the church will herself become more spiritual in her temper and ideas, more earnest in her proper work of moral reform and the nurture of the soul.   What has American experience to say on these four points?"

These are questions so pertinent to a right conception of the ecclesiastical side of American life that I cannot decline the duty of trying to answer them, though reluctant to tread on ground to which European conflicts give a controversial character.

1. To estimate the influence and authority of religion is not easy.   Suppose, however, that we take either the habit of attending church or the sale of religious books as evidences of its influence among the multitude ; suppose that as regards the more cultivated classes we look at the amount of respect paid to Christian precepts and ministers, the interest taken in theological questions, the connection of philanthropic reforms with religion.   Adding these various data together, we may get some sort of notion of the influence of religion on the American people as a whole.

Purposing to touch on these points in the chapter next following, I will here only say, by way of anticipation, that in all these respects the influence of Christianity seems to be, if we look not merely to the numbers, but also to the intelligence of the persons influenced, greater and more widespread in the United States than in any part of Western Continental Europe, and I think greater than in England.   In France, Italy, Spain, and the Catholic parts of Germany, as well as in German Austria, the authority of religion over the masses is of course great.   Its influence on the best educated classes — one must include all parts of society in order to form a fair judgment — is apparently smaller in France and Italy than in Great Britain, and I think distinctly smaller than in the United States. The country which most resembles America in this respect is Scotland, where the mass of the people enjoy large rights in the management of their church affairs, and where the interest of all classes has, ever since the Reformation, tended to run in ecclesiastical channels. So far from suffering from the want of state support, religion seems in the United States to stand all the firmer, because, standing alone, she is seen to stand by her own strength. No political party, no class in the community, has any hostility either to Christianity or to any particular Christian body. The churches are as thoroughly popular, in the best sense of the word, as any of the other institutions of the country.

2. The social and economic position of the clergy in the United States is above that of the priesthood, taken as a whole, in Roman Catholic countries, and of all denominations, Anglican and Nonconformist, in England. No American pastors enjoy such revenues as the prelates of England and Hungary; but the average income attached to the pastoral office is in America larger. The peculiar conditions of England, where one church looks down socially on the others, make a comparison in other respects difficult. The education of the American ministers, their manners, their capacity for spreading light among the people, seem superior to those of the seminarist priesthood of France and Italy (who are of course far more of a distinct caste), and equal to those of the Protestant pastors of Germany and Scotland.

3. Social jealousies connected with religion scarcely exist in America, and one notes a kindlier feeling between all denominations, Roman Catholics included, a greater readiness to work together for common charitable aims, than between Catholics and Protestants in France or Germany, or between Anglicans and Nonconformists in England. There is a rivalry between the leading denominations to extend

their bounds, to erect and fill new churches, to raise great sums for church purposes. But it is a friendly rivalry, which does not provoke bad blood, because the state stands neutral, and all churches have a free field. There is much less mutual exclusiveness than in any other country, except perhaps Scotland. An instance may be found in the habit of exchanging pulpits, another in the comparative frequency with which persons pass from one denomination to another, if a particular clergyman attracts them, or if they settle in a place distant from a church of their own body. One often finds members of the same family belonging to different denominations. Some of the leading bodies, and especially the Presbyterians and Congregationalists, between whose doctrines there exists practically no difference, have been wont, especially in the West, to co-operate for the sake of efficiency and economy in agreeing not to plant two rival churches in a place where one will suffice, but to arrange that one denomination shall set up its church, and the other advise its adherents to join and support that church.

4. To give an opinion on the three foregoing questions is incomparably easier than to say whether and how much Christianity has gained in spiritual purity and dignity by her severance from the secular power.

There is a spiritual gain in that diminution of envy, malice, and uncharitableness between the clergy of various sects which has resulted from their being all on the same legal level; and the absence both of these faults and of the habit of bringing ecclesiastical questions into secular politics, gives the enemy less occasion to blaspheme than he is apt to have in Europe. Church assemblies — synods, conferences, and conventions — seem on the whole to be conducted with better temper and more good sense than these bodies have shown in the Old World, from the Council of Ephesus down to and in our own day. But in America as elsewhere, some young men enter the clerical profession from temporal motives;

some laymen join a church to improve their social or even their business position; some country pastors look out for city cures, and justify their leaving a poorer flock for a richer by talking of a wider sphere of usefulness. The desire to push the progress of the particular church or of the denomination often mingles with the desire to preach the gospel more widely; and the gospel is sometimes preached, if not with "respect of persons," yet with less faithful insistence on unpalatable truths than the moral health of the community requires.

So far as I could ascertain, the dependence of the minister for his support on his congregation does not lower him in their eyes, nor make him more apt to flatter the leading members than he is in established churches. If he is personally dignified and unselfish, his independence will be in no danger. But whether the voluntary system, which no doubt makes men more liberal in giving for the support of religious ordinances among themselves and of missions elsewhere, tends to quicken spiritual life, and to keep the church pure and undefiled, free from the corrupting influences of the world, is another matter, on which a stranger may well hesitate to speak. All the Americans whose opinion I have inquired hold that in this respect also the fruits of freedom have been good; and I am inclined to believe that they are right.

CHAPTER VII.

THE INFLUENCE OF RELIGION

To convey some impression of the character and type which religion has taken in America, and to estimate its influence as a moral and spiritual force, is an infinitely harder task than to sketch the salient ecclesiastical phenomena of the country. I approach it with the greatest diffidence, and do not profess to give anything more than the sifted result of answers to questions addressed to many competent observers belonging to various churches or to none.

An obviously important point to determine is the extent to which the external ministrations of religion are supplied to the people and used by them. This is a matter on which no trustworthy statistics seem attainable, but on which the visitor's own eyes leave him in little doubt. There are churches everywhere, and everywhere equally, — in the cities and in the country, in the North and in the South, in the quiet nooks of New England, in the settlements which have sprung up along railroads in the West. It is only in the very roughest parts of the West, and especially in the region of mining camps, that they are wanting; and the want is but temporary, for " home missionary " societies are quickly in the field, and provide the ministrations of religion even to this migratory population. In many a town of moderate size one finds a church for every thousand inhabitants, as was the case with Dayton, in Ohio, which when it had 40,000 people had just forty churches. I remember to have seen, in Dakota, a young city which had three churches to its thirty houses.

Denominational rivalry has counted for something in the rapid creation of churches in the newly settled West and their multiplication everywhere else. Small churches are sometimes maintained out of pride when it would be better to let them be united with other congregations of the same body. But the attendance is generally good. In cities of moderate size, as well as in small towns and country places, a stranger is told that the bulk of the native American population go to church at least once every Sunday. In the great cities the proportion of those who attend is far smaller; but whether or no as small as in English cities, no one could tell me. One is much struck by the habit of church-going in the more settled parts of the Far West, where the people, being new-comers, might be supposed to be less under the sway of habit and convention. California is an exception, and is the State supposed to be least affected by religious influences. But in the chief city of Oregon I found that a person, and especially a lady, who did not belong to some church and attend it pretty regularly, would be looked askance on. She need not actually lose caste, but the fact would excite surprise and regret; and her disquieted friends would put some pressure upon her to enrol herself as a church-member.

The observance of the Sabbath, as it was, or the Sunday, as it is now more usually called, furnishes another test. Although the strictness of Puritan practice has disappeared, even in New England, the American part of the rural population, especially in the South, refrains from amusement as well as from work.* It is otherwise with the Germans; and

---

* An interesting summary of the laws for the observance of Sunday may be found in a paper read by Mr. Henry E. Young at the Third Annual meeting of the American Bar Association (1880). These laws, which seem to exist in every State, are in many cases very strict, forbidding all labor, except works of necessity and mercy, and in many cases forbidding also travelling, and nearly every kind of amusement. Vermont and South Carolina seem to go farthest in this direction. The former prescribes, under a fine of $2, that no one shall " visit from house to house,

in some parts of the country their example has brought in laxity as regards amusement. Such cities as Chicago, Cincinnati, New Orleans, and San Francisco have a Sunday quite unlike that of New England, and more resembling what one finds in Germany or France, although, in Chicago, the native Americans assure the stranger that their own more rigid practice continues unaffected by the habits of the Germans. Nowhere, however, does one see the shops open or ordinary work done. On many railroads there are few Sunday trains, and museums are in many cities closed. But in two respects the practice is more lax than in Great Britain. Most of the leading newspapers publish Sunday editions, which contain a great deal of general readable matter, stories, gossip, and so forth, over and above the news of the day; and in the great cities theatres are now open on Sunday evenings.*

The interest in theological questions is less keen than it was in New England a century ago, but keener than it has generally been in England since the days of the Commonwealth. A great deal of the ordinary reading of the average family has a religious tinge, being supplied in religious or

except from motives of humanity or charity, or travel from midnight of Saturday to midnight of Sunday, or hold or attend any ball or dance, or use any game, sport, or play, or resort to any house of entertainment for amusement or recreation."

In Indiana, where all labor and "engaging in one's usual avocation" are prohibited, it has been held by the courts that "selling a cigar to one who has contracted the habit of smoking is a work of necessity."

South Carolina winds up a minute series of prohibitions by ordering all persons to apply themselves to the observance of the day by exercising themselves thereon in the duties of piety and true religion. It need hardly be said that these laws are practically obsolete, except so far as they forbid ordinary and unnecessary traffic and labor. To that extent they are supported by public sentiment, and are justified, as being in the nature not so much of religious as of socially and economically useful regulations.

* One hears that it is now becoming the custom to make a week's engagement of an operatic or theatrical company — there are many traversing the country — begin on Sunday instead of, as formerly, on Monday night.

semi-religious weekly and monthly magazines.   In many parts of the West the old problems of predestination, reprobation, and election continue to be discussed by farmers and shopkeepers in their leisure moments with the old eagerness, and give a sombre tinge to their views of religion.   The ordinary man knows the Bible better, and takes up an allusion to it more quickly, than the ordinary Englishman, though perhaps not better than the ordinary Scotchman.   Indeed, I may say once for all that the native American in everything concerning theology reminds one much more of Scotland than of England, although in the general cast and turn of his mind he is far more English than Scotch.   It is hard to state any general view as to the substance of pulpit teaching, because the differences between different denominations are marked; but on the whole the tendency has been, alike among Congregationalists, Baptists, Northern Presbyterians, and Episcopalians, for sermons to be less metaphysical and less markedly doctrinal than formerly, and to become either expository, or else of a practical and hortatory character.   This is less the case among the Presbyterians of the South, who are more stringently orthodox, and in all respects more conservative, than their brethren of the North.   The discussion of the leading theological questions of the day, such as those of the authority of Scripture, the relation of natural science to the teachings of the Bible, the existence of rewards and punishments in a future state, goes on much as in England. Some of the leading reviews and magazines publish articles on these subjects, which are read more widely than corresponding articles in England, but do not, I think, absorb any more of the thought and attention of the average educated man and woman.

Whether scepticism makes any sensible advance either in affecting a larger number of minds, or in cutting more deeply at the roots of their belief in God and immortality, is a question which it is to-day extremely difficult for any one to

answer even as regards his own country. There are many
phenomena in every part of Europe which appear to indicate
that it does advance; there are others which point in the
opposite direction. Much more difficult, then, must it be for
a stranger to express a positive opinion as regards America
on this gravest of all subjects of inquiry. The conditions of
England and America appear to me very similar, and whatever tendency prevails in either country is likely to prevail in
the other. The mental habits of the people are the same;
their fundamental religious conceptions are the same, except
that those who prize a visible church and bow to her authority are relatively fewer among American Protestants; their
theological literature is the same. In discussing a theological
question with an American one never feels that slight difference of point of view, or, so to speak, of mental atmosphere,
which is sure to crop up in talking to a Frenchman or an
Italian, or even to a German. Considerations of speculative
argument, considerations of religious feeling, affect the two
nations in the same way; the course of their religious history
is not likely to diverge. If there be a difference at all in
their present attitude, it is perhaps to be found in this, that
whereas Americans are more frequently disposed to treat
minor issues in a bold and free spirit, they are more apt to
recoil from blank negation. As an American once said to
me, — they are apt to put serious views into familiar words,
— "We don't mind going a good way along the plank, but
we like to stop short of the jump-off."

Whether pronounced theological unbelief, which has latterly been preached by lectures and pamphlets with a freedom unknown even thirty years ago, has made substantial
progress among the thinking part of the working-class, is a
question on which one hears the most opposite statements. I
have seen statistics which purport to show that the proportion
of members of Christian churches to the total population has
risen in the Protestant churches from 1 in 14½ in A. D. 1800

to 1 in 5 in A. D. 1880; and which estimate the number of communicants in 1880 at 12,000,000, the total adult population in that year being taken at 25,000,000. But one also hears many lamentations over the diminished attendance at city churches; and in ecclesiastical circles people say, just as they say in England, that the great problem is how to reach the masses. The most probable conclusion seems to be that while in cities like New York and Chicago the bulk of the humbler classes (except the Roman Catholics) are practically heathen to the same extent as in London or Liverpool or Berlin, the proportion of working-men who belong to some religious body is rather larger in towns under 30,000 than it is in the similar towns of Great Britain or Germany.

In the cultivated circles of the great cities one finds a good many people, as one does in England, who have virtually abandoned Christianity; and in most of the smaller cities there is said to be a knot of men who profess agnosticism, and sometimes have a meeting-place where secularist lectures are delivered. Fifty years ago the former class would have been fewer and more reserved; the latter would scarcely have existed. But the relaxation of the old strictness of orthodoxy has not diminished the zeal of the various churches, nor their hold upon their adherents, nor their attachment to the fundamental doctrines of Christianity.

This zeal and attachment happily no longer show themselves in intolerance. Except in small places in the West or South, where aggressive scepticism would rouse displeasure and might affect a man's position in society, everybody is as free in America as in London to hold and express any views he pleases. Within the churches themselves there is an unmistakable tendency to loosen the bonds of subscription required from clergymen. Prosecutions for heresy of course come before church courts, since no civil court would take cognizance of such matters unless when invoked by some one alleging that a church court had given a decision, or a church authority had taken an executive step, which prejudiced him in some civil right, and was unjust because violating an obligation contracted with him.* Such prosecutions are not uncommon; but the sympathy of the public is usually with the accused minister, and the latitude allowed to divergence from the old standards becomes constantly greater. At present it is in the Congregationalist Church pretty much the same as in that church in England; in the Presbyterian Church of the North, and among Baptists and Methodists, about the same as in the unestablished Presbyterian Churches of Scotland. Speaking generally, no church allows quite so much latitude either in doctrine or in ritual as recent decisions of the courts of law, beginning from the " Essays and Reviews " case, have allowed to the clergy of the Anglican Establishment in England; but I could not gather that the clergy of the various Protestant bodies feel themselves fettered, or that the free development of religious thought is seriously checked, except in the South, where orthodoxy is rigid, and forbids a clergyman to hold Mr. Darwin's views regarding the descent of man. A pastor who begins to chafe under the formularies or liturgy of his denomination would be expected to leave the denomination and join some other in which he could feel more at home. He would not suffer socially by doing so, as an Anglican clergyman possibly might in the like case in England.

In what may be called the every-day religious life and usages of the United States there are differences from those of England or Scotland which it is easy to feel but hard to define or describe. There is rather less conventionalism or constraint in speaking of religious experiences, less of a formal separation between the church and the world, less disposition to treat the clergy as a caste and expect them to conform

---

* Including the case in which a church court had disregarded its own regulations, or acted in violation of the plain principles of judicial procedure.

to a standard not prescribed for the layman,* less reticence about sacred things, perhaps less sense of the refinement with which sacred things ought to be surrounded. The letting by auction of sittings in a popular church, though I think very rare, excites less disapproval than it would in Europe. Some fashionable churches are supplied with sofas, carpets, and the other comforts of a drawing-room; a well-trained choir is provided, and the congregation would not think of spoiling the performance by joining in the singing. The social side of church life is more fully developed than in Protestant Europe. A congregation, particularly among the Methodists, Baptists, and Congregationalists, is the centre of a group of societies, literary and recreative as well as religious and philanthropic, which not only stimulate charitable work, but bring the poorer and richer members into friendly relations, and form a large part of the social enjoyments of the young people, keeping them out of harm's way, and giving them a means of forming acquaintances. Often a sort of informal evening party, called a "sociable," is given once a month, at which all ages and classes meet on an easy footing.† Religion seems to associate itself better with the interests of the young in America, and to have come within the last forty years to wear a less forbidding countenance than it has generally done in Britain, or at least among English Nonconformists and in the churches of Scotland.

* Although total abstinence is much more generally expected from a clergyman than it would be in Great Britain. In most denominations, including Baptists and Methodists, Congregationalists and Presbyterians, it is practically universal among the clergy.

† Even dances may be given, but not by all denominations. When some years ago a Presbyterian congregation in a great Western city was giving a "reception" in honor of the opening of its new church building, — prosperous churches always have a building with a set of rooms for meetings, — the sexton (as he is called in America), who had come from a Protestant Episcopal church in the East, observed, as he surveyed the spacious hall, "What a pity you are not Episcopalians; you might have given a ball in this room!"

A still more peculiar feature of the American churches is the propensity to what may be called "revivalism" which some of them show. That exciting preaching and those external demonstrations of feeling which have occasionally appeared in Britain, have long been chronic there, appearing chiefly in the form of the camp-meeting, — a gathering of people, usually in the woods or on the sea-shore, where open-air preaching goes on perhaps for days together. One hears many stories about these camp-meetings, not always to their credit, which agree at least in this, that they exercise a powerful even if transient influence upon the classes who flock to them. In the West they have been serviceable in evangelizing districts where few regular churches had yet been established. In the East and South it is now chiefly among the humbler classes, and of course still more among the negroes, that they flourish. All denominations are more prone to emotionalism in religion, and have less reserve in displaying it, than in England or Scotland. I remember in 1870 to have been a passenger by one of the splendid steamers which ply along the Sound between New York and Fall River. A Unitarian congress was being held in New York, and a company of New England Unitarians were going to attend it. Now New England Unitarians are of all Americans perhaps the most staid and sober in their thoughts and habits, the least inclined to a demonstrative expression of their faith. This company, however, installed itself round the piano in the great saloon of the vessel and sang hymns, hymns full of effusion, for nearly two hours, many of the other passengers joining, and all looking on with sympathy. Our English party assumed at first that the singers belonged to some Methodist body, in which case there would have been nothing to remark except the attitude of the bystanders; but they were Unitarians.

European travellers have in one point greatly exaggerated the differences between their own continent and the United

States. They have represented the latter as pre-eminently a land of strange sects and abnormal religious developments. Such sects and developments there certainly are, but they play no greater part in the whole life of the nation than similar sects do in Germany and England, — far less than the various dissenting communities do in Russia. The Mormons have drawn the eyes of the world because they have attempted to form a sort of religious commonwealth, and have revived one ancient practice which modern ethics condemn. But the Mormon Church is chiefly recruited from Europe; one finds few native Americans in Salt Lake City, and those few from among the poor whites of the South.* The Shakers are an interesting and well-conducted folk, but there are very few of them; and of the other communistic religious bodies one hears more in Europe than in America. Here and there some strange little sect emerges and lives for a few years; † but in a country seething with religious emotion, and whose conditions seem to tempt to new departures and experiments of all kinds, the philosophic traveller may rather wonder that men have stood so generally upon the old path.

We have already seen that Christianity has in the United States maintained, so far as externals go, its authority and dignity, planting its houses of worship all over the country, and raising enormous revenues from its adherents. Such a position of apparent influence might, however, rest upon

---

* Some Southern States punish the preaching of Mormonism.

† Near Walla Walla in Washington Territory I came across a curious little sect formed by a Welshman who fell into trances and delivered revelations. He had two sons, and asserted one of them to be an incarnation of Christ, and the other of St. John Baptist, and gathered about fifty disciples, whom he endeavored to form into a society having all things in common. However, both the children died, and in 1881 most of his disciples had deserted him. Probably such phenomena are not uncommon; there is a good deal of proneness to superstition among the less-educated Westerns, especially the immigrants from Europe. They lead a solitary life in the midst of a vast nature.

ancient habit and convention, and imply no dominion over the souls of men. The Roman Empire in the days of Augustus was covered from end to end with superb temples to many gods; the priests were numerous and wealthy, and enjoyed the protection of the state; processions retained their pomp, and sacrifices drew crowds of admiring worshippers. But the old religions had lost their hold on the belief of the educated and on the conscience of all classes. If therefore we desire to know what place Christianity really fills in America, and how far it gives stability to the commonwealth, we must inquire how far it governs the life and moulds the mind of the people.

Such an inquiry may address itself to two points. It may examine into the influence which religion has on the conduct of the citizens, on their moral standard and the way they conform themselves thereto. And it may ask how far religion touches and gilds the imagination of the people, redeeming their lives from commonness, and bathing their souls in " the light that never was on sea or land."

In works of active beneficence no country has surpassed, perhaps none has equalled, the United States. Not only are the sums collected for all sorts of philanthropic purposes larger relatively to the wealth of America than in any European country, but the amount of personal interest shown in good works and personal effort devoted to them seems to a European visitor to exceed what he knows at home. How much of this interest and effort would be given were no religious motive present, it is impossible to say. Not quite all, but I think nearly all of it, is in fact given by religious people, and, as they themselves conceive, under a religious impulse. This religious impulse is less frequently than in England a sectarian impulse, for all Protestants, and to some extent Roman Catholics also, are wont to join hands for most works of benevolence.

The ethical standard of the average man is of course the

Christian standard, modified to some slight extent by the circumstances of American life, which have been different from those of Protestant Europe. The average man has not thought of any other standard, and religious teaching, though it has become less definite and less dogmatic, is still to him the source whence he believes himself to have drawn his ideas of duty and conduct. In Puritan days there must have been some little conscious and much more unconscious hypocrisy, the profession of religion being universal, and the exactitude of practice required by opinion, and even by law, being above what ordinary human nature seems capable of attaining. The fault of antinomianism, which used to be charged on High-Calvinists, is now sometimes charged on those who become, under the influence of revivals, extreme emotionalists in religion. But taking the native Americans as a whole, no people seems to-day less open to the charge of pharisaism or hypocrisy. They are perhaps more prone to the opposite error of good-natured indulgence to offences of which they are not themselves guilty.

That there is less crime among native Americans than among the foreign born is a point not to be greatly pressed, for it may be partly due to the fact that the latter are the poorer and more ignorant part of the population. If, however, we take matters which do not fall within the scope of penal law, the general impression of those who have lived long both in Protestant Europe and in America seems to be that as respects veracity, temperance, the purity of domestic life,* tenderness to children and the weak, and general kind-

---

* The alarming frequency of divorce in some States — there are spots where the proportion of divorces to marriages is 1 to 7 — does not appear to betoken immorality, but to be due to the extreme facility with which the law allows one or both of a married pair to indulge their caprice. Divorce prevails chiefly in the migratory and unsettled section of what would in Europe be called the lower middle class, and is rare both in the better part of the artisan and farming class and (except in one or two great cities) in the more cultivated class.

liness of behavior, the native American stands rather higher than either the English or the Germans.* And those whose opinion I am quoting seem generally, though not universally, disposed to think that the influence of religious belief, which may survive in its effect upon the character when a man has dropped his connection with any religious body, counts for a good deal in this, and is a more consciously present and active force than in the two countries I have referred to.

If we ask how far religion exerts a stimulating influence on the thought and imagination of a nation, we are met by the difficulty of determining what is the condition of mankind where no such influence is present. There has never been a civilized nation without a religion ; and though many highly civilized individual men live without it, they are so obviously the children of a state of sentiment and thought in which religion has been a powerful factor that no one can conjecture what a race of men would be like who had during several generations believed themselves to be the highest beings in the universe, or at least entirely out of relation to any other higher beings, and to be therewithal destined to no kind of existence after death. Some may hold that respect for public opinion, sympathy, an interest in the future of mankind, would do for such a people what religion has done in the past ; or that they might even be, as Lucretius expected, the happier for the extinction of possible supernatural terrors. Others may hold that life would seem narrow and insignificant, and that the wings of imagination would droop in a universe felt to be void. All that need be here said is that a people with comparatively little around it in the way of historic memories and associations to touch its emotion, a people whose energy is chiefly absorbed in commerce and the development of the material resources of its territory,

* This would not be said as regards commercial uprightness, in which respect the United States stand on no higher level than England and Germany, and possibly below France and Scandinavia.

a people consumed by a feverish activity that leaves few opportunities for reflection or for the contemplation of Nature, seems most of all to need to have its horizon widened, its sense of awe and mystery touched, by whatever calls it away from the busy world of sight and sound into the stillness of faith and meditation. A perusal of the literature which the ordinary American of the educated farming and artisan class reads, and a study of the kind of literature which those Americans who are least colored by European influences produce, lead me to think that the Bible and Christian theology altogether do more in the way of forming the imaginative background to an average American view of the world of man and Nature than they do in modern Protestant Europe.

No one is so thoughtless as not to sometimes ask himself what would befall mankind if the solid fabric of belief on which their morality has hitherto rested, or at least been deemed by them to rest, were suddenly to break up and vanish under the influence of new views of Nature, as the ice-fields split and melt when they have floated down into a warmer sea. Morality with religion for its sanction has hitherto been the basis of social polity, except under military despotisms : would morality be so far weakened as to make social polity unstable? and if so, would a reign of violence return? In Europe this question does not seem urgent, because in Europe the physical force of armed men which maintains order is usually conspicuous, and because obedience to authority is everywhere in Europe matter of ancient habit, having come down little impaired from ages when men obeyed without asking for a reason. But in America the whole system of government seems to rest, not on armed force, but on the will of the numerical majority, — a majority most of whom might well think that its overthrow would be for them a gain. So sometimes, standing in the midst of a great American city, and watching the throngs of eager figures streaming hither and thither, marking the sharp contrasts of poverty and wealth, an increasing mass of wretchedness and an increasing display of luxury, knowing that before long a hundred millions of men will be living between ocean and ocean under this one government, — a government which their own hands have made, and which they feel to be the work of their own hands, — one is startled by the thought of what might befall this huge yet delicate fabric of laws and commerce and social institutions, were the foundations it has rested on to crumble away. Suppose that all these men ceased to believe that there was any power above them, any future before them, anything in heaven or earth but what their senses told them of; suppose that their consciousness of individual force and responsibility, already dwarfed by the overwhelming power of the multitude, and the fatalistic submission it engenders, were further weakened by the feeling that their swiftly fleeting life was rounded by a perpetual sleep —

> " Soles occidere et redire possunt ;
> Nobis, quum semel occidit brevis lux
> Nox est perpetua una dormienda," —

would the moral code stand unshaken, and with it the reverence for law, the sense of duty towards the community, and even towards the generations yet to come? Would men say, " Let us eat and drink, for to-morrow we die"? Or would custom and sympathy and a perception of the advantages which stable government offers to the citizens as a whole, and which orderly self-restraint offers to each one, replace supernatural sanctions, and hold in check the violence of masses and the self-indulgent impulses of the individual? History, if she cannot give a complete answer to this question, tells us that hitherto civilized society has rested on religion, and that free government has prospered best among religious peoples.

America is no doubt the country in which intellectual movements work most swiftly upon the masses, and the country in which the loss of faith in the invisible might produce the completest revolution, because it is the country where men have been least wont to revere anything in the visible world.   Yet America seems as unlikely to drift from her ancient moorings as any country of the Old World.   It was religious zeal and the religious conscience which led to the founding of the New England colonies two centuries and a half ago, — those colonies whose spirit has in such a large measure passed into the whole nation.   Religion and conscience have been a constantly active force in the American commonwealth ever since, not indeed strong enough to avert many moral and political evils, yet at the worst times inspiring a minority with a courage and ardor by which moral and political evils have been held at bay, and in the long run generally overcome.

It is an old saying that monarchies live by honor, and republics by virtue.   The more democratic republics become, the more the masses grow conscious of their own power, the more do they need to live, not only by patriotism, but by reverence and self-control, and the more essential to their well-being are those sources whence reverence and self-control flow.

CHAPTER VIII.

THE POSITION OF WOMEN.

IT has been well said that the position which women hold in a country is, if not a complete test, yet one of the best tests of the progress it has made in civilization.   When one compares nomad man with settled man, heathen man with Christian man, the ancient world with the modern, the Eastern world with the Western, it is plain that in every case the advance in public order, in material comfort, in wealth, in decency and refinement of manners, among the whole population of a country, — for in these matters one must not look merely at the upper class, — has been accompanied by a greater respect for women, by a greater freedom accorded to them, by a fuller participation on their part in the best work of the world.   Americans are fond of pointing, and can with perfect justice point, to the position their women hold as an evidence of the high level their civilization has reached.   Certainly nothing in the country is more characteristic of the peculiar type their civilization has taken.

The subject may be regarded in so many aspects that it is convenient to take up each separately.

As respects the legal rights of women, these of course depend on the legislative enactments of each State of the Union, for in no case has the matter been left under the rigor of the common law.   With much diversity in minor details, the general principles of the law are in all or nearly all the States similar. Women have been placed in an equality with men as respects all private rights. Married as well as unmarried women have long since obtained full control of their property, whether obtained by gift or descent, or by their own labor. This has been deemed so important a point that, instead of being left to ordinary legislation, it has in several States been directly enacted by the people in the constitution. Women have in most, though perhaps not in all, States rights of guardianship over their children which the law of England denied to them till the Act of 1886. The law of divorce is in some States far from satisfactory, but it always aims at doing equal justice as between husbands and wives. Special protection as respects hours of labor is given to women by the laws of many States, and a good deal of recent legislation has been passed with intent to benefit them, though not always by well-chosen means.

Women have made their way into most of the professions more largely than in Europe. In many of the Northern cities they practise as physicians, and seem to have found little or no prejudice to overcome. Medical schools have been provided for them in some universities. It was less easy to obtain admission to the Bar, yet several have secured this, and the number seems to increase. They mostly devote themselves to the attorney's part of the work, rather than to court practice. One edits, or lately edited, the "Illinois Law Journal" with great acceptance. Several have entered the Christian ministry, though, I think, only in what may be called the minor sects, — not in any of the five or six great denominations, whose spirit is more conservative. Several have obtained success as professional lecturers. Less is heard of them in engineering and in journalism. They are seldom to be seen in the offices of hotels, but many, more than in England, are employed as clerks or secretaries, both in some of the Government departments, and by telegraphic and other companies, as well as in publishing houses and other kinds of business where physical strength is not needed. They form an overwhelming majority of the teachers in public schools for boys as well as for girls, and are thought to be better teachers, at least for the younger sort, than men are.* No class prejudice forbids the daughters of clergymen or lawyers of the best standing to teach in elementary schools. Taking one thing with another, it is easier for women to find a career, to obtain remunerative work of an intellectual as of a commercial or mechanical kind, than in any part of Europe. Popular sentiment is entirely in favor of giving them every chance, as witness the new constitutions of several Western States, which expressly provide that they shall be equally admissible to all professions or employments. In no other country have women borne so conspicuous a part in the promotion of moral and philanthropic causes. They were among the earliest, most zealous, and most effective apostles of the anti-slavery movement. They have taken an equally active share in the temperance agitation. Not only has the Women's Christian Temperance Union with its numerous branches been the most powerful agency directed against the traffic in intoxicants, particularly in the Western States, but individual women have thrown themselves into the struggle with extraordinary zeal. Some years ago, during what was called the Women's Whiskey War, they forced their way into the drinking-saloons, bearded the dealers, adjured the tipplers to come out. At elections in which the Prohibitionist issue is prominent, ladies will sometimes assemble outside the polls and sing hymns at the voters. Their services in dealing with pauperism, with charities and reformatory institutions, have been inestimable. In New York some few years ago, when an Act was needed for improving the administration of the charities, it was a lady (belonging to one of the oldest and most respected families

* The total number of teachers is given by the United States Bureau of Education Report for 1887 at 104,249 men and 191,439 women. As men are in a majority in the Southern States and in Indiana, the preponderance of women in the Northern States generally is very great.

in the country) who went to Albany, and by placing the case forcibly before the State legislature there, succeeded in obtaining the required measure. The Charity Organization societies of the great cities are very largely managed by ladies; and the freedom they enjoy, coupled with a knowledge of business less frequently found among European women, makes them invaluable agents in this work, which the growth of a pauper class renders daily more important. So too when it became necessary after the war to find teachers for the negroes in the institutions founded for their benefit in the South, it was chiefly Northern girls who volunteered for the duty, and discharged it with single-minded zeal.

American women take less part in politics than their English sisters do, although more than the women of Germany, France, or Italy. That they talk less about politics may be partly ascribed to the fact that politics come less into ordinary conversation in America (except during a presidential election) than in England. But the practice of canvassing at elections, recently developed by English ladies with eminent success, seems unknown. Ladies have never, I think, been chosen members of either Republican or Democratic conventions. However, at the two last National Conventions of the Prohibitionist party, in 1884 and 1888, a number of ladies presented credentials as delegates from local organizations, and were admitted to sit. One of the two secretaries of the Convention of 1884 was a woman. Several were placed on the Committee of Credentials. Here we are on the debatable ground between pure party politics and philanthropic agitation. Women have been so effective in the latter that they cannot easily be excluded when persuasion passes into constitutional action; and one is not surprised to find the Prohibition party declare in their platform of 1884 that " they alone recognize the influence of woman, and offer to her equal rights with man in the management of national affairs." Presidential candidates have often " receptions " given in their honor by ladies, and some of the letters which appear in the newspapers in advocacy of one or other party, bear female signatures. One hears of attempts made to establish political " salons " at Washington ; but neither there nor elsewhere has the influence of social gatherings attained the importance it has often possessed in France, though occasionally the wife of a politician makes his fortune by her tact and skill in winning support for him among professional politicians or the members of a State legislature. There is, however, another and less auspicious sphere of political action into which women have found their way at the national capital. The solicitation of members of a legislature with a view to the passing of bills, especially private bills, and to the obtaining of places, has become a profession there, and the persuasive assiduity which had long been recognized by poets as characteristic of the female sex, has made them widely employed and efficient in this work.

I have, in treating of the women's suffrage movement, referred to the various public offices which have been in many States thrown open to women. It is universally admitted that the gift of the suffrage must carry with it the right of obtaining any post in the service of the country for which votes are cast, up to and including the Presidency itself.

The subject of women's education opens up a large field. Want of space obliges me to omit a description, for which I have accumulated abundant materials, and to confine myself to a few concise remarks.

The public provision for the instruction of girls is quite as ample and adequate as that made for boys. Elementary schools are of course provided alike for both sexes, grammar-schools and high-schools are organized for the reception of girls, sometimes under the same roof or even in the same classes, sometimes in a distinct building, but always, I think, with an equally complete staff of teachers and equipment of educational appliances. The great majority of the daughters of mercantile and professional men, especially of course in the West,* receive their education in these public secondary schools; and, what is more remarkable, the number of girls who continue their education in the higher branches, including the ancient classics and physical science, up to the age of seventeen or eighteen, is as large, in many places larger, than that of the boys, the latter being drafted off into practical life, while the former indulge their more lively interest in the things of the mind. One often hears it charged as a fault on the American system that its liberal provision of gratuitous instruction in the advanced subjects tends to raise girls of the humbler classes out of the sphere to which their pecuniary means would destine them, makes them discontented with their lot, implants tastes which fate will forever forbid them to gratify.†

As stated in a previous chapter (Chapter V.), university education is provided for women in the Eastern States by colleges expressly erected for their benefit, and in the Western States by state universities, whose regulations usually provide for the admission of female equally with male students to a gratuitous instruction in all subjects. There are also some colleges of private foundation which receive young men and maidens together, teaching them in the same classes, but providing separate buildings for their lodging.

I must not attempt to set forth and discuss the evidence regarding the working of this system of co-education, interesting as the facts are, but be content with stating the general result of the inquiries I made.

* There are some private boarding-schools and many private day-schools for girls in the Eastern States. Comparatively few children are educated at home by governesses.

† A striking picture of such a case is given in a recent American tale called " The Breadwinners."

Co-education answers perfectly in institutions like Antioch and Oberlin in Ohio, where manners are plain and simple, where the students all come from a class in which the intercourse of young men and young women is easy and natural, and where there is a strong religious influence pervading the life of the place. No moral difficulties are found to arise. Each sex is said to improve the other; the men become more refined, the women more manly. Now and then students fall in love with one another, and marry when they have graduated. But why not? Such marriages are based upon a better reciprocal knowledge of character than is usually attainable in the great world, and are reported to be almost invariably happy. So also in the Western State universities co-education is well reported of. In these establishments the students mostly lodge where they will in the city, and are therefore brought into social relations only in the hours of public instruction; but the tendency of late years has been, while leaving men to find their own quarters, to provide places of residence for the women. The authorities have little to do in the way of discipline or supervision, and say they do not find it needed, and that they are not aware of any objections to the system. I did find, however, that the youths in some cases expressed aversion to it, saying they would rather be in classes by themselves; the reason apparently being that it was disagreeable to see a man whom men thought meanly of standing high in the favor of lady students. In these Western States there is so much freedom allowed in the intercourse of youths and girls, and girls are so well able to take care of themselves, that the objections which occur to a European arouse no disquietude. Whether a system which has borne good fruits in the primitive society of the West is fit to be adopted in the Eastern States, where the conditions of life approach nearer to those of Europe, is a question warmly debated in America. The need for it is at any rate not urgent, because the liberality of founders and benefactors has provided in at least four

women's colleges places where an excellent education, surpassing that of most of the Western universities, stands open
to women.   These colleges are at present so efficient and
popular, and the life of their students is in some respects so
much freer than it could well be, considering the etiquette of
Eastern society, in universities frequented by both sexes, that
they will probably continue to satisfy the practical needs of
the community and the wishes of all but the advocates of complete theoretical equality.

It will be seen from what has been said that the provision
for women's education in the United States is ampler and
better than that made in any European country, and that
the making of it has been far more distinctly recognized as a
matter of public concern.   To these advantages, and to the
spirit they proceed from, much of the influence which women
exert must be ascribed.   They feel more independent, they
have a fuller consciousness of their place in the world of
thought as well as in the world of action.   The practice of
educating the two sexes together in the same colleges
tends, in those sections of the country where it prevails,
in the same direction, placing women and men on a level
as regards attainments, and giving them a greater number
of common intellectual interests.   It does not, I think,
operate to make women either pedantic or masculine, or to
diminish the differences between their mental and moral
habits and those of men.   Nature is quite strong enough to
make the differences of temperament she creates persistent,
even under influences which might seem likely to diminish
them.

Custom allows to women a greater measure of freedom in
doing what they will and going where they please than they
have in any European country, except, perhaps, in Russia.
No one is surprised to see a lady travel alone from the
Atlantic to the Pacific, nor a girl of the richer class walking
alone through the streets of a city.   If a lady enters some

occupation heretofore usually reserved to men, she is subject to much less censorious remark than would follow her in Europe, though in this matter the society of Eastern cities is hardly so liberal as that of the West.

Social intercourse between youths and maidens is everywhere more easy and unrestrained than in England or Germany, not to speak of France. Yet there are considerable differences between the Eastern cities — whose usages have begun to approximate to those of Europe — and other parts of the country. In the rural districts, and generally all over the West, young men and girls are permitted to walk together, drive together, go out to parties, and even to public entertainments together, without the presence of any third person who can be supposed to be looking after or taking charge of the girl. So a girl may, if she pleases, keep up a correspondence with a young man, nor will her parents think of interfering. She will have her own friends, who when they call at her house ask for her, and are received by her, it may be alone; because they are not deemed to be necessarily the friends of her parents also, nor even of her sisters. In the cities of the Atlantic States it is beginning to be thought scarcely correct for a young man to take a young lady out for a solitary drive, and in few sets would he be now permitted to escort her alone to the theatre. But in some " good sets " girls still go without chaperons to dances, the hostess being deemed to act as chaperon for all her guests; and as regards both correspondence and the right to have one's own circle of acquaintances, the usage even of New York or Boston allows more liberty than does that of London or Edinburgh. It was at one time, and it may possibly still be, not uncommon for a group of young people who know one another well to make up an autumn " party in the woods." They choose some mountain and forest region, such as the Adirondack wilderness west of Lake Champlain, engage three or four guides, embark with guns and fishing-rods, tents, blankets, and a stock of groceries, and pass in boats up the rivers and across the lakes of this wild country through sixty or seventy miles of trackless forest to their chosen camping ground at the foot of some tall rock that rises from the still crystal of the lake. Here they build their bark hut, and spread their beds of the elastic and fragrant hemlock-boughs ; the youths roam about during the day, tracking the deer, the girls read and work and bake the corn-cakes ; at night there is a merry gathering round the fire, or a row in the soft moonlight. On these expeditions brothers will take their sisters and cousins, who bring perhaps some lady friends with them ; the brothers' friends will come too ; and all will live together in a fraternal way for weeks or months, though no elderly relative or married lady be of the party.

There can be no doubt that the pleasure of life is sensibly increased by the greater freedom which transatlantic custom permits ; and as the Americans insist that no bad results have followed, one notes with regret that freedom declines in the places which deem themselves most civilized. American girls have been, so far as a stranger can ascertain, less disposed to what are called " fast ways " than girls of the corresponding classes in England,* and exercise in this respect a pretty rigorous censorship over one another. But when two young people find pleasure in one another's company, they can see as much of each other as they please, can talk and walk together frequently, can show that they are mutually interested, and yet need have little fear of being misunderstood either by one another or by the rest of the world. It is all a matter of custom. In the West custom sanctions this easy friendship ; in the Atlantic cities, so soon as people have

* Between fastness and freedom there is in American eyes all the difference in the world ; but new-comers from Europe are startled. I remember to have once heard a German lady settled in a Western city characterize American women as "*furchtbar frei und furchtbar fromm*" (frightfully free, and frightfully pious).

come to find something exceptional in it, constraint is felt, and a conventional etiquette like that of the Old World begins to replace the innocent simplicity of the older time, the test of whose merit may be gathered from the universal persuasion in America that happy marriages are in the middle and upper ranks more common than in Europe, and that this is due to the ampler opportunities which young men and women have of learning one another's characters and habits before forming an engagement. Most girls have a larger range of intimate acquaintances than girls have in Europe, intercourse is franker, there is less difference between the manners of home and the manners of general society. The conclusions of a stranger are in such matters of no value, so I can only repeat that I have never met any judicious American lady who, however well she knew the Old World, did not think that the New World customs conduced more both to the pleasantness of life before marriage, and to constancy and concord after it.

In no country are women, and especially young women, so much made of. The world is at their feet. Society seems organized for the purpose of providing enjoyment for them. Parents, uncles, aunts, elderly friends, even brothers, are ready to make their comfort and convenience bend to the girls' wishes. The wife has fewer opportunities for reigning over the world of amusements, because, except among the richest people, she has more to do in household management than in England, owing to the scarcity of servants. But she holds in her own house a more prominent, if not a more substantially powerful, position than in England or even in France. With the German *Hausfrau*, who is too often content to be a mere housewife, there is of course no comparison. The best proof of the superior place American ladies occupy is to be found in the notions they profess to entertain of the relations of an English married pair. They talk of the English wife as little better than a slave, declaring that when they stay with English friends, or receive an English couple in America, they see the wife always deferring to the husband, and the husband always assuming that his pleasure and convenience are to prevail. The European wife, they admit, often gets her own way, but she gets it by tactful arts, by flattery or wheedling or playing on the man's weaknesses ; whereas in America the husband's duty and desire is to gratify the wife and render to her those services which the English tyrant exacts from his consort.* One may often hear an American matron commiserate a friend who has married in Europe, while the daughters declare in chorus that they will never follow the example. Laughable as all this may seem to Englishwomen, it is perfectly true that the theory as well as the practice of conjugal life is not the same in America as in England. There are overbearing husbands in America, but they are more condemned by the opinion of the neighborhood than in England. There are exacting wives in England, but their husbands are more pitied than would be the case in America. In neither country can one say that the principle of perfect equality reigns, for in America the balance inclines nearly, though not quite, as much in favor of the wife as it does in England in favor of the husband. No one man can have a sufficiently large acquaintance in both countries to entitle his individual opinion on the results to much weight. So far as I have been able to collect views from those observers who have lived in both countries, they are in favor of the American practice, — perhaps because the theory it is based on departs less from pure equality than does that of England. These observers do not mean that the recognition of women as equals or superiors makes them any better or sweeter or wiser than Englishwomen, but rather

---

* I have heard American ladies say, for instance, that they have observed that an Englishman who has forgotten his keys, sends his wife to the top of the house to fetch them ; whereas an American would do the like errand for his wife, and never suffer her to do it for him.

that the principle of equality, by correcting the characteristic faults of men, and especially their selfishness and vanity, is more conducive to the concord and happiness of a home. They conceive that to make the wife feel her independence and responsibility more strongly than she does in Europe, tends to brace and expand her character, while conjugal affection, usually stronger in her than in the husband, inasmuch as there are fewer competing interests, saves her from abusing the precedence yielded to her. This seems to be true ; but I have heard others maintain that the American system, since it does not require the wife habitually to forego her own wishes, tends, if not to make her self-indulgent and capricious, yet slightly to impair the more delicate charms of character ; as it is written, " It is more blessed to give than to receive."

A European cannot spend an evening in an American drawing-room without perceiving that the attitude of men to women is not that with which he is familiar at home. The average European man has usually a slight sense of condescension when he talks to a woman on serious subjects. Even if she is his superior in intellect, in character, in social rank, he thinks that as a man he is her superior, and consciously or unconsciously talks down to her. She is too much accustomed to this to resent it, unless it becomes tastelessly palpable. Such a notion does not cross an American's mind. He talks to a woman just as he would to a man, — of course with more deference of manner, and with a proper regard to the topics likely to interest her, but giving her his intellectual best, addressing her as a person whose opinion is understood by both to be worth as much as his own. Similarly an American lady does not expect to have conversation made to her. It is just as much her duty or pleasure to lead it as it is the man's, and more often than not she takes the burden from him, darting along with a gay vivacity which puts to shame his slower wits.

It need hardly be said that in all cases where the two sexes come into competition for comfort, provision is made first for women.   On some railroads the end car of the train, being that farthest removed from the smoke of the locomotive, is reserved for them (though men accompanying a lady are allowed to enter it), and at hotels their sitting-room is the best, and perhaps the only available public room, ladyless guests being driven to the bar or the hall.   In omnibuses and street-cars it was formerly the custom for a gentleman to rise and offer his seat to a lady if there were no vacant place.   This is now less universally done.   In several cities I have seen the men keep their seats when ladies entered; and I recollect one occasion when the offer of a seat to a lady was declined by her, on the ground that as she had chosen to enter a full car she ought to take the consequences.   It was (I was told in Boston) a feeling of this kind that had led to the discontinuance of the old courtesy.   When ladies constantly pressed into the already crowded vehicles, the men, who could not secure the enforcement of the regulations against overcrowding, tried to protect themselves by refusing to rise.   It is sometimes said that the privileges yielded to American women have disposed them to claim as a right what was only a courtesy, and have told unfavorably upon their manners.   I know of several instances, besides this one of the street-cars, which might seem to support the criticism, but cannot on the whole think it well founded.   The better-bred women do not presume on their sex; and the area of good breeding is always widening.   It need hardly be said that the community at large gains by the softening and restraining influence which the reverence for womanhood diffuses.   Nothing so quickly incenses the people as any insult offered to a woman.   Wife-beating, and indeed any kind of rough violence offered to women, is far less common among the rudest class than it is in England.   Field work or work at the pit-mouth of mines is seldom or never done by women in America; and the American traveller who in some parts of Europe finds women performing severe manual labor is revolted by the sight in a way which Europeans find surprising.

In the farther West — that is to say, beyond the Mississippi, in the Rocky Mountain and Pacific States — one is much struck by what seems the absence of the humblest class of women. The trains are full of poorly-dressed and sometimes (though less frequently) rough-mannered men. One discovers no women whose dress or air marks them out as the wives, daughters, or sisters of these men, and wonders whether the male population is celibate, and if so, why there are so many women. Closer observation shows that the wives, daughters, and sisters are there, only their attire and manner are those of what Europeans would call middle-class and not working-class people. This is partly due to the fact that Western men affect a rough dress. Still, one may say that the remark so often made that the masses of the American people correspond to the middle class of Europe is more true of the women than of the men, and is more true of them in the rural districts and in the West than it is of the inhabitants of Atlantic cities. I remember to have been dawdling in a book-store in a small town in Oregon when a lady entered to inquire if a monthly magazine, whose name was unknown to me, had yet arrived. When she was gone I asked the salesman who she was, and what was the periodical she wanted. He answered that she was the wife of a railway workman, that the magazine was a journal of fashions, and that the demand for such journals was large and constant among women of the wage-earning class in the town. This set me to observing female dress more closely, and it turned out to be perfectly true that the women in these little towns were following the Parisian fashions very closely, and were, in fact, ahead of the majority of English ladies belonging to the professional and mercantile

classes.* Of course in such a town as I refer to there are no
domestic servants except in the hotels (indeed, almost the
only domestic service to be had in the Pacific States is that
of Chinese), so these votaries of fashion did all their own
housework and looked after their own babies.

Three causes combine to create among American women an
average of literary taste and influence higher than that of
women in any European country. These are, the educational
facilities they enjoy, the recognition of the equality of the
sexes in the whole social and intellectual sphere, and the leisure which they possess as compared with men. In a country
where men are incessantly occupied at their business or profession, the function of keeping up the level of culture devolves
upon women. It is safe in their hands. They are quick and
keen-witted, less fond of open-air life and physical exertion
than Englishwomen are, and obliged by the climate to pass a
greater part of their time under shelter from the cold of winter
and the sun of summer. For music and for the pictorial arts
they do not yet seem to have formed so strong a taste as for
literature, partly perhaps owing to the fact that in America the
opportunities of seeing or hearing masterpieces, except indeed operas, are rarer than in Europe. But they are eager and
assiduous readers of all such books and periodicals as do not
presuppose special knowledge in some branch of science or
learning, while the number who have devoted themselves to
some special study and attained proficiency in it is large.
The fondness for sentiment, especially moral and domestic
sentiment, which is often observed as characterizing American taste in literature, seems to be mainly due to the influence
of women ; for they form not only the larger part of the reading public, but an independent-minded part, not disposed to
adopt the canons laid down by men, and their preferences

* The above of course does not apply to the latest immigrants from
Europe, who are still European in their dress and ways, though in a town
they become quickly Americanized.

count for more in the opinions and predilections of the whole nation than is the case in England. Similarly the number of women who write is infinitely larger in America than in Europe. Fiction, essays, and poetry are naturally their favorite provinces. In poetry more particularly, many whose names are quite unknown in Europe have attained widespread fame.

Some one may ask how far the differences between the position of women in America and their position in Europe are due to democracy? Or if not to this, then to what other cause?

They are due to democratic feeling in so far as they spring from the notion that all men are free and equal, possessed of certain inalienable rights, and owing certain corresponding duties. This root-idea of democracy cannot stop at defining men as male human beings, any more than it could ultimately stop at defining them as white human beings. For many years the Americans believed in equality with the pride of discoverers as well as with the fervor of apostles. Accustomed to apply it to all sorts and conditions of men, they were naturally the first to apply it to women also, — not, indeed, as respects politics, but in all the social as well as legal relations of life. Democracy is in America more respectful of the individual, less disposed to infringe his freedom or subject him to any sort of legal or family control, than it has shown itself in Continental Europe ; and this regard for the individual inured to the benefit of women. Of the other causes that have worked in the same direction, two may be mentioned. One is the usage of the Congregationalist, Presbyterian, and Baptist churches, under which a woman who is a member of the congregation has the same rights in choosing a deacon, elder, or pastor as a man has. Another is the fact that among the westward-moving settlers women were at first few in number, and were therefore treated with special respect. The habit then formed was retained as the communities grew, and propagated itself all over the country.

What have been the results on the character and usefulness of women themselves?

Favorable. They have opened to them a wider life and more variety of career. While the special graces of the feminine character do not appear to have suffered, there have been produced a sort of independence and a capacity for self-help which are increasingly valuable as the number of unmarried women increases. More resources are open to an American woman who has to lead a solitary life, not merely in the way of employment, but for the occupation of her mind and tastes, than to a European spinster or widow ; while her education has not rendered the American wife less competent for the discharge of household duties.

How has the nation at large been affected by the development of this new type of womanhood, or rather perhaps of this variation on the English type?

If women have on the whole gained, it is clear that the nation gains through them. As mothers they mould the character of their children ; while the function of forming the habits of society and determining its moral tone rests greatly in their hands. But there is reason to think that the influence of the American system tells directly for good upon men as well as upon the whole community. Men gain in being brought to treat women as equals rather than as graceful playthings or useful drudges. The respect for women which every American man either feels or is obliged by public sentiment to profess, has a wholesome effect on his conduct and character, and serves to check the cynicism which some other peculiarities of the country foster. The nation as a whole owes to the active benevolence of its women, and their zeal in promoting social reforms, benefits which the customs of Continental Europe would scarcely have permitted women to confer. Europeans have of late years begun to render a well-deserved admiration to the brightness and vivacity of American ladies. Those who know the work they have done and are doing in many a noble cause will admire still more their energy, their courage, their self-devotion. No country seems to owe more to its women than America does, nor to owe to them so much of what is best in social institutions and in the beliefs that govern conduct.

CHAPTER IX.

EQUALITY.

THE United States are deemed all the world over to be pre-eminently the land of equality. This was the first feature which struck Europeans when they began, after the peace of 1815 had left them time to look beyond the Atlantic, to feel curious about the phenomena of a new society. This was the great theme of Tocqueville's description, and the starting-point of his speculations; this has been the most constant boast of the Americans themselves, who have believed their liberty more complete than that of any other people, because equality has been more fully blended with it. Yet some philosophers say that equality is impossible, and others, who express themselves more precisely, insist that distinctions of rank are so inevitable that however you try to expunge them, they are sure to reappear. Before we discuss this question, let us see in what senses the word is used.

First there is legal equality, including both what one may call passive, or private equality, — *i. e.*, the equal possession of private civil rights by all inhabitants, — and active, or public equality, the equal possession by all of rights to a share in the government, such as the electoral franchise and eligibility to public office. Both kinds of political equality exist in America in the amplest measure, and may be dismissed from the present discussion.

Next there is the equality of material conditions, — that is, of wealth, and all that wealth gives; there is the equality of education and intelligence; there is the equality of social status or rank; and there is (what comes near to, but is not exactly the same as, this last) the equality of estimation, — *i. e.*, of the value which men set upon one another, whatever be the elements that come into this value, whether wealth, or education, or official rank, or social rank, or any other species of excellence. In how many and which of these senses of the word does equality exist in the United States?

Clearly not as regards material conditions. Sixty years ago there were no great fortunes in America, few large fortunes, no poverty. Now there is some poverty (though only in a few places can it be called pauperism), many large fortunes, and a greater number of gigantic fortunes than in any other country of the world. The class of persons who are passably well off but not rich, — a class corresponding in point of income to the lower middle class of England or France, but superior in manners to that class, — is much larger than in the great countries of Europe. Between the houses, the dress, and the way of life of these persons, and those of the richer sort, there is less difference than in Europe. The very rich do not (except in a few places) make an ostentatious display of their wealth, because they have no means of doing so; and a visitor is therefore apt to overrate the extent to which equality of wealth, and of material conditions generally, still prevails. The most remarkable phenomenon of the last twenty-five years has been the appearance, not only of those few colossal millionnaires who fill the public eye, but of many millionnaires of the second order, — men with fortunes ranging from $5,000,000 to $15,000,000. At a seaside resort like Newport, where one sees the finished luxury of the villas and counts the well-appointed equipages, with their superb horses, which turn out in the afternoon, one gets some impression of the vast and growing wealth of the Eastern cities. But through the country generally there is little to mark out the man with an income of $100,000 a year from the man of

$10,000, as he is marked out in England by his country house with its park, or in France by the opportunities for display which Paris affords. The number of these fortunes seems likely to go on increasing; for they are due not merely to the sudden development of the West, with the chances of making vast sums by land speculation or in railway construction, but to the field for doing business on a great scale which the size of the country presents. Where a merchant or manufacturer in France or England could realize thousands, an American, operating more boldly, and on this far wider theatre, may realize tens of thousands. We may therefore expect these inequalities of wealth to grow. Nor will even the habit of equal division among children keep them down; for families are often small, and though some of those who inherit wealth may renounce business, others will pursue it, since the attractions of other kinds of life are fewer than in Europe. Politics are less exciting; there is no great land-holding class, with the duties towards tenants and neighbors which an English squire may, if he pleases, usefully discharge; the pursuit of collecting pictures or other objects of curiosity implies frequent visits to Europe; and although the killing of birds prevails in the Middle States, and the killing of deer in the West, this barbarous form of pleasure is likely in time to die out from a civilized people. Other kinds of what is called "sport" no doubt remain, such as horse-racing, — eagerly pursued in the form of trotting matches,* — and the manlier amusements of yacht-racing, rowing, and base-ball; but these can only be followed during part of the year, and some of them only by the young. A life of so-called pleasure is certainly harder to follow in an American city than in Paris or Vienna or London. Accordingly, while great fortunes will continue to be made, they will be less easily and quickly spent than in Europe, and one may sur-

* The trotting-horse is driven, not ridden, — a return to the earliest forms of horse-racing we know of.

mise that the equality of material conditions, almost universal in last century, still general sixty years ago, will more and more diminish by the growth of a very rich class at one end of the line, and of a very poor class at the other end.

As respects education, the profusion of superior as well as elementary schools tends to raise the mass to a somewhat higher point than in Europe, while the stimulus of life being keener and the habit of reading more general, the number of persons one finds on the same general level of brightness, keenness, and a superficially competent knowledge of common facts, whether in science, history, geography, or literature, is extremely large. This general level tends to rise. But the level of exceptional attainment in that small but increasing class who have studied at the best native universities or in Europe, and who pursue learning and science either as a profession or as a source of pleasure, rises faster than does the general level of the multitude, so that in this regard also it appears that equality has diminished, and will diminish further.

So far we have been on comparatively smooth and easy ground. Equality of wealth is a concrete thing; equality of intellectual possession and resource is a thing which can be perceived and gauged. Of social equality, of distinctions of standing and estimation in private life, it is far more difficult to speak; and in what follows I speak with some hesitation.

One thing, and perhaps one thing only, may be asserted with confidence. There is no rank in America, — that is to say, no external and recognized stamp, marking one man as entitled to any social privileges, or to deference and respect from others. No man is entitled to think himself better than his fellows, or to expect any exceptional consideration to be shown by them to him. There is no such thing as a recognized order of precedence, either on public occasions or at a private party, except that yielded to a few official persons, such as the governor and chief judges of a State within that

State, as well as to the President and Vice-President, the Speaker of the House, the Federal senators, the judges of the Supreme Federal Court, and the members of the President's cabinet everywhere through the Union. In fact, the idea of a regular " rule of precedence " displeases the Americans,* and one finds them slow to believe that the existence of such a rule in England, entitling the youthful daughter of a baronet, for instance, to go first out of the room at a dinner party on the host's arm, although there may be present married ladies both older and of some personal distinction, is not felt as a mortification by the latter ladies, because it is a mere matter of convention and usage which does not prevent the other guests from respecting these wives of ordinary commoners much more than they may respect the baronet's daughter. That an obscure earl should take precedence of a prime minister who happens to be a commoner, shocks Americans out of measure.

What then is the effect or influence for social purposes of such distinctions as do exist between men, — distinctions of birth, of wealth, of official position, of intellectual eminence?

To be sprung from an ancient stock, or from a stock which can count persons of eminence among its ancestors, is of course a satisfaction to the man himself. There is at present almost a passion among Americans for genealogical researches. A good many families can trace themselves back to English families of the sixteenth or seventeenth century, and of course a great many more profess to do so. For a man's ancestors to have come over in the " Mayflower " is in

---

* In private parties, so far as there is any rule of precedence, it is that of age, with a tendency to make an exception in favor of clergymen or of any person of special eminence. It is only in Washington, where senators, judges, ministers, and congressmen are sensitive on these points, that such questions seem to arise, or to be regarded as deserving the attention of a rational mind.

America much what their having come over with William the Conqueror used to be in England. The descendants of any of the revolutionary heroes, such as John Adams, Edmund Randolph, Alexander Hamilton, and the descendants of any famous man of colonial times, such as the early governors of Massachusetts, from William Endicott downwards, or of Jonathan Edwards, or of Eliot, the Apostle of the Indians, are regarded by their neighbors with a certain amount of interest, and their legitimate pride in such an ancestry excites no disapproval.* In the Eastern cities and at watering-places like Newport one begins to see carriages with armorial bearings on their panels; but most people appear to disapprove or ridicule this as a piece of Anglomania more likely to be practised by a *parvenu* than by the scion of a really old family. Virginians used to set much store by their pedigrees, and the letters F. F. V. (First Families of Virginia) had become a sort of jest against persons pluming themselves on their social position in the Old Dominion.† Since the war, however, which has shattered old Virginian society from its foundations, one hears little of such pretensions.‡

The fault which Americans are most frequently accused of is the worship of wealth. The amazing fuss which is made

* In all the cases mentioned in the text I remember to have been told by others, but never by the persons concerned, of the ancestry. This is an illustration of the fact that while such ancestry is felt to be a distinction, it would be thought bad taste for those who possess it to mention it unless they were asked.

† An anecdote is told of the captain of a steamer plying at a ferry from Maryland into Virginia, who being asked by a needy Virginian to give him a free passage across, inquired if the applicant belonged to one of the F. F. V. "No," answered the man, "I can't exactly say that, — rather to one of the second families." "Jump on board," said the captain; "I never met one of your sort before."

‡ A few years ago a club was formed in New York to include only persons who could prove that their progenitors were settled in the State before the Revolution; and I daresay clubs exist elsewhere making similar claims to exclusiveness.

about very rich men, the descriptions of their doings, the
speculation as to their intentions, the gossip about their
private life, lend color to the reproach. He who builds up
a huge fortune, especially if he does it suddenly, is no doubt
a sort of hero, because an enormous number of men have the
same ambition. Having done best what millions are trying
to do, he is discussed, admired, and envied in the same way as
the captain of a cricket eleven is at a large English school, or
the stroke of the university boat at Oxford or Cambridge.
If he be a great financier, or the owner of a great railroad or
a great newspaper, he exercises vast power, and is therefore
well worth courting by those who desire his help or would
avert his enmity. Admitting all this, it may seem a paradox
to observe that a millionnaire has a better and easier social
career open to him in England than in America. Nevertheless there is a sense in which this is true. In America, if
his private character be bad, if he be mean, or openly immoral, or personally vulgar, or dishonest, the best society
will keep its doors closed against him. In England, great
wealth, skilfully employed, will more readily force these
doors to open. For in England great wealth can, by using
the appropriate methods, practically buy rank from those
who bestow it ; or by obliging persons whose position enables
them to command fashionable society, can induce them to
stand sponsors for the upstart and force him into society, —
a thing which no person in America has the power of doing.
To effect such a stroke in England the rich man must of
course have stopped short of positive frauds ; that is, of such
frauds as can be proved in a court of law. But he may be
still distrusted and disliked by the *élite* of the commercial
world, he may be vulgar and ill-educated, and indeed have
nothing to recommend him except his wealth and his willingness to spend it in providing amusement for fashionable people.
All this will not prevent him from becoming a baronet, or
possibly a peer, and thereby acquiring a position of assured

dignity which he can transmit to his offspring. The existence of a system of artificial rank enables a stamp to be given to base metal in Europe which cannot be given in a thoroughly republican country.* The feeling of the American public towards the very rich is, so far as a stranger can judge, one of curiosity and wonder rather than of respect. There is less snobbishness shown towards them than in England. They are admired as a famous runner or a jockey is admired, but do not seem to receive either flattery or social deference. When a man has won great wealth by the display of remarkable talents, as is the case with some of the manufacturers and railroad kings, the case is rather different, for it is felt that his gifts are a credit to the nation.

The persons to whom official rank gives importance are very few indeed, being for the nation at large only about one hundred persons at the top of the Federal Government, and in each State less than a dozen of its highest state functionaries. For these state functionaries, indeed, the respect shown is extremely scanty, and much more official than personal. A high Federal officer, a senator, or justice of the Supreme Court, or cabinet minister, is conspicuous while he holds his place, and is of course a personage in any private society he may enter, but less so than a corresponding official would be in Europe. A simple member of the House of Representatives is nobody. Even men of the highest official rank do not give themselves airs on the score of their position. Some years ago, being in Washington, I was taken by a friend to be presented to the Commander-in-chief of the United States army, — a great soldier, whose fame all the world knows. We

---

* The English system of hereditary titles tends to maintain the distinction of ancient lineage far less perfectly than that simple use of a family name which prevailed in ancient Rome, and in Italy during the Middle Ages. A Colonna or a Doria, like a Cornelius or a Valerius, carried the glory of his nobility in his name, whereas any upstart may be created a duke.

found him standing at a desk in a bare room in the War
Department, at work with one clerk. While he was talking
to us the door of the room was pushed open, and there appeared the figure of a Western tourist, belonging to what
Europeans would call the lower middle class, followed by his
wife and sister, who were " doing" Washington. Perceiving
that the room was occupied, they began to retreat; but the
Commander-in-chief called them back. " Walk in, ladies,"
he said. " You can look around; you won't disturb me.
Make yourselves at home."

Intellectual attainment does not excite much notice till it
becomes eminent, — that is to say, till it either places its possessor in a conspicuous position, such as that of president of
one of the greatest universities, or till it has made him well
known to the world as a preacher, or writer, or scientific
discoverer. When this kind of eminence has been reached,
it receives more respect than anywhere in Europe, except
possibly in Italy, where the interest in learned men, or
poets, or artists, seems to be greater than anywhere else in
Europe.* A famous writer or divine is known by name to
a far greater number of persons in America than would
know a similar person in any European country. He is
one of the glories of the country. There is no artificial
rank to cast him into the shade. He is possibly less
famous than the railroad kings or manipulators of the stock-
markets; but he excites a different kind of sentiment, and
people are willing to honor him in a way, sometimes dis-
tasteful to himself, which would not be applied to the
millionnaire except by those who sought to gain something
from him.

* In Germany great respect is no doubt felt for the leaders of learning
and science ; but they are regarded as belonging to a world of their own,
separated by a wide gulf from the territorial aristocracy, which still deems
itself (as in the days of Candide) a different form of mankind from those
who have not sixteen quarterings to show.

Perhaps the best way of explaining how some of the differences above mentioned, in wealth or official position or intellectual eminence, affect social equality is by reverting to what was called, a few pages back, Equality of Estimation, — the idea which men form of other men as compared with themselves. It is in this that the real sense of equality comes out. In America men hold others to be at bottom exactly the same as themselves. If a man is enormously rich like A. T. Stewart or William H. Vanderbilt, or if he is a great orator like Daniel Webster or Henry Ward Beecher, or a great soldier like Ulysses S. Grant, or a great writer like R. W. Emerson, or President of the United States, so much the better for him. He is an object of interest, perhaps of admiration, possibly even of reverence. But he is deemed to be still of the same flesh and blood as other men. The admiration felt for him may be a reason for going to see him, and longing to shake hands with him. But it is not a reason for bowing down to him, or addressing him in deferential terms, or treating him as if he was porcelain and yourself only earthenware.* In this respect there is, I think, a difference, slight but perceptible, between the sentiment of equality as it exists in the United States and as one finds it in France and Switzerland, the countries of the Old World where (if we except Norway, which has never had a titled aristocracy) social equality has made the greatest progress. In France and Switzerland there lingers a kind of feeling as if the old *noblesse*

* This is seen even in the manner of American servants. Although there is an aversion among native Americans to enter domestic service, the temporary discharge of such duties does not necessarily involve any loss of caste. Twenty years ago I remember to have found all the waiting in a large hotel in the White Mountains done by the daughters of respectable New England farmers in the low country, who had come up for their summer change of air to this place of resort, and were earning their board and lodging by acting as waitresses. They were treated by the guests as equals, and were indeed educated and well-mannered young women.

were not quite like other men. The Swiss peasant, with all his manly independence, has in many cantons a touch of instinctive reverence for the old families ; or perhaps, in some other cantons, a touch of jealousy which makes him desire to exclude their members from office, because he feels that they still think themselves better than he is. Nothing like this is possible in America, where the very notion of such distinctions excites a wondering curiosity as to what sort of creature the titled noble of Europe can be.

The total absence of rank and the universal acceptance of equality do not however prevent the existence of grades and distinctions in society which, though they may find no tangible expression, are sometimes as sharply drawn as in Europe. Except in the newer parts of the West, those who deem themselves ladies and gentlemen draw just the same line between themselves and the multitude as is drawn in England, and draw it in much the same way. The nature of a man's occupation, his education, his manners and breeding,* his income, his connections, all come into view in determining whether he is in this narrow sense of the word " a gentleman," almost as they would in England, though in most parts of the United States personal qualities count for rather more than in England, and occupation for rather less. The word is equally indefinable in both countries, but in America the expression " not quite a lady" seems to be less frequently employed. One is told, however, that the son of cultivated parents would not like to enter a retail store ; and even in a Western city like Detroit the best people will say of a party that it was " very mixed." In some of the older cities society is as

---

* On the New York Elevated Railroad smoking is not permitted in any car. When I asked a conductor how he was able to enforce this rule, considering that on every other railway smoking was practised, he answered, "I always say when any one seems disposed to insist, ' Sir, I am sure that if you are a gentleman you will not wish to bring me into a difficulty ; ' and then they always leave off."

exclusive as in the more old-fashioned English counties, the
" best set" considering itself very select indeed.   In such a
city I remember to have heard a family belonging to the best
set, which is mostly to be found in a particular quarter of the
city, speak of the inhabitants of a handsome suburb two miles
away just as Belgravians might speak of Islington ; and the
son of the family, who, having made in Europe the acquaintance of some of the dwellers in this suburb, had gone to a
ball there, was questioned by his sisters about their manners
and customs much as if he had returned from visiting a tribe
in Central Africa.   On inquiry I discovered that these North
Shore people were as rich and doubtless thought themselves as
cultivated as the people of my friend's quarter.   But all the
city knew that the latter were the " best set."   One is told
that this exclusiveness spreads steadily from East to West,
and that before long there will be such sets in all the greater
cities.

Europeans have been known to ask whether the United
States do not suffer from the absence of a hereditary nobility.
As may be supposed, such a question excites mirth in America : it is as if you were to offer them a Court and an Established Church.   They remark, with truth, that since Pitt in
England and the Napoleons in France prostituted hereditary
titles, these have ceased to be either respectable or useful.
" They do not," say the Americans, " suggest antiquity, for
the English families that enjoy them are mostly new ; they
are not associated, like the older and now extinct titles, with
the history of your nation : they are merely a prize offered to
wealth, the expression of a desire for gilding that plutocracy
which has replaced the ancient aristocracy of your country.
Seeing how little service hereditary nobility renders in maintaining the standard either of manners or morals * or honor or

* The moral and social standard which American society enforces is in
some respects more exacting than that of England.   I have frequently
heard Americans express surprise at the reception accorded by fashionable

public duty, few sensible men would create it in any European country where it did not exist. Much less then should we dream of creating it in America, which possesses none of the materials or conditions which could make it tolerable. If a peerage is purchasable even in England, where the dignity of the older nobility might have suggested some care in bestowal, purchasable not so openly as in Portugal or a German principality, but practically purchasable by party services and by large subscriptions to public purposes, much more would it be purchasable here, where there are no traditions to break down, where wealth accumulates rapidly, and the wealthy seek every avenue for display. Titles in this country would be simply an additional prize offered to wealth and ambition. They could not be respected. They would make us as snobbish as you are. They would be an unmixed evil." A European observer will not quarrel with this judgment. There is already a disposition in America, as everywhere else, to relish and make the most of such professional or official titles as can be had: it is a harmless way of trying to relieve the monotony of the world. If there be, as no doubt there is, less disposition than in England to run after and pay court to the great or the fashionable, this is perhaps due, not to any superior virtue, but to the absence of those opportunities and temptations which their hereditary titles and other social institutions set before the English. It would be the very wantonness of folly to create in the new country what most thinking people would gladly be rid of in the old one.

Another question is more serious and less easily answered: What is the effect of social equality upon manners? Many causes go to the making of manners, as one may see by noting how much better they are in some parts of Europe than in other parts, where nevertheless the structure of society is equally aristocratic, or democratic, as the case may be. One

London to Americans whom they held cheap, or to persons, whether English or foreign, whose transgressions had become matter of notoriety.

must therefore be careful not to ascribe to this source alone such peculiarities as America shows. On the whole, bearing in mind that the English race has less than some other races of that quickness of perception and sympathy which goes far to make manners good, the Americans have gained more than they have lost by equality. I do not think that the upper class loses in grace, I am sure that the humbler class gains in independence. The manners of the "best people" are exactly those of England, with a thought more of consideration towards inferiors and of frankness towards equals. Among the masses there is, generally speaking,* as much real courtesy and good-nature as anywhere else in the world. There is less outward politeness than in some parts of Europe, — Portugal, for instance, or Tuscany, or Sweden. There is a certain coolness or off-handedness which at first annoys the European visitor who still thinks himself "a superior;" but when he perceives that it is not meant for insolence, and that native Americans do not notice it, he learns to acquiesce. Perhaps the worst manners are those of persons dressed in some rag of authority. The railroad car-conductor has a bad name; but personally I have always been well treated by him, and remember with pleasure one on a Southern railroad (an ex-Confederate soldier) who did the honors of his car with a dignified courtesy worthy of those Hungarian nobles who are said to have the best manners in Europe. The hotel clerk is supercilious, but if one frankly admits his superiority, his patronage becomes friendly, and he may even condescend to interest himself in making your stay in the city agreeable. One finds

---

* There are parts of the West which still lack polish; and the behavior of the whites to the Chinese often incenses a stranger from the Atlantic States or Europe. I remember in Oregon to have seen a huge navvy turn an inoffensive Chinaman out of his seat in a railway car; and when I went to the conductor and endeavored to invoke his interference, he calmly remarked, " Yes, I know those things do make the English mad." On the other hand, on the Pacific slope colored people often sit down to table with whites.

most courtesy among the rural population of New England and the Middle States, least among the recent immigrants in the cities and the unsettled population of the West. However, the most material point to remark is the improvement of recent years. The concurrent testimony of European travellers, including both admirers and detractors of democracy, proves that manners must have been disagreeable forty years ago; and one finds nowadays an equally general admission that the Americans are as pleasant to one another and to strangers as are the French or the Germans or the English. The feature least agreeable to the visitors of former years, — an incessant vaunting of their own country, and disparagement of others, — has disappeared, and the tinge of self-assertion which the sense of equality used to give is now but faintly noticeable.

CHAPTER X.

THE INFLUENCE OF DEMOCRACY ON THOUGHT.

Two opposite theories regarding the influence of democratic institutions on intellectual activity have found currency. One theory extols them because they stimulate the mind of a people, not only sharpening men's wits by continual struggle and unrest, but giving to each citizen a sense of his own powers and duties in the world, which spurs him on to exertions in ever-widening fields. This theory is commonly applied to Athens and other democracies of the ancient world, as contrasted with Sparta and the oligarchic cities, whose intellectual production was scanty or altogether wanting. It compares the Rome of Cicero, Lucretius, and Catullus, and the Augustan age, whose great figures were born under the Republic, with the vaster but comparatively sterile Roman world of Marcus Aurelius or Constantine, when freedom had long since vanished. It notes the outburst of literary and artistic splendor that fell in the later age of the republics of mediæval Italy, and dwells with especial pleasure on the achievements of Florence, — the longest-lived and the most glorious of the free commonwealths of Italy.

According to the other theory, Democracy is the child of ignorance, the parent of dulness and conceit. The opinion of the greatest number being the universal standard, everything is reduced to the level of vulgar minds. Originality is stunted, variety disappears, no man thinks for himself, or, if he does, fears to express what he thinks. A drear pall of monotony covers the sky.

"Thy hand, great Anarch, lets the curtain fall,
  And universal darkness buries all."

This doctrine seems to date from the appearance of Toc-queville's book, though his professed disciples have pushed it much farther than his words warrant. It is really an à priori doctrine, drawn from imagining what the consequences of a complete equality of material conditions and political powers ought to be. But it claims to rest upon the observed phenomena of the United States, which, thirty years ago, were still the only great modern democracy; and it was with reference to the United States that it was enunciated by Mr. Robert Lowe, in one of those speeches of 1866 which so greatly impressed his contemporaries.

Both these theories will be found on examination to be baseless. Both, so far as they are à priori theories, are fan-ciful; both, in so far as they purport to rest upon the facts of history, err by regarding one set of facts only, and ignoring a great number of concomitant conditions which have prob-ably more to do with the result than the few conditions which have been arbitrarily taken to be sufficient causes. None of the Greek republics was a democracy in the modern sense, for all rested upon slavery; nor, indeed, can the name be applied, except at passing moments, to the Italian cities. Many circumstances besides their popular government com-bined to place the imperishable crown of literary and artistic glory upon the brows of the city of the Violet and the city of the Lily. So also the view that a democratic land is neces-sarily a land of barren monotony, while unsound even as a deduction from general principles, is still more unsound in its assumption of certain phenomena as true of America, and in the face it puts on the phenomena it has assumed. The theorists who have propounded it give us, like Daniel, the dream as well as their interpretation of it. But the dream is one of their own inventing; and such as it is, it is wrongly interpreted.

Few mistakes are more common than that of exaggerating the influence of forms of government. As there are historians and politicians who, when they come across a trait of national character for which no obvious explanation presents itself, set it down to " race," so there are writers and speakers who, too indolent to examine the whole facts of the case, or too ill-trained to feel the need of such examination, pounce upon the political institutions of a country as the easiest way to account for its social and intellectual, perhaps even for its moral and religious, peculiarities. Few problems are in reality more complex than the relation between the political and the intellectual life of a country; few things more difficult to distinguish than the influences respectively attributable to an equality of political rights and powers on the one hand, an equality of material and social conditions on the other. It is commonly assumed that Democracy and Equality go hand in hand; but as one may have popular government along with enormous differences of wealth and dissimilarities in social usage, so also one may have social equality under a despot. Doubtless, when social and political equality go hand in hand they intensify one another; but when inequality of material conditions becomes marked, social life changes, and as social phenomena become more complex, their analysis becomes more difficult.

Reverting to the two theories from which we set out, it may be said that the United States furnish little support to either. American democracy has certainly produced no age of Pericles. Neither has it dwarfed literature and led a wretched people, so dull as not even to realize their dulness, into a barren plain of featureless mediocrity. To ascribe the deficiencies, such as they are, of art and culture in America, solely or even mainly to her form of government, is not less absurd than to ascribe, as many Americans of what I may call the trumpeting school do, her marvellous material progress to the same cause. It is not Democracy that has paid off a gigantic debt and raised Chicago out of a swamp; neither is it Democracy that has denied her philosophers like Burke and poets like Wordsworth.

Most writers who have dealt with these matters have not only laid more upon the shoulders of democratic government than it ought to bear, but have preferred abstract speculations to the humbler task of ascertaining and weighing the facts. They have spun ingenious theories about democracy as the source of this or that, or whatever it pleased them to assume; they have not tried to determine by a wide induction what specific results appear in countries which, differing in other respects, agree in being democratically governed. If I do not follow these time-honored precedents, it is not because the process is difficult, but because it is unprofitable. These speculations have perhaps had their use in suggesting to us what phenomena we ought to look for in democratic countries; but if positive results are to be reached, they must be reached by carefully verifying the intellectual phenomena of more than one country, and establishing an unmistakable relation between them and the political institutions under which they prevail.

If some one, starting from the current conception of democracy, were to say that in a democratic nation we should find a disposition to bold and unbridled speculations, sparing neither theology nor morals, a total absence of rule, tradition, and precedent, each man thinking and writing as responsible to no criticism, "every poet his own Aristotle," a taste for strong effects and garish colors, valuing force rather than fineness, grandeur rather than beauty, a vigorous, hasty, impetuous style of speaking and writing, a grandiose and perhaps sensational art, — he would say what would be quite as natural and reasonable à *priori* as most of the pictures given us of democratic societies. Yet many of the suggested features would be the opposite of those which America presents.

Every such picture must be fanciful. He who starts from so simple and (so to speak) bare a conception as that of equal civil rights and equal political powers vested in every member of the community cannot but have recourse to his fancy in trying to body forth the results of this principle. Let any one study the portrait of the democratic man and democratic city which the first and greatest of all the hostile critics of democracy has left us,* and compare it with the very different descriptions of life and culture under a popular government in which European speculation has disported itself since Tocqueville's time : he will find each theory plausible in the abstract, and each equally unlike the facts which contemporary America sets before us.

Let us then bid farewell to fancy, and endeavor to discover what are now the salient intellectual features of the mass of the native population in the United States.

As there is much difference of opinion regarding them, I present with diffidence the following list : —

1. A desire to be abreast of the best thought and work of the world everywhere, to have every form of literature and art adequately represented and excellent of its kind, so that America shall be felt to hold her own among the nations.

2. A fondness for bold and striking effects, a preference for large generalizations and theories which have an air of completeness.

3. An absence among the multitude of refined taste, and disposition to be attracted rather by general brilliance than by delicacy of workmanship ; a want of mellowness and inadequate perception of the difference between first-rate work in a quiet style and mere flatness.

* Plato indeed indulges his fancy so far as to describe the very mules and asses of a democracy as prancing along the roads, scarcely deigning to bear their burdens. The passion for unrestrained license, for novelty, for variety, is to him the note of democracy ; whereas monotony, and even obstinate conservatism, are the faults which the latest European critics bid us expect.

4. Little respect for canons or traditions, accompanied by the notion that new conditions must of necessity produce new ideas.

5. An undervaluing of special knowledge or experience, except perhaps in the sphere of applied science and commerce, an idea that an able man can do one thing pretty much as well as another, — as Dr. Johnson thought that if he had taken to politics he would have been as distinguished therein as he was in poetry.

6. An admiration for literary or scientific eminence, an enthusiasm for anything that can be called genius, with an over readiness to discover it.

7. A love of intellectual novelties.

8. An intellectual impatience, and desire for quick and patent results.

9. An over-valuing of the judgments of the multitude; a disposition to judge by the test of success work which has not been produced for the sake of success.

10. A tendency to mistake bigness for greatness.

Contrariwise, if we regard, not the people generally, but the most cultivated class, we shall find, together with some of the above-mentioned qualities, others which indicate a reaction against the popular tendencies. This class has a strong relish for subtlety of thought and highly finished art, whether in literature or painting. It is so much afraid of crudity and vagueness as to be prone to devote itself to minute and careful study of subjects unattractive to the masses.

Of these characteristics of the people at large some may at first sight seem inconsistent with others; as, for instance, the admiration for intellectual gifts, with the undervaluing of special knowledge: nevertheless it could be shown that both are discoverable in Americans as compared with Englishmen. The former admire intelligence more than the latter do; but they defer less to special competence. However, assuming for the moment that there is something true in these suggestions, which it would take too long to attempt to establish one by one, be it observed that very few of them can be directly connected with democratic government. Even these few might take a different form in a differently situated democracy. The seventh and eighth seem due to the general intelligence and education of the people; while the remainder, though not wholly uninfluenced by the habits which popular government tends to breed, must be mainly ascribed to the vast size of the country, the vast numbers and homogeneity of its native white population, the prevalence of social equality, a busy industrialism, a restless changefulness of occupation, and the absence of a leisured class dominant in matters of taste, — conditions that have little or nothing to do with political institutions. The prevalence of evangelical Protestantism has been quite as important a factor in the intellectual life of the nation as its form of government.

Some one may say — I wish to state the view fairly, though I do not entirely agree with it — that, assuming the foregoing analysis to be correct, the influence of democracy, apart from its tendency to secure an ample provision of education, is discernible in two points. It produces self-confidence and self-complacency, national and personal, with the result both of stimulating a certain amount of thought, and of preventing the thought that is so produced from being subjected to proper tests. Ambition and self-esteem will call out what might have lain dormant; but they will hinder a nation, as they do a man, from duly judging its own work, and in so far will retard its progress. Those who are naturally led to trust and obey common-sense and the numerical majority in matters of state, overvalue the judgment of the majority in other matters. Now the judgment of the masses is a poor standard for the thinker or the artist to set before him. It may narrow his view and debase his style. He fears to tread in new paths or express unpopular opinions; or if he despises the multitude, he may take refuge in an acrid cynicism. Where the masses rule, a writer cannot but think of the masses; and as they do not appreciate refinements, he will eschew these, making himself at all hazards intelligible to the common mind, and seeking to attract by broad, perhaps coarsely broad, effects, the hasty reader, who at the circulating libraries passes by Walter Scott or Thackeray to fasten on the latest sketch of fashionable life or mysterious crime.

I do not deny that there is some force in this way of putting the case. Democracy tends to produce a superficially active public, and perhaps also a jubilant and self-confident public. But it is quite possible to have a democratic people which shall be neither fond of letters nor disposed to trust its own judgment and taste in judging them. Much will depend on the other features of the situation. In the United States the cultivated public increases rapidly, and the very reaction which goes on within it against the defects of the multitude becomes an important factor. All things considered, I doubt whether democracy tends to discourage originality, subtlety, refinement, in thought and in expression, whether literary or artistic. I doubt if there be any solid ground for expecting monotony or vulgarity under one form of government more than another. The causes lie deeper. Art and literature have before now been base and vulgar under absolute monarchies and under oligarchies. One of the most polished and aristocratic societies in Europe has for two centuries been that of Vienna; yet what society could have been intellectually duller or less productive? Moreover, it must not be forgotten that the habits of popular government which open a career to talent in public life, open it in literature also. No man need lean on a faction or propitiate a coterie. A pure, clear voice, with an unwonted message, may at first fail to make itself heard over the din of competitors for popular favor; but once heard, it and its message will probably be judged on their own merits.

Passing away from this question as to the supposed nar-
cotic power of democracy, the further question may be asked,
What is the distinctive note of democratic thought and art as
they actually appear in the United States? What is the peculiar quality or flavor which springs from this political element
in their condition? I cannot tell. I find no such note. I
have searched for it, and, as the Americans say, it is hard
work looking for what is not there. Some Europeans and
many Americans profess to have found it, and will tell you
that this or that peculiarity of American literature is due to
democracy. No doubt, if you take individual writers you
may discover in several of them something, though not
always the same thing, which savors of democratic feeling,
and tinges their way of regarding human life. But that is
not enough. What must be shown is a general quality running through the majority of these writers, — a quality which
is at once recognized as racy of the soil, and which can be
traced back to the democratic element which the soil un-
doubtedly contains. No such quality seems to have been
shown. That there is a distinctive note in many — not, perhaps, in all — of the best American books may be admitted.
It may be caught by ears not the most delicate. But is this
note the voice of democracy? Is it even the voice of democracy and equality combined? There is a difference, slight
yet perceptible, in the part which both sentiment and humor
play in American books, when we compare them with English
books of equivalent strength. The humor has a vein of
oddity, and the contrast between the soft copiousness of the
sentiment and the rigid lines of lingering Puritanism which
it suffuses, is rarely met with in England. Perhaps there is
less repose in the American style; there is certainly a curious
unrestfulness in the effort, less common in English writers,
to bend metaphors to unwonted uses. But are these differences, with others I might mention — and, after all, they are
slight — due to any cause connected with politics? Are they

not rather due to a mixed and curiously intertwined variety
of other causes which have moulded the American mind during the last two centuries?   American imagination has produced nothing more conspicuously original than the romances
of Hawthorne.   If any one says that he finds something in
them which he remembers in no previous English writer, we
know what is meant, and probably agree.   But can it be said
that there is anything distinctively American in Hawthorne,
— that is to say, that his specific quality is of a kind which
reappears in other American writers?   Few will affirm this.
The most peculiar, and therefore I suppose the most charac-
teristically American, school of thought, has been what used
to be called the Concord or Transcendental school of forty
years ago, among the writings produced by which, those of
Emerson are best known in Europe.   Were the authors of
that school distinctively democratic either in the color of
their thought, or in its direction, or in the style which expresses it?   And if so, can the same democratic tinge be
discerned in the authors of to-day?   I doubt it; but such
matters do not admit of proof or disproof.   One must leave
them to the literary feeling of the reader.

A very distinguished American man of letters once said to
me that he hated nothing so much as to hear people talk
about American literature.   He meant, I think, that those
who did so were puzzling themselves unnecessarily to find
something which belonged to a new country, and a democratic country, and were forgetting or ignoring the natural
relation of works of imagination and thought produced in
America to books written by men of the same race in the Old
World before and since 1776.

So far, then, as regards American literature generally, I do
not believe that there is in it anything specifically democratic.
Nor if we look at the various departments of speculative
thought, such as metaphysics and theology, or at those which
approach nearer to the exact sciences, such as economics and

jurisprudence, shall we find that the character and substance of the doctrines propounded bear marked traces of a democratic influence. Why should we be surprised at this, seeing that the influence of a form of government is only one among many influences, even where a nation stands alone, and creates a literature distinctively local? But can books written in the United States be deemed to constitute a literature locally American in the same sense as the literatures of France and Germany, of Italy and Russia, belong to those countries? For the purposes of thought and art, the United States are a part of England, and England is a part of America. Many English books are more widely read and strike deeper to the heart in America than in England. Some American books have a like fortune in England. Differences there are, but differences how trivial compared with the resemblances in temper, in feeling, in susceptibility to certain forms of moral and physical beauty, in the general view of life and nature, in the disposition to revere and be swayed by the same matchless models of that elder literature which both branches of the English race can equally claim. American literature does not to-day differ more from English literature than the Scottish writers of eighty or a hundred years ago — Burns, Scott, Adam Smith, Reid, Hume, Robertson — differed from their English contemporaries. There was a fondness for abstractions and generalizations in the Scottish prose writers; there was in the Scottish poets a bloom and fragrance of mountain heather which gave to their work a charm of freshness and singularity, like that which a faint touch of local accent gives to the tongue of an orator. But they were English as well as Scottish writers; they belong to English literature, and make part of its glory to the world beyond. So Fenimore Cooper, Hawthorne, Emerson, Longfellow, and those on whom their mantle has fallen, belong to England as well as to America; and English writers, as they more and more realize the vastness of the American public they address, will more and more feel themselves to be American as well as English, and will often find in America not only a larger but a more responsive audience.

We have been here concerned not to discuss the merits and estimate the place of American thinkers and writers, but only to examine the relation in which they stand to their political and social environment. That relation, however, sets before us one more question. The English-speaking population of the United States is one third larger than that of the United Kingdom. It is a more educated population, in which a greater number of persons come under the influence of books, and might therefore be stirred up to intellectual production. Why then does it not make more important contributions to the common literary wealth of the race? Is there a want of creative power? and if so, to what is the want due?

This is a question frequently propounded. I propose to consider it in the chapter which follows.

CHAPTER XI.

CREATIVE INTELLECTUAL POWER.

THERE is a street in Florence on each side of which stand statues of the famous Florentines of the fourteenth and fifteenth centuries, — Dante, Giotto, Petrarch, Boccaccio, Ghiberti, Machiavelli, Michael Angelo, and others scarcely less illustrious, all natives of the little city which in their days had never a population of more than sixty thousand souls.* No one can walk between these rows of world-famous figures, matched by no other city of the modern world, without asking himself what cause determined so much of the highest genius to this one spot; why in Italy herself populous Milan and Naples and Venice have no such list to show; why the succession of greatness stopped with the beginning of the sixteenth century and has never been resumed? Questions substantially the same constantly rise to the mind in reading the history of other countries. Why did England produce no first-rate poet in the two stirring centuries between Chaucer and Shakspeare, and again in the century and a half between Milton's birth and Wordsworth's? Why have epochs of comparative sterility more than once fallen upon Germany and France? And why has music sometimes reached its highest pitch of excellence at moments when the other arts were languishing? Why does the sceptre of intellectual and artistic leadership pass now to one great nation, now to another, inconstant and unpredictable as are the shifting winds?

* Petrarch saw the light in Arezzo, but his family was Florentine, and it was by a mere accident that he was born away from his own city.

These questions touch the deepest and most complex problems of history, and neither historian nor physiologist has yet been able to throw any real light upon them. Even the commonplace remark that times of effort and struggle tend to develop an unusually active intellectual movement, and therewith to awaken or nourish rare geniuses, is not altogether true; for some of the geniuses have arisen at moments when there was no excitement to call them forth, and at other times seasons of storm and stress have raised up no one capable of directing the efforts or interpreting the feelings of his generation. One thing, however, is palpable: numbers have nothing to do with the matter. There is no average of a man of genius to so many thousands or millions of persons. Out of the sixty thousand of Florence there arise during two centuries more men of undying fame than out of huge London during the last three centuries. Even the stock of solid second-class ability does not necessarily increase with increasing numbers; while as to those rare combinations of gifts which produce poetry or philosophy of the first order, they are revealed no more frequently in a great European nation now than they were in a Semitic tribe or a tiny Greek city twenty-five or thirty centuries ago.

There is therefore no reason why the absence of brilliant genius among the sixty millions in the United States should excite any surprise; we might as well wonder that there is no Goethe or Schiller or Kant or Hegel in the Germany of to-day, so much more populous and better educated than the Germany of their birth-time. It is not to be made a reproach against America that men like Tennyson or Darwin have not been born there. "The wind bloweth where it listeth;" the rarest gifts appear no one can tell why or how. In broad France a century ago no man was found able to spring upon the neck of the Revolution and turn it to his will. Fate brought her favorite from a wild Italian island that had but just passed under the yoke of the nation to which it gave a master.

The question we have to ask as regards the United States is therefore not why it has given us few men of the highest and rarest distinction, but whether it has failed to produce its fair share of talents of the second rank ; that is, of men capable of taking the lead in all the great branches of literary or artistic or scientific activity, men who instruct and delight their own generation, though possibly future generations may not hold all of them in remembrance.

Have fewer men of this order adorned the roll of fame in the United States, during the century of their independence, than in England or France or Germany during the same period? Obviously this is the fact as regards art in all its branches, and also as regards physical and mathematical science. In literature the disparity is less evident; yet most candid Americans will agree with Englishmen that it is greater than those who know the education and intelligence of the younger people would have expected. · I pass by oratory and statesmanship, because comparison is in these fields very difficult. The fact therefore being admitted, we have to endeavor to account for it.

If the matter were one of numerical averages, it would be pertinent to remark that of the sixty millions of people in the United States seven or eight millions are negroes, at present altogether below the stratum from which production can be expected ; that of the whites there may be nearly two millions to whom English is a foreign language, and that several millions are recent immigrants from Europe. This diminishes the contrast between numbers and intellectual results. But numbers have so little to do with the question that the point deserves no more than a passing reference.

Those who have discussed the conditions of intellectual productivity have often remarked that epochs of stir and excitement are favorable, because they stimulate men's minds, setting new ideas afloat and awakening new ambitions. It is also true that vigorous, unremitting labor is, speaking generally, needed for the production of good work, and that one is therefore less entitled to expect it in an indolent time and from members of the luxurious classes. But it is not less true, though less frequently observed, that tranquillity and repose are necessary to men of the kind we are considering, and often helpful even to the highest geniuses, for the evolving of new thoughts and the creation of forms of finished and harmonious beauty. He who is to do such work must have time to meditate, and pause, and meditate again. He must be able to set his creation aside, and return to it after days or weeks to look at it with fresh eyes. He must be neither distracted from his main purpose, nor hurried in effecting it. He must be able to concentrate the whole force of his reason or imagination on one subject, to abstract himself when needful from the flitting sights and many-voiced clamor of the outer world. Juvenal said this long ago about the poet; it also applies, though possibly in a lower degree, both to the artist and to the serious thinker or delicate workman in any field of literature, to the metaphysician, the theologian, the philosophic historian, the economist, the philologist, even the novelist and the statesman. I have heard men who had gone from a quiet life into politics complain that they found their thinking powers wither, and that while they became far more expert in getting up subjects and speaking forcibly and plausibly, they found it harder and harder to form sound general views and penetrate beneath the superficialities of the newspaper and the platform. Interrupted thought, trains of reflection or imaginative conceptions constantly broken by a variety of petty, transient calls of business, claims of society, matters passing in the world to note and think of, not only tire the mind, but destroy its chances of attaining just and deep views of life and nature, as a wind-ruffled pool ceases to reflect the rocks and woods around it. Mohammed falling into trances on the mountain above Mecca, Dante in the sylvan solitudes of Fonte Avellana, Cervantes and Bunyan in the enforced seclusion of a prison, Hegel so

rapt and lost in his speculations that, taking his manu-
script to the publisher in Jena on the day of the great battle,
he was surprised to see French soldiers in the streets : these
are types of the men and conditions which give birth to
thoughts that occupy succeeding generations ; and what is
true of these greatest men is perhaps even more true of men
of the next rank.　Doubtless many great works have been
produced among inauspicious surroundings, and even under
severe pressure of time ; but it will, I think, be almost invariably found that the producer had formed his ideas or conceived his creations in hours of comparative tranquillity,
and had turned on them the full stream of his powers,
to the exclusion of whatever could break or divert its
force.

In Europe men call this a century of unrest.　But the
United States is more unrestful than Europe, more unrestful
than any country we know of has yet been.　Nearly every one
is busy ; those few who have not to earn their living, and do
not feel called to serve their countrymen, find themselves out
of place, and have been wont either to make amusement into
a business, or to transfer themselves to the ease of France
or Italy.　The earning of one's living is not, indeed, incompatible with intellectually creative work, for many of those
who have done such work best have done it in addition to
their gainful occupation, or have earned their living by it.
But in America it is unusually hard for any one to withdraw
his mind from the endless variety of external impressions and
interests which daily life presents, and which impinge upon the
mind, I will not say to vex it, but to keep it constantly vibra-
ting to their touch.　Life is that of the squirrel in his revolv-
ing cage, never still even when it does not seem to change.
It becomes every day more and more so in England, and English literature and art show increasing marks of haste.　In
the United States the ceaseless stir and movement, the constant presence of newspapers, the eagerness which looks

through every pair of eyes, even that active intelligence and
sense of public duty, strongest in the best minds, which make
a citizen feel that he ought to know what is passing in the
wider world as well as in his own, — all these render life more
exciting to the average man than it is in Europe, but chase
away from it the opportunities for repose and meditation
which art and philosophy need, as growing plants need the
coolness and darkness of night no less than the blaze of day.
The type of mind which American conditions have evolved is
quick, vigorous, practical, versatile; but it is unfavorable to
the natural germination and slow ripening of large and lumi-
nous ideas, it wants the patience that will spend weeks or
months in bringing details to an exquisite perfection. And
accordingly we see that the most rich and finished literary
work America has given us has proceeded from the older
regions of the country, where the pulsations of life are slower
and steadier than in the West or in the great commercial
cities. It was from New England that nearly all the best
books of the last generation came; and that not solely because the English race has been purest there, and education
most generally diffused, for the New Englanders who have
gone West, though they have carried with them their moral
standard and their bright intelligence, seem either to have
left behind their gift for literary creation, or to care to
employ it only in teaching and in journalism.

It may be objected to this view that some of the great
literary ages, such as the Periclean age at Athens, the Medi-
cean age at Florence, the age of Elizabeth in England, have
been ages full of movement and excitement. But the unrestfulness which prevails in America is altogether different
from the large variety of life, the flow of stimulating ideas
and impressions, which marked those ages. Life is not as
interesting in America, except as regards commercial speculation, as it is in Europe, because society and the environment of man are too uniform. It is hurried and bustling;

it is filled with a multitude of duties and occupations and transient impressions. In the ages I have referred to, men had time enough for all there was to do; and the very scantiness of literature and rarity of news made that which was read and received tell more powerfully upon the imagination.

Nor is it only the distractions of American life that clog the wings of invention. The atmosphere is over-full of all that pertains to material progress. Americans themselves say, when excusing the comparative poverty of learning and science, that their chief occupation is at present the subjugation of their continent; that it is an occupation large enough to demand most of the energy and ambition of the nation; but that presently, when this work is done, the same energy and ambition will win similar triumphs in the fields of abstract thought, while the gifts which now make them the first nation in the world for practical inventions, will then assure to them a like place in scientific discovery.* There is evidently much truth in this. The attractions of practical life are so great to men conscious of their own vigor, the development of the West and the vast operations of commerce and finance which have accompanied that development have absorbed so many strenuous talents, that the supply of ability available, not only for pure science (apart from its applications) and for philosophical and historical studies, but even for statesmanship, has been proportionately reduced. But besides this withdrawal of an unusually large part of the nation's force, the predominance of material and practical interests has turned men's thoughts and conversation into a channel unfavorable to the growth of the higher and more solid kinds of literature, perhaps still more unfavorable to art. Goethe said, à propos of the good work produced by such men as

* "Chicago." A citizen of that exultant city is said to have remarked, "Chicago has not had time yet for culture, but when she takes it up she will make it hum."

Ampère and Mérimée at a very early age, "If a talent is to be speedily and happily developed, the chief point is that a great deal of intellect and sound culture should be current in a nation." There is certainly a great deal of intellect current in the United States; but it is chiefly directed to business, that is, to railways, to finance, to commerce, to inventions, to manufactures (as well as to practical professions like law), — things which play a relatively larger part than in Europe, as subjects of universal attention and discussion. There is abundance of sound culture, but it is so scattered about in divers places and among small groups which seldom meet one another that no large cultured society has arisen similar to that of European capitals or to that which her universities have created for Germany. In Boston twenty years ago a host could have brought together round his table nine men as interesting and cultivated as Paris or London would have furnished. But a similar party of eighteen could not have been collected; nor perhaps even the nine anywhere except in Boston. At present, culture is more diffused; there are many cities where men of high attainments and keen intellectual interests are found, and associate themselves in literary or scientific clubs. Societies for the study of particular authors are not uncommon among women. I remember to have been told of a Homer club and an Æschylus club formed by the ladies of St. Louis, and of a Dante club in some Eastern city. Nevertheless, a young talent gains less than it would gain in Europe from the surroundings into which it is born. The atmosphere is not charged with ideas as in Germany, nor with critical *finesse* as in France. Stimulative it is, but the stimulus drives eager youth away from the groves of the Muses into the struggling throng of the market-place.

It may be thought fanciful to add that in a new country one whole set of objects which appeal to the imagination are absent, — no castles gray with age; no solemn cathedrals whose altering styles of architecture carry the mind up or down the long stream of history from the eleventh to the seventeenth century; few spots or edifices consecrated by memories of famous men or deeds, and among these none of remote date. There is certainly no want of interest in those few spots: the warmth with which Americans cherish them puts to shame the indifference of the British Parliament to the historic and prehistoric sites and buildings of Britain. But not one American youth in a thousand comes under the spell of any such associations. In the city or State where he lives there is nothing to call him away from the present. All he sees is new, and has no glories to set before him save those of accumulated wealth and industry skilfully applied to severely practical ends.

Some one may say that if (as was observed in last chapter) English and American literature are practically one, there is no need to explain the fact that one part of a race undivided for literary purposes leaves the bulk of literary production to be done by the other part, seeing that it can enter freely into the labors of the latter and reckon them its own. To argue thus would be to push the doctrine of the unity of the two branches rather too far, for, after all, there is much in American conditions and life which needs its special literary and artistic interpretations; and the question would still confront us, why the transatlantic branch, nowise inferior in mental force, contributes less than its share to the common stock. Still it is certainly true that the existence of a great body of producers of literature in England, as in France of pictures, diminishes the need for production in America. Or, to put the same thing in another way, if the Americans did not speak English, they would evidently feel called on to create more high literature for themselves. Many books which America might produce are not produced because the men qualified to write them know that there are already English books on the same subject; and the higher such men's standard is, the more apt are they to overrate the advantages which English authors enjoy as compared with themselves. Many feelings and ideas which now find adequate expression through the English books which Americans read would then have to be expressed through American books, and their literature would be not only more individual, but more copious and energetic. If it lost in breadth, it would gain in freshness and independence. American authors conceive that even the non-recognition of international copyright has told for evil on their profession. Since the native writer has been undersold by reprints of English and French books, which, paying nothing to the European author, can be published at the cost of the paper and printing only, native authorship is discouraged, native talent diverted into other fields, while at the same time the intellectual standard of the public is lowered and its taste vulgarized. It might be thought that the profusion of cheap reprints would tend to quicken thought and diffuse the higher kinds of knowledge among the masses. But experience proves that by far the largest part of these reprints, and the part which is most extensively read, are novels, and among them many flimsy novels, which drive better books, including some of the best American fiction, out of the market, and tend to Europeanize the American mind in the worst way. One may smile at the suggestion that the allegiance of the working-classes to their democratic institutions will be seduced by descriptions of English duchesses; * yet it is probably true that the profusion of new frothy or highly-spiced fiction offered at twenty or twenty-five cents a volume tends to spoil the popular palate for the enjoyment of more wholesome and nutritious food. And if it injures the higher literature by diminishing the demand, it may further injure it by creating an atmosphere unfavorable to the growth of pure and earnest native literary talent.

* I have seen this argument advanced.

What then of the newspapers? The newspapers are too large a subject for this chapter, and their influence as organs of opinion has been already discussed. The vigor and brightness of many among them are surprising. Nothing escapes them ; everything is set in the sharpest, clearest light. Their want of reticence and delicacy is regretfully admitted by all educated Americans, — the editors included. The cause of this deficiency is probably to be found in the fact that whereas the first European journals were written for the polite world of large cities, American journals were early in their career, if not at its very beginning, written for the bulk of the people, and published in communities still so small that everybody's concerns were already pretty well known to everybody else. They had attained no high level of literary excellence when, some forty years ago, an enterprising man of unrefined taste created a new type of " live " newspaper, which made a rapid success by its smartness, copiousness, and variety, while addressing itself entirely to the multitude. Other papers were almost forced to shape themselves on the same lines, because the class which desired something more choice was still relatively small ; and now the journals of the chief cities have become such vast commercial concerns that they still think first of the mass, and are controlled by its tastes, which they have themselves done so much to create. There are cities where the more refined readers, who dislike flippant personalities, are counted by tens of thousands ; but in such cities competition is now too severe to hold out much prospect of success to a paper which does not expect the support of hundreds of thousands. It is not, however, with the æsthetic or moral view of the newspaper that we are here concerned, but with the effect on the national mind of the enormous ratio which the reading of newspapers bears to all other reading, — a ratio higher than even in France or England. A famous Englishman, himself a powerful and fertile thinker, contrasted the value of the history of Thucydides with that of a single number of the "Times" newspaper, — greatly to the advantage of the latter. Others may conceive that a thoughtful study of Thucydides, or, not to go beyond our own tongue, of Bacon, Milton, Locke, or Burke, — perhaps even of Gibbon, Grote, or Macaulay, — will do more to give keenness to the eye and strength to the wings of the mind than a whole year's reading of the best daily newspaper. It is not merely that the matter is of more permanent and intrinsic worth, nor that the manner and style form the student's taste; it is not merely that in the newspaper we are in contact with persons like ourselves, in the other case with rare and splendid intellects. The whole attitude of the reader is different. His attention is loose, his mind unbraced, so that he does not stop to scrutinize an argument, and forgets even valuable facts as quickly as he has learnt them. If he read Burke as he reads the newspaper, Burke would do him little good. And therefore the habit of mind produced by a diet largely composed of newspapers is adverse to solid thinking, and dulling to the sense of beauty. Scorched and stony is the soil which newspaper reading has prepared to receive the seeds of genius.

Does the modern world really gain, so far as creative thought is concerned, by the profusion of cheap literature? It is a question one often asks in watching the passengers on an American railway. A boy walks up and down the car scattering newspapers and books in paper covers right and left as he goes. The newspapers are glanced at, though probably most people have read several of the day's papers already. The books are nearly all novels. They are not usually bad in tone, and sometimes they give incidentally a superficial knowledge of things outside the personal experience of the reader; while from their newspapers the passengers draw a stock of information far beyond that of a European peasant, or even of an average European artisan. Yet one feels that this constant succession of transient ideas, none of them impressively though many of them startlingly stated, all of them flitting swiftly past the mental sight as the trees flit past the eyes when one looks out of the car window, is no more favorable to the development of serious intellectual interests and creative intellectual power than is the limited knowledge of the European artisan.

Most of the reasons I have hazarded to account for a phenomenon surprising to one who recognizes the quantity of intellect current in America, and the diffusion, far more general than in any other country, of intellectual curiosity, are reasons valid in the Europe of to-day as compared with the Europe of last century, and still more true of the modern world as compared with the best periods of the ancient. Printing is by no means pure gain to the creative faculties, whatever it may be to the acquisitive; even as a great ancient thinker seems to have thought that the invention of writing in Egypt had weakened the reflective powers of man. The question follows, Are these causes, supposing them to be true causes, likely to be more or less operative in the America of next century than they now are? Will America become more what Europe is now, or will she be even more American?

I have elsewhere thrown out some conjectures on this point. Meantime it is pertinent to ask what are the most recent developments of American thought and research; for this will help us to see whether the tide of productive endeavor is rising or falling.

The abundant and excellent work done in fiction need be mentioned only for the sake of calling attention to the interest it has, over and above its artistic merit, as a record of the local manners and usages and types of character in various parts of the Union, — types which are fast disappearing. The Creoles of Louisiana, the negroes under slavery, with African tales still surviving in their memories, the rough but kindly backwoodsmen of Indiana forty years ago, the strange, half-civilized mountain land of Tennessee and North Carolina, the humors of the Mississippi steamboat and the adventurous life of the Far West, are all known to Europe through the tales of writers now living, as the Indians of eighty years ago became known through the romances of Fenimore Cooper. However, this is familiar ground to European readers, so I pass to work of a less generally attractive order.

Thirty years ago the standard of classical scholarship was low, and even the school commentaries on classical authors fell far short of those produced in Germany or England. Nowadays both in classical and in Oriental philology admirably thorough and painstaking work is produced. I have heard high European authorities observe that there is an almost excessive anxiety among American scholars to master all that has been written, even by third-rate Germans, and that the desire they evince to overtake Germany in respect of knowledge betrays some among them into the German fault of neglecting merits of form and style. In the sciences of nature, especially in those of observation, remarkable advances have been made. Dr. Asa Gray, whom the eldest American university has lately lost, was one of the two or three greatest botanists of his age. Much excellent work has been done in geology and palæontology, particularly in exploring the Rocky Mountain regions. Both for the excellence of their instruments and the accuracy of their observations, the astronomers stand in the front rank : nor do they fall behind Europe in the theoretical part of this science. In some branches of physics and chemistry, such as spectrum analysis, American investigators have won like fame. Competent authorities award the highest praise to their recent contributions to biology and to medical science. In economics they seem to stand before either England or France, both as regards the extent to which the subject is studied in universities and as regards the number of eminent persons whom it occupies. In jurisprudence and law, American text-books are at least as good as those produced in England ; * and one author, the late Mr. Justice Story, deserves, looking to the quantity as well as to the quality of his work, to be placed at the head of all who have handled those topics in the English tongue during the last sixty years. Political science has begun to be studied more energetically than in England, where, to be sure, it is scarcely studied at all ; and every year sees treatises and articles of permanent value added to the scanty modern literature which our language possesses on this subject. Similarly there is great activity in the field of both secular and ecclesiastical history, though as the work done has largely taken the direction of inquiries into the early history of institutions, and has altogether been more in the nature of research than of treatises attractive to the general public, its quantity and its merits have not yet been duly appreciated even at home, much less in Europe. Indeed, it is remarkable how far from showy and sensational is the bulk of the work now done in America. It is mostly work of the German type, — solid, careful, exact ; not at all the sort of work which theorists about democracy would have looked for, since it appeals rather to the learned few than to the so-called general reader. One receives the impression that the class of intellectual workers, who until recently wanted institutions in which the highest and fullest training could be had, have now become sensible that their country, occupied in developing its resources and educating its ordinary citizens, had fallen behind Europe in learning and science, and that they are therefore the more eager to accumulate knowledge and spend their energy in minutely laborious special studies.†

* The number of legal journals and magazines in the United States is very much larger than in England, and the average level of workmanship in them seems to be higher.

† The extreme pains taken in America to provide every library with a classified catalogue directing readers to the books on each subject, seems to illustrate this tendency. Such catalogues would be still more serviceable

I may be reminded that neither in the departments above mentioned, nor in statesmanship, can one point to many brilliant personalities. The men whose names rise to the lips of a European are all advanced in life. Perhaps this is true of Europe also ; perhaps the world has entered on an age of mediocrities. Some one lately said that there was now nobody in Paris, Berlin, or London under sixty years of age whom one would cross the street to look at. If this be so, it is not merely because length of years has given better chances of winning fame, for nearly all the men now famous in Europe had won fame before they were forty. There have been periods in history when striking figures were lacking, although great events seemed to call for them. As regards America, if there be few persons of exceptional gifts, it is significant that the number of those who are engaged in scientific work, whether in the investigation of nature or in the moral, political, and historical sciences, is larger, relatively to the population of the country, than it was thirty years ago, the methods better, the work done more solid, the spirit more earnest and eager. Nothing more strikes a stranger who visits the American universities than the ardor with which the younger generation has thrown itself into study, even kinds of study which will never win the applause of the multitude. There is more zeal and heartiness among these men, more freshness of mind, more love of learning for its own sake, more willingness to forego the chances of fame and wealth for the sake of adding to the stock of human knowledge, than is to be found to-day in Oxford or Cambridge or in the universities of Scotland. One is reminded of the scholars of the Renaissance flinging themselves into the study of re-discovered philology, or of the German universi-

if they discriminated between the good books and the uncritical compilations or superficial popularizations which have latterly become common.

ties after the War of Liberation. And under the impressions formed in mingling with such men, one learns to agree with the conviction of the Americans that for a nation so abounding in fervid force there is reserved a fruitful career in science and letters no less than in whatever makes material prosperity.

CHAPTER XII.

THE RELATION OF THE UNITED STATES TO EUROPE.

ONE cannot discuss American literature and thought without asking, What is the intellectual relation of the United States to Europe? Is it that of an equal member of the great republic of letters; or is it that of a colony towards the mother-country, or of a province towards a capital? Is it, to take instances from history, such a relation as was that of Rome to Greece in the second and first centuries before Christ; or of Northern and Western Europe to Italy in the fifteenth; or of Germany to France in the eighteenth? — in all of which cases there was a measure of intellectual dependence on the part of a nation which felt itself in other respects as strong as, or stronger than, that whose models it followed, and from whose hearth it lighted its own flame.

To answer this question we must first answer another, — How do the Americans themselves conceive their position towards Europe? And this, again, suggests a third, — What does the American people think of itself?

Fifty, or even forty, years ago the conceit of this people was a byword. It was not only self-conscious, but obtrusive and aggressive. Every visitor satirized it, Dickens most keenly of all, in forgiving whom the Americans gave the strongest proof of their good-nature. Doubtless all nations are either vain, or proud, or both; and those not least who, like the Danes and the Portuguese, receive least recognition from their neighbors. A nation could hardly stand without this element to support its self-reliance; though when pushed to an extreme it may, as happens with the Turks, make national ruin the more irretrievable. But American conceit has been steadily declining as the country has grown older, more aware of its true strength, more respected by other countries.* There was less conceit after the Civil War than before, though the Civil War had revealed elements of greatness unexpected by foreigners; there is less now than there was at the close of the Civil War. An impartially rigorous censor from some other planet might say of the Americans that they are at this moment less priggishly supercilious than the Germans, less restlessly pretentious than the French, less pharisaically self-satisfied than the English. Among the upper or better-educated classes glorification has died out, except, of course, in Fourth of July and other public addresses, when the scream of the national eagle must be heard. One sometimes finds it replaced by undue self-depreciation, with lamentations over the want of culture, the decline of faith, or the corruption of politics. Among the masses it survives in an exultation over the size and material resources of the country, — the physically large is to them the sublime, — in an over-estimate of men and events in American history, in a delight — strongest, of course, among the recent immigrants — in the completeness of social equality, and a corresponding contempt for the " serfs of Europe " who submit to be called " subjects " of their sovereign, in a belief in the superior purity of their domestic life and literature, and in the notion that they are the only people who enjoy true political liberty,† — liberty far fuller

* Tocqueville complains that the Americans would not permit a stranger to pass even the smallest unfavorable criticism on any one of their institutions, however warmly he might express his admiration of the rest.

† It must, however, be admitted that this whimsical idea is not confined to the masses. I find, for instance, in an address delivered by an eminent man to a distinguished literary fraternity, in October, 1887, the following passage : " They (*i. e.* 'the immortal periods of the Declaration of Independence') have given political freedom to America and France, unity

than that of England, far more orderly than that of France. Taking all classes together, they are now not more sensitive to external opinion than the nations of Western Europe, and less so than the Russians, though they are still a trifle more apt to go through Europe comparing what they find with what they left at home. A foreign critic who tries to flout or scourge them no longer disturbs their composure; his jeers are received with amusement or indifference. Their patriotism is in one respect stronger than that of Frenchmen or Englishmen, because it is less broken by class feeling; but it has ceased to be aggressive.

Accordingly, the attitude of thoughtful Americans to Europe has no longer either the old open antagonism or the old latent self-distrust. It is that of a people which conceives itself to be intellectually the equal of any other people, but to have taken upon itself for the time a special task which impedes it in the race of literary and artistic development. Its mission is to reclaim the waste lands of a continent, to furnish homes for instreaming millions of strangers, to work out a system of harmonious and orderly democratic institutions. That it may fulfil these tasks it has for the moment postponed certain other tasks which it will in due time resume. Meanwhile it may, without loss of dignity or of faith in itself, use and enjoy the fruits of European intellect which it imports until it sees itself free to rival them by native growths. If I may

and nationality to Germany and Italy, emancipated the Russian serf, relieved Prussia and Hungary from feudal tenures, *and will in time free Great Britain and Ireland also*"!

I have often asked Americans wherein they consider their freedom superior to that of the British, but have never found them able to indicate a single point in which the individual man is worse off in Great Britain as regards either his private civil rights, or his political rights, or his general liberty of doing and thinking as he pleases. They generally turn the discussion to social equality, the existence of a monarchy and of hereditary titles, and so forth, — matters which are, of course, quite different from freedom in its proper sense.

resort to a homely comparison, the Americans are like a man whose next-door neighbor is in the habit of giving musical parties in the summer evenings. When one of these parties comes off, he sits with his family in the balcony to enjoy the quartettes and solos which float across to him through the open windows. He feels no inferiority, knowing that when he pleases he can have performers equally good to delight his own friends, though for this year he prefers to spend his surplus income in refurnishing his house or starting his son in business.

There is of course a difference in the view of the value of European work, as compared with their own, taken by the more-educated and by the less-educated classes. Of the latter some fail to appreciate the worth of culture and of science, even for practical purposes, as compared with industrial success, — though in this respect they are no more obtuse than the bulk of Englishmen; and they accordingly underrate their obligations to Europe. Others, knowing that they ought to admire works of imagination and research, but possessed of more patriotism than discernment, cry up second or third rate fiction, poetry, and theology because it is American, and try to believe that their country gives as much to Europe as she receives. Taste for literature is so much more diffused than taste in literature that a certain kind of fame is easily won. There are dozens of poets and scores of poetesses much admired in their own State, some even beyond its limits, with no merit but that of writing verse which can be scanned and will raise no blush on the most sensitive cheek. Criticism is lenient, or rather it does not exist; for the few journals which contain good reviews are little read except in four or five Northern Atlantic States and several inland cities. A really active and searching criticism, which should appraise literary work on sound canons, not caring whether it has been produced in America or in Europe, by a man or by a woman, in the East or in the West, is one of the things most needed in America. Among highly educated men this extravagant appreciation of native industry produces a disgust expressing itself sometimes in sarcasm, sometimes in despondency. Many deem their home-grown literature trivial, and occupy themselves with European books, watching the presses of England, France, and Germany more carefully than almost any one does in England. Yet even these, I think, cherish silently the faith that when the West has been settled and the railways built, and possibilities of sudden leaps to wealth diminished, when culture has diffused itself among the classes whose education is now superficial, and their love of art extended itself from furniture to pictures and statuary, American literature will in due course flower out with a brilliance of bloom and a richness of fruit rivalling the Old World.

The United States are therefore, if this account be correct, in a relation to Europe for which no exact historical parallel can be found. They do not look up to her, nor seek to model themselves after her. They are too proud for a province, too large for a colony. They certainly draw from Europe far more thought than they send to her, while of art they produce comparatively little and export nothing. Yet they cannot be said to be led or ruled by Europe, because they apply their own standards and judgment to whatever they receive.

Their special relations to the leading European countries are worth noting. In old colonial days England was everything. The revolt of 1776 produced an estrangement which might have been healed after 1783, had England acted with courtesy and good sense, but which was embittered by her scornful attitude. Wounds which were just beginning to scar over were reopened by the war of 1812; and the hostility continued as long as the generation lived whose manhood saw that war. Tocqueville in 1833 says he can imagine no hatred more venomous than that between the Americans and the English. The generation which remembered 1812 was disappearing when the sympathy of the English upper classes for the Southern Confederacy in 1861-65 lit up the almost extinguished flames. These have been nearly if not quite entirely quenched, so far as the native Americans are concerned, by the settlement of the Alabama claims, which impressed the United States not merely as a concession to themselves, but as an evidence of the magnanimity of a proud country. There is still a certain amount of rivalry with England, together with a strange idea, fostered by the protective tariff, that England's gain means America's loss, and conversely. There is also a certain suspicion that the English are trying to patronize even when the latter are innocent of such intentions. Now and then an Englishman who, feeling himself practically at home, speaks with the same freedom as he would use there, finds himself misunderstood. But these lingering touches of jealousy are slight compared with the growing sympathy felt for " the old country," as it is still called. It is the only European country in which the American people can be said to feel any personal interest, or towards an alliance with which they are drawn by any sentiment. For a time, however, the sense of gratitude to France for her aid in the War of Independence was very strong. It brought French literature as well as some French usages into vogue, and increased the political influence which France exercised during the earlier years of her own Revolution. Still, that influence did not go far beyond the sphere of politics ; one feels it but slightly in the literature of the half century from 1780 to 1830.

During the reign of Louis Napoleon wealthy Americans resorted largely to Paris ; and there, living often for years together in a congenial atmosphere of display and amusement, imbibed undemocratic tastes and ideas, which through them found their way back across the ocean and colored certain sections of American society, particularly in New York.

Although there is still an American colony in Paris, Parisian influence seems no longer to cross the Atlantic. French books, novels excepted, and these in translations, are not largely read; French politics excite little interest: France is practically not a factor at all in the moral or intellectual life of the country. Over art, however, especially painting and decoration, she has still great power. Many American artists study in Paris, — indeed all resort thither who do not go to Rome or Florence; French pictures enjoy such favor with American dealers and private buyers as to make the native artists complain, not without reason, that equally good home-made work receives no encouragement; * and house-decoration, in which America seems to stand before England, particularly in the skilful use of wood, is much affected by French designs and methods.

The enormous German immigration of the last thirty years might have been expected to go far towards Germanizing the American mind, giving it a taste for metaphysics on the one hand, and for minutely patient research on the other. It does not seem to have had either the one result or the other, or indeed any result whatever in the field of thought. It has enormously stimulated the brewing industry, it has retarded the progress of Prohibitionism, it has introduced more out-door life than formerly existed, it has increased the taste for music, it has broken down the strictness of Sabbath observance, and has indeed in some cities produced what is commonly called "a Continental Sunday." But the vast majority of German immigrants belong to the humbler classes. There have been among them extremely few *savants*, or men likely to become *savants*, nor have

---

* There is a heavy customs duty on foreign works of art; but this does not greatly help the native artist, for the men who buy pictures can usually buy notwithstanding the duty, while it prevents the artist from furnishing himself with the works he needs to have around him for the purposes of his own training.

these played any conspicuous part in the universities or in literature.*

Nevertheless the influence of Germany has been of late years powerfully stimulative upon the cultivated classes, for not only are German treatises largely read, but many of the most promising graduates of the universities proceed to Germany for a year or two to complete their studies, and there become imbued with German ideas and methods. The English universities have, by their omission to develop advanced instruction in special branches of knowledge, lost a golden opportunity of coming into relation with and influencing that academic youth of America in whose hands the future of American science and learning lies. This German strain in American work has however not tended towards the propagation of metaphysical schools, metaphysics themselves being now on the ebb in Germany. It appears in some departments of theology, and is also visible in historical and philological studies, in economics, and in the sciences of nature.

On the more popular kinds of literature, as well as upon manners, social usages, current sentiment generally, England and her influences are of course nearer and more potent than those of any other European country, seeing that English books go everywhere among all classes, and that they work upon those who are substantially English already in their fundamental ideas and habits. Americans of the cultivated order, and especially women, are more alive to the movements and changes in the lighter literature of England, and more curious about those who figure in it, especially the rising poets and essayists, than equally cultivated English men and women. I have been repeatedly surprised to find books and men that had made no noise in London well known in the Atlantic

* Mr. Andrew D. White, in an interesting article on the influence of German thought in the United States, cites only Francis Lieber and Mr. Carl Schurz. In public life two or three Germans have attained high distinction.

States, and their merits canvassed with more zest and probably more acuteness than a London drawing-room would have shown. The verdicts of the best circles were not always the same as those of similar circles in England, but they were nowise biassed by national feeling, and often seemed to proceed from a more delicate and sympathetic insight. I recollect, though I had better not mention, instances in which they welcomed English books which England had failed to appreciate, and refused to approve American books over which English reviewers had become ecstatic.

Transient English fashions in social customs and in such things as games sometimes spread to America, — possibly more often than similar American fashions do to England, — but sometimes encounter ridicule there. The Anglomaniac is a familiar object of good-humored satire. As for those large movements of opinion or taste or practical philanthropy in which a parallelism or correspondence between the two countries may often be discerned, this correspondence is more frequently due to the simultaneous action of the same causes than to any direct influence of the older country. In theology, for instance, the same relaxation of the rigid tests of orthodoxy has been making way in the churches of both nations. In the Protestant Episcopal Church there has been a similar, though less pronounced, tendency to the development of an ornate ritual. The movement for dealing with city pauperism by voluntary organizations began later than the Charity Organization societies of England, but would probably have begun without their example. The rapidly growing taste for beauty in house decoration and in street architecture is a birth of the time rather than of Old World teaching, though it owes something to Mr. Ruskin's books, which have been more widely read in America than in England.*

* America has produced of late years at least one really distinguished architect, now unhappily lost to her; and this art — as, indeed, art in general — seems to be making rapid progress.

In political matters the intellectual sympathy of the two countries is of course less close than in the matters just described, because the difference between institutions and conditions involves a diversity in the problems which call for a practical solution. Political changes in England affect American opinion less than such changes in France affect English opinion, although the Americans know more and care more and judge more soundly about English affairs than the French do about English or the English about French. The cessation of bitterness between Great Britain and the Irish would make a difference in American politics ; but no political event in England less serious than, let us say, the establishment of a powerful Socialist party, would sensibly tell on American opinion, just as no event happening beyond the Atlantic, except the rise and fall of the Southern Confederacy, has influenced the course of English political thought. However, the wise men of the West watch English experiments for light and guidance in their own troubles. A distinguished American who came a few years ago to London to study English politics, told me that he did so in the hope of finding conservative institutions and forces from which lessons might be learned that would be, as he thought, very serviceable to the United States. After a fortnight, however, he concluded that England was in a state of suppressed revolution, and departed sorrowful.

On a review of the whole matter it will appear that although as respects most kinds of intellectual work America is rather in the position of the consumer, Europe, and especially England, in that of the producer ; although America is more influenced by English, French, and German books and by French art than these countries are influenced by her, — still she does not look for initiative to them, or hold herself in any way their disciple. She is in many points independent, and in all fully persuaded of her independence.

Will she then in time develop a new literature, bearing the

stamp of her own mint? She calls herself a new country: will she give the world a new philosophy, new views of religion, a new type of life, in which plain living and high thinking may be more happily blended than we now see them in the Old World, — a life in which the franker recognition of equality will give a freshness to ideas, and to manners a charm of simplicity which the aristocratic societies of Europe have failed to attain?

As regards manners and life, she has already approached nearer this happy combination than any society of the Old World. As regards ideas, I have found among the most cultivated Americans a certain cosmopolitanism of view, and detachment from national or local prejudice, superior to that of the same classes in France, England, or Germany. In the ideas themselves there is little one can call novel or distinctively American, though there is a kind of thoroughness in embracing or working out certain political and social conceptions which is less common in England. As regards literature, nothing at present indicates the emergence of a new type. The influence of the great nations on one another grows always closer, and makes new national types less likely to appear. Science, which has no nationality, exerts a growing sway over men's minds, and exerts it contemporaneously and similarly in all civilized countries. For the purposes of thought, at least, if not of literary expression, the world draws closer together, and becomes more of a homogeneous community.

A visitor doubts whether the United States are, so far as the things of the mind are concerned, " a new country." The people have the hopefulness of youth. But their institutions are old, though many have been remodelled or new faced; their religion is old; their views of morality and conduct are old; their sentiments in matters of art and taste have not greatly diverged from those of the parent stock. Is the mere fact that they inhabit new territories, and that the conditions of life there have trained to higher efficiency certain gifts, and have left others in comparative quiescence, is this fact sufficient so to transform the national spirit as to make the products of their creative power essentially diverse from those of the same race abiding in its ancient seats? A transplanted tree may bear fruit of a slightly different flavor, but the apple remains an apple, and the pear a pear.

However, it is still too early in the growth of the United States to form any conclusions on these high matters, almost too soon to speculate regarding them. There are causes at work which may in time produce a new type of intellectual life; but whether or not this come to pass, it can hardly be doubted that when the American people give themselves some repose from their present labors, when they occupy themselves less with doing and more with being, there will arise among them a literature and a science, possibly also, though later, an art, which will tell upon Europe with a new force. It will have behind it the momentum of hundreds of millions of men.

CHAPTER XIII.

THE ABSENCE OF A CAPITAL

THE United States are the only great country in the world which has no capital. Germany and Italy were long without one, because the existence of the mediæval empire prevented the growth in either country of a national monarchy. But the wonderfully reconstructive age we live in has now supplied the want; and although Rome and Berlin still fall short of being to their respective states what Paris and London are to France and England, what Vienna and Pesth are to the Dual Monarchy, they bid fair to attain a similar rank * in their respective nations. By a capital I mean a city which is not only the seat of political government, but is also by the size, wealth, and character of its population the head and centre of the country, a leading seat of commerce and industry, a reservoir of financial resources, the favored residence of the great and powerful, the spot in which the chiefs of the learned professions are to be found, where the most potent

* Athens, Lisbon, Copenhagen, Stockholm, Brussels, are equally good instances among the smaller countries. In Switzerland, Bern has not reached the same position, because Switzerland is a federation, and, so to speak, an artificial country made by history. Zurich, Lausanne, and Geneva are intellectually quite as influential. So Holland retains traces of her federal condition in the relatively less important position of Amsterdam. Madrid, being a modern city placed in a country more recently and less perfectly consolidated than most of the other states of Europe, is less of a capital to Spain than Lisbon is to Portugal or Paris to France.

and widely-read journals are published, whither men of
literary and scientific capacity are drawn. The heaping together in such a place of these various elements of power,
the conjunction of the forces of rank, wealth, knowledge, intellect, naturally makes such a city a sort of foundry in which
opinion is melted and cast, where it receives that definite
shape in which it can be easily and swiftly propagated and
diffused through the whole country, deriving not only an
authority from the position of those who form it, but a momentum from the weight of numbers in the community whence
it comes. The opinion of such a city becomes powerful politically because it is that of the persons who live at headquarters, who hold the strings of government in their hands, who
either themselves rule the state, or are in close contact with
those who do. It is true that under a representative government power rests with those whom the people have sent up
from all parts of the country. Still, these members of the
legislature reside in the capital, and cannot but feel the
steady pressure of its prevailing sentiment, which touches
them socially at every point. It sometimes happens that the
populace of the capital by their power of overawing the rulers,
or perhaps of effecting a revolution, are able to turn the fortunes of the state. But even where no such peril is to be
apprehended, any nation with the kind of a capital I am describing, acquires the habit of looking to it for light and
leading, and is apt to yield to it an initiative in political
movements.

In the field of art and literature the influence of a great
capital is no less marked. It gathers to a centre the creative
power of the country, and subjects it to the criticism of the
best-instructed and most-polished society. The constant
action and reaction upon one another of groups of capable
men in an atmosphere at once stimulative to invention and
corrective of extravagance, may give birth to works which
isolated genius could hardly have produced. Goethe made

this observation as regards Paris, contrasting the centralized society of France with the dispersion of the elements of culture over the wide area of his own Germany.

"Now conceive a city like Paris, where the highest talents of a great kingdom are all assembled in a single spot, and by daily intercourse, strife, and emulation mutually instruct and advance each other; where the best works, both of nature and art, from all kingdoms of the earth, are open to daily inspection, — conceive this metropolis of the world, I say, where every walk across a bridge or across a square recalls some mighty past, and where some historical event is connected with every corner of a street. In addition to all this, conceive, not the Paris of a dull, spiritless time, but the Paris of the nineteenth century, in which, during three generations, such men as Molière, Voltaire, Diderot, and the like have kept up such a current of intellect as cannot be found twice in a single spot on the whole world, and you will comprehend that a man of talent like Ampère, who has grown up amid such abundance, can easily be something in his four and twentieth year." *

The same idea of the power which a highly-polished and strenuously active society has to educe and develop brilliant gifts underlies the memorable description which Pericles gives of Athens, in a speech preserved for us by Thucydides. And the influence of such a society may be contemplated with the greater satisfaction because it does not necessarily impoverish the rest of a country. The centralization of intellectual life may tend to diminish the chances of variability, and establish too uniform a type; but it probably gives a higher efficiency to the men of capacity whom it draws into its own orbit, than they could have attained in the isolation of their natal spot.

In the case both of politics and of literature, the existence of a capital tends to strengthen the influence of what is called Society; that is to say, of the men of wealth and leisure who have time to think of other matters than the needs of daily

* Conversations with Eckermann.

life, and whose company and approval are apt to be sought by the men of talent. Thus where the rich and great are gathered in one spot to which the nation looks, they effect more in the way of guiding its political thought and training its literary taste than is possible where they are dispersed over the face of a large country. In both points, therefore, it will evidently make a difference to a democratic country whether it has a capital, and what degree of deference that capital receives. Paris is the extreme case of a city which has latterly been everything to the national literature and art, and has sought to be everthing in national politics also. London, since the decline of Dublin and of Edinburgh, has stood without a British rival in the domain of art and letters; and although one can hardly say that a literary society exists in London, most of the people who employ themselves in writing books, and nearly all those who paint pictures, live in or near it. Over politics London has less authority than Paris has exerted in France, — doubtless because parts of the North and West of Britain are more highly vitalized than the provinces of France, while the English city is almost too populous to have a common feeling. Its very hugeness makes it amorphous.

What are the cities of the United States which can claim to approach nearest to the sort of capital we have been considering? Not Washington, though it is the meeting-place of Congress and the seat of Federal administration. It has a relatively small population (in 1890, 230,392, of whom one third were negroes). Society consists of congressmen (for about half the year), officials, diplomatists, and some rich and leisured people who come to spend the winter. The leaders of finance, industry, commerce, and the professions are absent; there are few men of letters, no artists, hardly any journalists. What is called the " society " of Washington, which, being small, polished, and composed of people who constantly meet one another, is agreeable, and not the less agreeable because it has a peculiar flavor, is so far from aspiring to political authority as to deem it " bad form " to talk politics.*

Not New York, though she is now by far the most populous city. She is the centre of commerce, the sovereign of finance ; but New York has no special political influence or power beyond that of casting a large vote, which is an important factor in determining the thirty-six presidential votes of the State. Business is her main occupation : the representatives of literature are few ; the journals, although certainly among the ablest and most widely read in the country, are, after all, New York journals, and not, like those of Paris, London, or even Berlin, professedly written for the whole nation. Next comes Philadelphia, once the first city in the Union, but now standing below New York in all the points just mentioned, with even less claim to be deemed a centre of art or opinion. Boston was for a time the chosen home of letters and culture, and still contains, in proportion to her population, a larger number of men and women capable of making or judging good work than any other city. But she can no longer be said to lead abstract thought, much less current opinion. Chicago combines a vast and growing population with a central position ; she is in some respects more of a typical American city than any of the others I have named. But Chicago, so far as political initiative goes, has no more weight than what the number of her voters represents, and in art and literature is nowhere. Nor does any one of these cities seem on the way to gain a more commanding position. New York will probably retain her pre-eminence in population and commercial consequence, but she does not rise proportionately in

* Washington, being situated in the Federal District of Columbia, is not a part of any State, and therefore enjoys no share in the Federal government. A resident in it is unenfranchised for all but certain local purposes. He can vote neither for a member of Congress nor for presidential electors, and the city is governed by a Federal Commission.

culture, while the centre of political gravity, shifting ever more and more to the West, will doubtless finally fix itself in the Mississippi valley.*

It deserves to be remarked that what is true of the whole country is also true of the great sections of the country. Of the cities I have named, none, except possibly Boston and San Francisco, can be said to be even a local capital, either for purposes of political opinion or of intellectual movement and tendency. Boston retains her position as the literary centre of New England; San Francisco by her size has a preponderating influence on the Pacific coast. But no other great city is regarded by the inhabitants of her own and the adjoining States as their natural head, to which they look for political guidance, or from which they expect any intellectual stimulance. Even New Orleans, though by far the largest place in the South, is in no sense the metropolis of the South, and does little more for the South than set a conspicuous example of municipal misgovernment to the surrounding commonwealths. Though no Paris, no Berlin stands above them, these great American cities are not more important in the country, or even in their own sections of the country, than Lyons and Bordeaux are in France, Hamburg and Cologne in Germany. Even as between municipal communities, even in the sphere of thought and literary effort, equality and local independence have in America their perfect work.

The geographical as well as political causes that have produced this equality are obvious enough, and only one needs

---

* A leading New York paper says (March, 1888), " In no capital that we know of does the cause of religion and morality derive so little support against luxury from intellectual interest or activity of any description. This interest has its place here, but it leads a sickly existence as yet, under the shadow of great wealth which cares not for it." This remark applies with equal force to Chicago and San Francisco, possibly less to Baltimore, and still less to Boston and some of the smaller cities.

special mention. The seat of Federal government was in 1790 fixed at a place which was not even a village, but a piece of swampy woodland,* not merely for the sake of preventing the national legislature from being threatened by the mob of a great city, but because the jealousies of the States made it necessary to place the legislature in a spot exempt from all State influence or jurisdiction. So too in each State the seat of government is rarely to be found in the largest city. Albany, not New York, is the capital of New York State; Springfield, not Chicago, of Illinois; Sacramento, not San Francisco, of California; Columbus, not Cincinnati, of Ohio; Harrisburg, not Philadelphia, of Pennsylvania; Columbia, not Charleston, of South Carolina. And this has been so ordered, less from fear of the turbulence of a vast population, than from the jealousy which the rural districts and smaller cities feel of the place which casts the heaviest vote, and is likely to seek to use the State resources for its own benefit.

It is a natural result of the phenomena described that in the United States public opinion crystallizes both less rapidly and in less sharp and well-defined forms than happens in those European countries which are led by the capital. The temperature of the fluid in which opinion takes shape (if I may venture to pursue the metaphor) is not so high all over a large country as in the society of a city, where the minds that make opinion are in daily contact, and the process by which opinion is made is therefore slower, giving a

* Congress, however, did not remove from Philadelphia to the banks of the Potomac until 1800. Thomas Moore's lines on Washington, as he saw it in 1804, deserve to be quoted:—

> " An embryo capital, where Fancy sees
> Squares in morasses, obelisks in trees;
> Where second-sighted seers the plain adorn
> With fanes unbuilt and heroes yet unborn,
> Though nought but woods and Jefferson they see
> Where streets should run, and sages ought to be."·

somewhat more amorphous product. I do not mean that a European capital generates opinion of one type only, but that each doctrine, each programme, each type of views, whether political or economic or religious, is likely to assume in a capital its sharpest and most pronounced form, that form being taken up and propagated from the capital through the country. And this is one reason why Americans were the first to adopt the system of Conventions, — mass meetings of persons belonging to a particular party or advocating a particular cause, gathered from every corner of the country to exchange their ideas and deliberate on their common policy.

It may be thought that in this respect the United States suffer from the absence of a centre of light and heat. Admitting that there is some loss, there are also some conspicuous gains. It is a gain that the multitude of no one city should be able to overawe the executive and the legislature, perhaps even to change the form of government, as Paris has so often done in France. It is a gain, for a democratic country, that the feeling of what is called Society — that is to say, of those who toil not, neither do they spin, who are satisfied with the world, and are apt to regard it as a place for enjoyment — should not become too marked and palpable in its influence on the members of the legislature and the administration, that it should rather be diffused over the nation and act insensibly upon other classes through the ordinary relations of private life than take visible shape as the voice of a number of wealthy families gathered in one spot, whose luxury may render them the objects of envy and the target for invective. And although types of political view may form themselves less swiftly, though doctrines may be less systematic, programmes less fully reasoned out, than when the brisk intelligence of groups gathered in a capital labors to produce them, they may, when they do finally emerge from the mind of the whole people, have a breadth and solidity proportioned to the slowness of their growth, and be more truly representative of all the classes, interests, and tendencies that exist within the nation.

How far the loss exceeds the gain as respects the speculative and artistic sides of intellectual effort, it is too soon to determine; for American cities are all creatures of the last sixty years. That which Goethe admired in Paris is evidently impossible to the dispersed geniuses of America. On the other hand, that indraught of talent from the provinces to Paris which many thoughtful Frenchmen deplore, and which has become more unfortunate since Paris has grown to be the centre of amusement for the dissipated classes of Europe, is an experience which no other country need wish to undergo. Germany has not begun to produce more work or better work since she has given herself a capital; indeed, he who looks back over her annals since the middle of last century will think that so far as scholarship, metaphysics, and possibly even poetry are concerned, she gained from that very want of centralization which Goethe regretted. Great critics realize so vividly the defects of the system they see around them that they sometimes underrate the merits that go with those defects, — as a late distinguished English man of letters wished that England possessed an Academy of Letters, at the absence of which most Englishmen, knowing how such an institution is apt to be perverted, are disposed to rejoice. It may be that in the next age American cities will profit by their local independence to develop varieties greater than they now exhibit, and will evolve diverse types of literary and artistic production. Europe will watch with curiosity the progress of an experiment which it is now too late for any of her great countries to try.

CHAPTER XIV.

AMERICAN ORATORY.

ORATORY is an accomplishment in which Europeans believe that Americans excel; and that this is the opinion of the Americans themselves, although they are too modest to express it, may be gathered from the surprise they betray when they find an Englishman fluent before an audience. Fifty years ago they had the advantage (if it is an advantage) of much more practice than any European nation; but now, with democracy triumphant in England and France, the proportion of speeches and speaking to population is probably much the same in all three countries. Some observations on a form of effort which has absorbed a good deal of the talent of the nation, seem properly to belong to an account of its intellectual life.

Oratorical excellence may be said to consist in the combination of five aptitudes, —

Invention; that is to say, the power of finding good ideas and weaving effective arguments.

Skill and taste in the choice of appropriate words.

Readiness in producing appropriate ideas and words at short notice.

Quickness in catching the temper and tendencies of the particular audience addressed.

Weight, animation, and grace in delivery.

Such excellence as the Americans possess, such superiority as they may claim over Englishmen, consists rather in the three latter of these than in the two former.

The substance of their speeches is not better than one finds in other countries, because substance depends on the intellectual resources of the speaker and on the capacity of the audience for appreciating worthy matter. Neither is the literary form better; that is to say, the ideas are not clothed in any choicer language. But there is more fluency, more readiness, more self-possession. Being usually quicker and nimbler in mind than an Englishman, and feeling less embarrassed on his legs, an American is apt to see his point more clearly, and to get at it by a more direct path. He is less frequently confused and clumsy, less prosy also, because his sympathy with the audience tells him when they begin to tire, and makes him sensible of the necessity of catching and holding their attention. I do not deny that American speakers sometimes weary the listener; but when they do so it is rather because the notions are commonplace and the arguments unsound than because, as might often happen in England, ideas of some value are tediously and pointlessly put. The English race has in America acquired a keener sensitiveness of sympathy. That habit of deference to others, and that desire to be in accord with the sentiments of others, which equality and democratic institutions foster, make the American feel himself more completely one of the audience and a partaker of its sentiments than an average English speaker does. This may have the consequence, if the audience be ignorant or prejudiced, of dragging him down to its level; but it makes him more effective. Needless to add that humor, which is a commoner gift in America than elsewhere, often redeems an otherwise uninteresting address, and is the best means of keeping speaker and audience in touch with one another.

A deliberate and even slow delivery is the rule in American public speaking, as it is in private conversation. This has the advantage of making a story or jest tell with more effect. There is also, I think, less stiffness and hesitation among American than among English speakers, greater skill in managing the voice, because more practice in open-air meetings, greater clearness of enunciation. But as regards grace, either in action or in manner, the Teutonic race shows no more capacity on the other side of the Atlantic than it has generally done in England for rivalling the orators of Italy, Spain, and France.

The commonest American defect is a turgid and inflated style. The rhetoric is Rhodian rather than Attic, overloaded with tropes and figures, apt to aim at concealing poverty or triteness in thought by exaggeration of statement, by a profusion of ornament, by appeals to sentiments too lofty for the subject or the occasion. The florid diction of the debating club or the solemn pomp of the funeral oration is frequently invoked when nothing but clearness of exposition or cogency of argument is needed. These faults have probably sprung from the practice of stump oratory, in which the temptation to rouse a multitude by declamation is specially strong. A man straining his voice in the open air is apt to strain his phrases also, and command attention by vehemence. They have been increased by the custom of having orations delivered on certain anniversaries, and especially on the Fourth of July, for on these great occasions the speaker feels bound to talk " his very tallest." Public taste, which was high in the days after the Revolution, when it was formed and controlled by a small number of educated men, began to degenerate in the first half of this century. Despite the influence of several orators of the first rank, incessant stump speaking and the inordinate vanity of the average audience brought a florid or inflated style into fashion, which became an easy mark for European satire. Of late years a reaction for the better seems to have set in. There are indeed still those who imitate Macaulay or Webster, without the richness of the one or the stately strength of the other. The newspapers, in acknowledging that a lecturer is fluent or lucid, still complain if he is not also " eloquent." Commemorative addresses, which are far more abundant than in Europe, usually sin by over-finish of composition. But on the whole there is a manifest and steady improvement in the taste of listeners and in the style of speeches. Such improvement would be more rapid were it not for the enormous number of speeches by people who have really nothing to say, as well as by able men on occasions when there is nothing to be said which has not been said hundreds of times before. This is, of course, almost equally true of England, and indeed of all popularly governed countries. Those who run down popular government may fairly count profusion of speech as one of the drawbacks to democracy, and a drawback which shows no signs of disappearing.

As respects the different kinds of oratory, that of the pulpit seems to show an average slightly higher than in England. The visitor naturally hears the best preachers, for these are of course drawn to the cities ; but whether he takes cities or rural districts, he forms the impression that mere dulness and commonplace are less common than in Great Britain, though high excellence may be equally rare. Even when the discourse is read, it is read in a less mechanical way, and there is altogether more sense of the worth of vivacity and variety. The average length of sermons is a mean between the twenty minutes of an English Episcopalian minister and the fifty minutes of Scotland. The manner is perhaps a trifle less conventional, because the American clergyman is less apt than his European brother to feel himself a member of a distinct caste.

Forensic oratory seems to stand neither higher nor lower than it does in England, whose Bar is not at this moment adorned by any speakers whom men go to hear simply for the sake of their eloquence, as men flocked to listen to Erskine or Brougham or Follett. In America, as in England, there are many powerful advocates, but no consummate artist. Whether this is due to the failure of Nature to produce persons specially gifted, or to the absence of trials whose issues and circum-

stances are calculated to rouse forensic ability to exceptional
efforts, or to a change in public taste and a disposition to
prefer the practical to the showy, is a question which is often
asked in England, and is no easier to answer in America.

Congress, for reasons explained in the chapter treating of
it, is a less favorable theatre for oratory than the great representative assemblies of Europe. The House of Representatives has at no period of its history shone with lights of
eloquence, though a few of Clay's great speeches were delivered in it.   There is some good short brisk debating in Committee of the Whole, but the set speeches are mostly pompous
and heavy. The Senate has maintained a higher level, partly
from the smaller size of its chamber, partly from its greater
leisure, partly from the superior ability of its members.
Webster's and Calhoun's greatest efforts were made on its
floor, and produced an enormous effect on the nation.   At
present, however, the " full-dress debates " in the Senate are
apt to want life, the long set speeches being fired off rather
with a view to their circulation in the country than to any
immediate effect on the assembly. But the ordinary discussions of bills, or questions of policy, reveal plenty of practical
speaking power.   If there be little passion and no brilliancy,
there is strong common-sense put in a telling way.

Of the forty-seven State and Territorial legislatures not
much need be said. In them, as in the House of Representatives, the bulk of the work is done in committees, and the
opportunities for a display of eloquence are limited, — which
it is well should be the case. They are good enough schools
to form a practical business speaker, and they do form many
such.   But the characteristic merits and defects of transatlantic oratory are more fully displayed on the stump and
in those national and State nominating conventions whereof
I have already spoken. So far as the handling great assemblies is an art attainable by a man who does not possess the
highest gifts of thought and imagination, it has been brought

to perfection by the heroes of these mass meetings. They have learned how to deck out commonplaces with the gaudier flowers of eloquence; how to appeal to the dominant sentiment of the moment; above all, how to make a strong and flexible voice the means of rousing enthusiasm. They scathe the opposite party by vigorous invective; they interweave stories and jokes with their declamatory passages, so as to keep the audience constantly amused; They deliver clap-trap with an air of hearty conviction. The party men who listen, — because there are few present at a mass meeting, and still fewer at a convention, except members of the speaker's party, — are better pleased with themselves than ever, and go away roused to effort in the party cause. But there has been little argument all through, little attempt to get hold of the reason and judgment of the people. Stimulation, and not instruction or conviction, is the aim which the stump orator sets before himself; and the consequence is that an election campaign is less educationally valuable than one conducted in England, by men much less practised and skilful in speaking, commonly proves to English electors. It is worth remarking that the custom which in England requires a representative to deliver at least once a year an address to his constituents, setting forth his view of the political situation, and explaining his own speeches and votes during the preceding session, does not seem to exist in the United States. In fact the people of the Northern States receive less political instruction by the living voice than do those of England. When an instructive address has to be given, it takes the form of a lecture, and is usually delivered by some well-known public man, who receives a fee for it.

There are three kinds of speech which, though they exist in most European countries, have been so much more fully developed beyond the Atlantic as to deserve some notice.

The first of these is the Oration of the Occasion. When an anniversary comes round — and celebrations of an anniversary are very common in America — or when a sort of festival is held in honor of some public event, — such for instance as the unveiling of a statue, or the erection of a monument on a battle-field, or the opening of a city hall or State capitol, or the driving the last spike of a great railroad, — a large part of the programme is devoted to speaking. The chief speech is intrusted to one eminent person, who is called the Orator of the Day, and from whom is expected a long and highly-finished harangue, the length and finish of which are wearisome to a critical outsider, though the people of the locality are flattered. Sometimes these speeches contain good matter, — I could mention instances where they have embodied personal recollections of a distinguished man in whose honor the celebration was being held,'— but the sort of artificial elevation at which the speaker usually feels bound to maintain himself is apt to make him pompous and affected.

Although public dinners are less frequent than in England, speeches of a complimentary and purely " epideictic " nature of the English public banquet type are very common. There is scarcely an occasion in life which brings forty or fifty people together on which a prominent citizen or a stranger from Europe is not called upon " to offer a few remarks." No subject is prescribed for him, often no toast has to be proposed or responded to ;* he is simply put on his legs to talk upon anything in heaven or earth which may rise to his mind. The European, who is at first embarrassed by this unchartered freedom, presently discovers its advantages, for it enables him so to construct his speech as to lead up to whatever joke, or point, or complimentary observations he has ready at hand. There is also more opening for variety than the conventional uniformity of an English toast-list permits.

---

* Of course there are often toasts given at public dinners ; but they seem to be fewer in number than in England, and more varied, more judiciously adapted to the special occasion.

The third form of discourse specially characteristic of the United States is the Lecture. It is less frequent and less fashionable now than thirty years ago, partly from the rise of monthly magazines full of excellent matter, partly because other kinds of evening entertainment have become more accessible to people outside the great cities. But it is still far more frequent, and more valuable as a means of interesting people in literary, scientific, and political questions, than anywhere in Europe, except possibly in Edinburgh. And the art of lecturing has been developed in a corresponding measure. A discourse of this kind, whatever the merits of its substance, is usually well arranged, well composed to meet the taste of the audience, and above all, well delivered. Eminent Englishmen who go to lecture in America are frequently criticised as ignorant of what may be called the technical part of their business. They may know a great deal, it is said, but they do not know how much the audience knows, and assume a lower level of intelligence and knowledge than exists, with the result of displeasing the latter. They are monotonous in manner, and unskilled in elocution. The European lecturer, on the other hand, has been known to confess himself annoyed, not only by the irreverent comments of the press, but by the apparent coldness of the audience, which, though it will applaud heartily at the end if well satisfied, refuses him the running encouragement of cheers, even when he invites them by pausing to drink a glass of water.

This grave reserve in American listeners surprises Europeans,* especially those who have observed the excitability shown on presidential campaigns. It seems to arise from the practical turn of their minds as well as from their intelligence. In an election campaign it is necessary and expe-

---

* A story is told of Edmund Kean acting before an audience in New England which he found so chilling that at last he refused to come on for the next scene unless some applause were given, observing that such a house was enough to put out Etna.

dient to give vent to one's feelings ; in listening to a lecture it is not.   One comes to be instructed or entertained, and comes with a critical habit formed by hearing many lectures as well as reading many books.   Something may also be due to the large proportion of women in an American audience at lectures or other non-political occasions.

A stranger is on the whole inclined to think that the kind of oratory in which the Americans show to most advantage is neither the political kind, abundant as it is, nor the commemorative oration, assiduously as it is cultivated, but what may be called the lighter ornamental style, such as the after-dinner speech.   The fondness of the people for anecdotes, and their skill in telling them, the general diffusion of humor, the readiness in catching the spirit of an occasion, all contribute to make their efforts in this direction more easy and happy than those of the English, while furnishing less temptation for the characteristic fault of a straining after effect. I have already observed that they shine in stump speaking, properly so called ; that is, in speaking which rouses an audience but ought not to be reported.   The reasons why their more serious platform and parliamentary oratory remains somewhat inferior to that of Europe are, over and above the absence of momentous issues, probably the same as those which have affected the average of newspaper writing.   In Europe the leading speakers and writers have nearly all belonged to the cultivated classes ; and feeling themselves raised above their audiences, have been in the habit of obeying their own taste and that of their class rather than the appetite of those whom they addressed.   In England, for instance, the standard of speaking by public men has been set by parliamentary debate, because till within the last few decades the leading men of the country had won their reputation in parliament.   They carried their parliamentary style with them into popular meetings, and aspirants of all classes imitated this style.   It sometimes erred in being too formal and too prolix ; but its taste was good, and its very plainness obliged the speaker to have solid matter. In America, on the other hand, stump oratory is older than congressional oratory, and the latter has never gained that hold on the ideas and habits of the people which parliamentary debate held in England. Hence speaking has generally moved on a somewhat lower level; not but what there were brilliant popular orators in the first days of the Republic, like Patrick Henry, and majestic parliamentary orators, like Daniel Webster, in the next generation, but that the volume of stump speaking was so much greater than in England that the fashion could not be set by a few of the greatest men, but was determined by the capacities of the average man. The taste of the average man was not raised by the cultivated few to their own standard, but tended to lower the practice, and to some extent even the taste, of the cultivated few. To seem wiser or more refined than the multitude, to incur the suspicion of talking down to the multitude, would have offended the sentiment of the country and injured the prospects of a statesman. It is perhaps a confirmation of this view that, while pompousness has flourished in the West, the most polished speakers have generally belonged to New England, where the level of average taste and knowledge was exceptionally high. One of these speakers, the late Mr. Wendell Phillips, was, in the opinion of competent critics, — an opinion which those who remember his conversation will be inclined to agree with, — one of the first orators of the present century, and not more remarkable for the finish than for the transparent, though studied, simplicity of his style, which attained its highest effects by the most direct and natural methods.

CHAPTER XV.

THE PLEASANTNESS OF AMERICAN LIFE.

I HAVE never met a European of the upper or middle classes who did not express astonishment when told that America was a more agreeable place than Europe to live in. "For working-men," he would answer, " yes ; but for men of education or property, how can a new rough country, where nothing but business is talked, and the refinements of life are only just beginning to appear, how can such a country be compared with England or France or Italy?"

It is nevertheless true that there are elements in the life of the United States which may well make a European of any class prefer to dwell there rather than in the land of his birth. Let us see what they are.

In the first place there is the general prosperity and material well-being of the mass of the inhabitants. In Europe, if an observer takes his eye off his own class and considers the whole population of any one of the greater countries (for I except Switzerland and parts of Scandinavia and Portugal), he will perceive that by far the greater number lead very laborious lives, and are, if not actually in want of the necessaries of existence, yet liable to fall into want, — the agriculturists when Nature is harsh, the wage-earners when work is scarce. In England the lot of the laborer has been hitherto a hard one, — incessant field-toil, with rheumatism at fifty and the workhouse at the end of the vista ; while the misery massed in such cities as London, Liverpool, and Glasgow is only too well known.   In France there is less pauperism, but nothing can be more pinched and sordid than the life of the bulk of the peasantry.   In the great towns of Germany there is constant distress and increasing discontent.   The riots of 1886 in Belgium told an even more painful tale of the wretchedness of the miners and artisans there.   In Italy the condition of the rural population of Lombardy and Venetia, as well as of the southern provinces, seems to grow worse, and fills statesmen with alarm.   Of Russia, with her eighty millions of ignorant peasants living in half barbarism, there is no need to speak.   Contrast any one of these countries with the United States, where the working-classes are as well fed, clothed, and lodged as the lower middle-class in Europe, and the farmers who till their own land (as nearly all do) much better, where a good education is within the reach of the poorest, where the opportunities for getting on in one way or another are so abundant that no one need fear any physical ill but disease or the results of his own intemperance.   Pauperism already exists, and increases in some of the larger cities, where drink breeds misery, and where recent immigrants, with the shiftlessness of Europe still clinging round them, are huddled together in squalor.   But outside these few cities one sees nothing but comfort.   In Connecticut and Massachusetts the operatives in many a manufacturing town lead a life far easier, far more brightened by intellectual culture and by amusements, than that of the clerks and shopkeepers of England or France.   In cities like Cleveland or Chicago one finds miles on miles of suburb filled with neat wooden houses, each with its tiny garden plot, owned by the shop-assistants and handicraftsmen who return on the horse-cars in the evening from their work. All over the wide West, from Lake Ontario to the Upper Missouri, one travels past farms of two to three hundred acres, in every one of which there is a spacious farmhouse among orchards and meadows, where the farmer's children

grow up strong and hearty on abundant food, the boys full
of intelligence and enterprise, ready to push their way on
farms of their own, or enter business in the nearest town,
the girls familiar with the current literature of England as
well as of America. The life of the new emigrant in the
farther West has its privations in the first years, but it is
brightened by hope, and has a singular charm of freedom
and simplicity. The impression which this comfort and
plenty makes is heightened by the brilliance of the air
and by the look of freshness and cleanness which even the
cities wear, — all of them except the poorest parts of those
few I have referred to above. The fog and soot-flakes of an
English town, as well as its squalor, are wanting; you are
in a new world, and a world which knows the sun. It is
impossible not to feel warmed, cheered, invigorated, by the
sense of such material well-being all around one, impossible
not to be infected by the buoyancy and hopefulness of the
people. The wretchedness of Europe lies far behind; the
weight of its problems seems lifted from the mind. As a
man suffering from depression feels the clouds roll away
from his spirit when he meets a friend whose good-humor
and energy present the better side of things and point the
way through difficulties, so the sanguine temper of the
Americans, and the sight of the ardor with which they pursue
their aims, stimulates a European, and makes him think the
world a better place than it had seemed amid the entangle-
ments and sufferings of his own hemisphere.

To some Europeans this may seem fanciful. I doubt if
any European can realize till he has been in America how
much difference it makes to the happiness of any one not
wholly devoid of sympathy with his fellow-beings, to feel
that all round him, in all classes of society and all parts
of the country, there exist in such ample measure so many
of the external conditions of happiness, — abundance of the
necessaries of life, easy command of education and books,

amusements and leisure to enjoy them, comparatively few temptations to intemperance and vice.

The second charm of American life is one which some Europeans will smile at. It is social equality. To many Europeans the word has an odious sound. It suggests a dirty fellow in a blouse elbowing his betters in a crowd, or an ill-conditioned villager shaking his fist at the parson and the squire; or, at any rate, it suggests obtrusiveness and bad manners. The exact contrary is the truth. Equality improves manners, for it strengthens the basis of all good manners, — respect for other men and women simply as men and women, irrespective of their station in life. Probably the assertion of social equality was one of the causes which injured American manners forty years ago; for that they were then bad, at least among townsfolk, can hardly be doubted, in face of the testimony, not merely of sharp tongues like Mrs. Trollope's, but of calm observers like Sir Charles Lyell and sympathetic observers like Richard Cobden. In those days there was an obtrusive self-assertiveness among the less refined classes, especially towards those who, coming from the Old World, were assumed to come in a patronizing spirit. Now, however, social equality has grown so naturally out of the circumstances of the country, has been so long established, and is so ungrudgingly admitted, that all excuse for obtrusiveness has disappeared. People meet on a simple and natural footing, with more frankness and ease than is possible in countries where every one is either looking up or looking down.* There is no ser-

* A trifling anecdote may illustrate what I mean. In a small Far Western town the station-master lent me a locomotive to run a few miles out along the railway to see a remarkable piece of scenery. The engine took me and dropped me there, as I wished to walk back, — much to the surprise of the driver and stoker, for in America no one walks if he can help it. The same evening, as I was sitting in the hall of the hotel, I was touched on the arm, and turning round found myself accosted by a well-mannered man, who turned out to be the engine-driver. He expressed

vility on the part of the humbler, and if now and then a little of the "I am as good as you" rudeness be perceptible, it is almost sure to proceed from a recent immigrant, to whom the attitude of simple equality has not yet become familiar as the evidently proper attitude of one man to another. There is no condescension on the part of the more highly placed, nor is there even that sort of scrupulously polite coldness which one might think they would adopt in order to protect their dignity. They have no cause to fear for their dignity, so long as they do not themselves forget it. And the fact that your shoemaker or your factory hand addresses you as an equal does not prevent him from respecting, and showing his respect for, all such superiority as your birth or education or eminence in any line of life may entitle you to receive.

This naturalness of intercourse is a distinct addition to the pleasure of social life. It enlarges the circle of possible friendship, by removing the *gêne* which in most parts of Europe persons of different ranks feel in exchanging their thoughts on any matters save those of business. It raises the humbler classes without lowering the upper, — indeed, it improves the upper no less than the lower, by expunging that latent insolence which deforms the manners of so many of the European rich or great. It relieves women in particular, who in Europe are specially apt to think of class distinctions, from that sense of constraint and uneasiness which is produced by the knowledge that other women with whom they come in contact are either looking down on them, or at any rate trying to gauge and determine their social position. It expands the range of a man's sympathies, and makes it easier for him to

his regret that the locomotive had not been cleaner and better "fixed up," as he would have liked to make my trip as agreeable as possible, but the notice given him had been short. He talked with intelligence, and we had some pleasant chat together. It was fortunate that I had resisted in the forenoon the British impulse to bestow a gratuity.

enter into the sentiments of other classes than his own. It gives a sense of solidarity to the whole nation, cutting away the ground for all sorts of jealousies and grudges which distract people, so long as the social pretensions of past centuries linger on, to be resisted and resented by the levelling spirit of a revolutionary age. And I have never heard native Americans speak of any drawbacks corresponding to and qualifying these benefits.

There are, moreover, other rancors besides those of social inequality whose absence from America brightens it to a European eye. There are no quarrels of churches and sects. Judah does not vex Ephraim, nor Ephraim envy Judah. No Established Church looks down scornfully upon Dissenters from the height of its titles and endowments, and talks of them as hindrances in the way of its work. No Dissenters pursue an Established Church in a spirit of watchful jealousy, nor agitate for its overthrow. One is not offended by the contrast between the theory and the practice of a religion of peace, between professions of universal affection in pulpit addresses and forms of prayer, and the acrimony of clerical controversialists. Still less, of course, is there that sharp opposition and antagonism of Christians and anti-Christians which lacerates the private as well as public life of France. Rivalry between sects appears only in the innocent form of the planting of new churches and raising of funds for missionary objects, while most of the Protestant denominations, including the four most numerous, constantly fraternize in charitable work. Between Roman Catholics and Protestants there is little hostility, and sometimes even co-operation for a philanthropic purpose. The sceptic is no longer under a social ban, and discussions on the essentials of Christianity and of theism are conducted with good temper. There is not a country in the world where Frederick the Great's principle, that every one should be allowed to go to heaven his own way, is so fully applied. This sense of religious peace as well as religious freedom all around one is soothing to the weary European, and contributes not a little to sweeten the lives of ordinary people.

I come last to the character and ways of the Americans themselves, in which there is a certain charm, hard to convey by description, but felt almost as soon as one sets foot on their shore, and felt constantly thereafter. They are a kindly people. Good-nature, heartiness, a readiness to render small services to one another, an assumption that neighbors in a country, or persons thrown together in travel, or even in a crowd, were meant to be friendly rather than hostile to one another, seem to be everywhere in the air, and in those who breathe it. Sociability is the rule, isolation and moroseness the rare exception. It is not that people are more vivacious or talkative than an Englishman expects to find them, for the Western man is often taciturn, and seldom wreathes his long face into a smile. It is rather that you feel that the man next you, whether silent or talkative, does not mean to repel intercourse, or convey by his manner his low opinion of his fellow-creatures. Everybody seems disposed to think well of the world and its inhabitants, — well enough at least to wish to be on easy terms with them and serve them in those little things whose trouble to the doer is small in proportion to the pleasure they give to the receiver. To help others is better recognized as a duty than in Europe. Nowhere is money so readily given for any public purpose ; nowhere, I suspect, are there so many acts of private kindness done, — such, for instance, as paying the college expenses of a promising boy, or aiding a widow to carry on her husband's farm ; and these are not done with ostentation. People seem to take their own troubles more lightly than they do in Europe, and to be more indulgent to the faults by which troubles are caused. It is a land of hope, and a land of hope is a land of good-humor. And they have also — though this is a quality more perceptible in women than in men — a remarkable faculty for enjoyment, a power of drawing more happiness from obvious pleasures, simple and innocent pleasures, than one often finds in over-burdened Europe.

As generalizations like this are necessarily comparative, I may be asked with whom I am comparing the Americans. With the English, or with some attempted average of European nations? Primarily I am comparing them with the English, because they are the nearest relatives of the English. But there are other European countries, such as France, Belgium, Spain, in which the sort of cheerful friendliness I have sought to describe is less common than it is in America. Even in Germany and German Austria, simple and kindly as are the masses of the people, the upper classes have that *roideur* which belongs to countries dominated by an old aristocracy, or by a plutocracy trying to imitate aristocratic ways. The upper class in America (if one may use such an expression) has not in this respect differentiated itself from the character of the nation at large.

If the view here presented be a true one, to what causes are we to ascribe this agreeable development of the original English type, — a development in whose course the sadness of Puritanism seems to have been shed off?

Perhaps one of them is the humorous turn of the American character. Humor is a sweetener of temper, a copious spring of charity, for it makes the good side of bad things even more visible than the weak side of good things; but humor in Americans may be as much a result of an easy and kindly turn as their kindliness is of their humor. Another is the perpetuation of a habit of mutual help formed in colonial days. Colonists need one another's aid more constantly than the dwellers in an old country, are thrown more upon one another, even when they live scattered in woods or prairies, are more interested in one another's welfare. When you have only three neighbors within five miles, each of them covers a large part of your horizon. You want to borrow a plough from one; you get another to help you to roll your logs; your children's delight is to go over for an evening's merrymaking to the lads and lasses of the third. It is much pleasanter to be on good terms with these few neighbors; and when others come one by one, they fall into the same habits of intimacy. Any one who has read those stories of rustic New England or New York life which delighted the English children of thirty years ago — I do not know whether they delight children still, or have been thrown aside for more highly-spiced food— will remember the warm-hearted simplicity and atmosphere of genial goodwill which softened the roughness of peasant manners and tempered the sternness of a Calvinistic creed. It is natural that the freedom of intercourse and sense of interdependence which existed among the early settlers, and which have existed ever since among the pioneers of colonization in the West as they moved from the Connecticut to the Mohawk, from the Mohawk to the Ohio, from the Ohio to the Mississippi, should have left on the national character traces not effaced even in the more artificial civilization of our own time. Something may be set down to the feeling of social equality, creating that respect for a man as a man, whether he be rich or poor, which was described a few pages back, and something to a regard for the sentiment of the multitude, — a sentiment which forbids any man to stand aloof in the conceit of self-importance, and holds up geniality and good fellowship as almost the first of social virtues. I do not mean that a man consciously suppresses his impulses to selfishness or gruffness because he knows that his faults will be ill regarded, but that, having grown up in a society which is infinitely powerful as compared with the most powerful person in it, he has learned to realize his individual insignificance as members of the upper class in Europe never do, and has become permeated by the feeling which this society entertains, — that each one's duty is not only to accept equality, but also to relish equality and to make himself pleasant to his equals. Thus the habit is formed even in natures of no special sweetness, and men become kindly by doing kindly acts.

Whether, however, these suggestions be right or wrong, there is, I think, no doubt as to the fact which they attempt to explain. I do not, of course, give it merely as the casual impression of European visitors, whom a singularly frank and ready hospitality welcomes and makes much of; I base it on the reports of European friends who have lived for years in the United States, and whose criticism of the ways and notions of the people is keen enough to show that they are no partial witnesses.

CHAPTER XVI.

THE UNIFORMITY OF AMERICAN LIFE.

To the pleasantness of American life there is one, and only one, serious drawback, — its uniformity. Those who have been struck by the size of America, and by what they have heard of its restless excitement, may be surprised at the word. They would have guessed that an unquiet changefulness and turmoil were the disagreeables to be feared. But uniformity, which the European visitor begins to note when he has travelled for a month or two, is the feature of the country which Englishmen who have lived long there, and Americans who are familiar with Europe, most frequently revert to when asked to say what is the " crook in their lot."

It is felt in many ways. I will name a few.

It is felt in the aspects of Nature. All the natural features of the United States are on a larger scale than those of Europe. The four great mountain chains are each of them longer than the Alps.* Of the gigantic rivers and of those inland seas we call the Great Lakes one need not speak. The centre of the continent is occupied by a plain larger than the western half of Europe. In the Mississippi valley, from the Gulf of Mexico to Lake Superior, there is nothing deserving to be called a hill, though as one moves westward from the great river, long, soft undulations in the prairie begin to appear. Through vast stretches of country one finds the same

* The Alleghanies, continued in the Green and White Mountains; the Rocky Mountains; the Sierra Nevada, continued in the Cascade Range; and the Coast Range, which borders the Pacific.

physical character maintained with little change, — the same strata, the same vegetation, a generally similar climate. From the point where you leave the Alleghanies at Pittsburg until, after crossing the Missouri, you approach the still untilled prairie of the West, a railway run of some thousand miles, there is a uniformity of landscape greater than could be found along any one hundred miles of railway run in Western Europe. Everywhere the same nearly flat country, over which you cannot see far, because you are little raised above it, the same fields and crops, the same rough wooden fences, the same thickets of the same bushes along the stream edges, — with here and there a bit of old forest, — the same solitary farm-houses and straggling wood-built villages. And when one has passed beyond the fields and farm-houses, there is an even more unvaried stretch of slightly rolling prairie, smooth and bare, till after five hundred miles the blue line of the Rocky Mountains rises upon the western horizon.

There are some extraordinary natural phenomena, — such as Niagara, the Yellowstone Geysers, and the great cañon of the Colorado River, — which Europe cannot equal. But taking the country as a whole, and remembering that it is a continent, it is not more rich in picturesque beauty than the much smaller western half of Europe. There is a good deal of pretty scenery and a few really romantic spots in the long Alleghany range, but hardly anything so charming as the best bits of Scotland or southern Ireland, or the English lakes. The Rocky Mountains are pierced by some splendid gorges, such as the famous cañon of the Arkansas River above South Pueblo, and show some very grand prospects, such as that over the Great Salt Lake from the Mormon capital. But neither the Rocky Mountains, with their dependent ranges, nor the Sierra Nevada, can be compared for variety of grandeur and beauty with the Alps ; for although each chain nearly equals the Alps in height, and covers a greater area, they have little snow, no glaciers,* and a singular uniformity of character. One finds, I think, less variety in the whole chain of the Rockies than in the comparatively short Pyrenees. There are indeed in the whole United States very few quite first-rate pieces of mountain scenery rivalling the best of the Old World. The most impressive are, I think, two or three of the deep valleys of the Sierra Nevada (of which the Yo-semite is the best known) and the superb line of extinct volcanoes, bearing snow-fields and glaciers, which one sees, rising out of vast and sombre forests, from the banks of the Columbia River and the shores of Puget Sound.† So the Atlantic coast, though there are pretty bits between Newport and the New Brunswick frontier, — particularly in Mount Desert island, — cannot vie with the coasts of Scot-land, Ireland, or Norway; while southward from New York to Florida it is everywhere flat, and generally dreary. In the United States people take journeys proportionate to the size of the country. A family thinks nothing of going twelve hundred miles, from St. Louis to Cape May (near Philadelphia), for a seaside holiday. But even journeys of twelve hundred miles do not give an American so much

---

* There are a few inconsiderable glaciers in the northernmost part of the Rocky Mountains, and a small one on Mount Shasta. In the Cana-dian Rockies, and of course in Alaska, the glaciers are of great size.

† I have been obliged, by want of space, to omit the chapters which were intended to describe the scenery of the United States and to conjec-ture its probable future influence on the character of the people.

Nothing is further from my mind than to attempt to disparage the scenery of the Great West, which contains, from the eastern slope of the Rocky Mountains to the Pacific, many very striking and impressive points. I only say that they are less beautiful than the Alps, just as the mountains of Asia Minor, even when equal or superior in height, are less beautiful, and largely for the same reason. They are much drier, and have therefore fewer streams and less variety and wealth of vegetation, the upper zone of the Sierra Nevada excepted; and the Rockies, as they run north and south, present less of a contrast between their two sides than do the northern and southern declivities of the Alps or the Caucasus.

change of scene and variety of surroundings as a Parisian has when he goes to Nice, or a Berliner to Berchtesgaden. The man who lives in the section of America which seems destined to contain the largest population — I mean the States on the Upper Mississippi — lives in the midst of a plain wider than the plains of Russia, and must travel hundreds of miles to escape from its monotony.

When we turn from the aspects of Nature to the cities of men, the uniformity is even more remarkable. With five or six exceptions, to be mentioned presently, American cities differ from one another only herein, that some of them are built more with brick than with wood, and others more with wood than with brick. In all else they are alike, both great and small. In all the same wide streets, crossing at right angles, ill-paved, but planted along the side-walks with maple-trees whose autumnal scarlet surpasses the brilliance of any European foliage. In all the same shops, arranged on the same plan, the same Chinese laundries, with Li Kow visible through the window, the same ice-cream stores, the same large hotels with seedy men hovering about in the dreary entrance-hall, the same street-cars passing to and fro, with passengers clinging to the doorstep, the same locomotives ringing their great bells as they clank slowly down the middle of the street. I admit that in external aspect there is a sad monotony in the larger towns of England also. Compare English cities with Italian cities, and most of the former seem like one another, incapable of being, so to speak, individualized as you individualize a man with a definite character and aspect unlike that of other men. Take the Lancashire towns, for instance, — large and prosperous places. You cannot individualize Bolton or Wigan, Oldham or Bury, except by trying to remember that Bury is slightly less rough than Oldham, and Wigan a thought more grimy than Bolton. But in Italy every city has its character, its memories, its life and achievements wrought into the pillars of its churches and the towers that stand

along its ramparts.   Siena is not like Perugia, nor Perugia like
Orvieto ; Ravenna, Rimini, Pesaro, Fano, Ancona, Osimo,
standing along the same coast within seventy miles of one
another, have each of them a character, a sentiment, what one
may call an idiosyncrasy, which comes vividly back to us at
the mention of its name.   Now, what English towns are to
Italian, that American towns are to English.   They are in
some ways pleasanter ; they are cleaner, there is less poverty,
less squalor, less darkness.   But their monotony haunts one
like a nightmare.   Even the irksomeness of finding the streets
named by numbers becomes insufferable.*   It is doubtless
convenient to know by the number how far up the city the
particular street is.   But you cannot give any sort of character to Twenty-ninth Street, for the name refuses to lend itself
to any association.   There is something wearisomely hard
and bare in such a system.

I return joyfully to the exceptions.   Boston has a character
of her own, with her beautiful common, her smooth, environ-
ing waters, her Beacon Hill, crowned by the gilded dome of
the State House, and Bunker Hill, bearing the monument of
the famous fight.   New York, besides a magnificent position,
has in the loftiness of the buildings and the tremendous rush
of men and vehicles along the streets, as much the air of a
great capital as London itself.   Chicago, with her enormous size
and the splendid warehouses that line her endless thorough-
fares, leaves a strong, though not wholly agreeable impression.
Richmond and Charleston have a quaint, old-world look which
dwells in the memory ; few cities can show a sea-front equal
in beauty to the lake-front of Cleveland.   Washington, with its
wide and beautifully-graded avenues, and the glittering white

* In the newer cities one set of parallel streets is named by numbers,
the others, which cross them at right angles, are in some instances, as in
New York, called avenues, and so numbered.   In Washington the avenues
are called after States, and of the two sets of streets (which the avenues
cross obliquely), one is called by numbers, the other by the letters of the
alphabet.

of the stately Capitol, has become within the last twenty years
a singularly handsome city.   And New Orleans — or rather
the Creole quarter of New Orleans, for the rest of the city is
commonplace — is delicious, suggesting old France and Spain,
yet a France and Spain strangely transmuted in this new
clime. I have seen nothing in America more picturesque than
the Rue Royale, with its houses of all heights, often built round
a courtyard, where a magnolia or an orange-tree stands in
the middle, and wooden external staircases lead up to wooden
galleries, the house-fronts painted of diverse colors, and carrying double rows of balconies decorated with pretty ironwork,
the whole standing languid and still in the warm, soft air, and
touched with the subtle fragrance of decay. Here in New
Orleans the streets and public buildings, and specially the
old City Hall, with the arms of Spain still upon it, speak of
history.   One feels, in stepping across Canal Street from the
Creole quarter to the business parts of the town, that one
steps from an old nationality to a new one, that this city
must have had vicissitudes, that it represents something, and
that something one of the great events of history, — the sur-
render of the northern half of the New World by the Romano-
Celtic races to the Teutonic.   Quebec, and to a less degree
Montreal, fifteen hundred miles away, tell the same tale;
Santa Fé in New Mexico repeats it.

It is the absence in nearly all the American cities of anything that speaks of the past that makes their external aspect
so unsuggestive. In pacing their busy streets and admiring
their handsome city halls and churches, one's heart sinks at
the feeling that nothing historically interesting ever has happened here, perhaps ever will happen. In many an English
town, however ugly with its smoke and its new suburbs, one
sees at least an ancient church, one can discover some frag-
ments of a castle or a city wall.   Even Wigan and Northampton have ancient churches, though Northampton lately allowed
the North-Western Railway to destroy the last traces of the

castle where Henry II. issued his Assize. But in America hardly any public building is associated with anything more interesting than a big party convention; and nowadays even the big conventions are held in temporary structures, whose materials are sold when the politicians have dispersed. Nowhere, perhaps, does this sense of the absolute novelty of all things strike one so strongly as in San Francisco. Few cities in the world can vie with her either in the beauty or in the natural advantages of her situation; indeed, there are only two places in Europe — Constantinople and Gibraltar — that combine an equally perfect landscape with what may be called an equally imperial position. Before you there is the magnificent bay, with its far-stretching arms and rocky isles, and beyond it the faint line of the Sierra Nevada, cutting the clear air like mother-of-pearl; behind there is the roll of the ocean; to the left the majestic gateway between mountains through which ships bear in commerce from the farthest shores of the Pacific; to the right, valleys rich with corn and wine, sweeping away to the southern horizon. The city itself is full of bold hills, rising steeply from the deep water. The air is keen, dry, and bright, like the air of Greece, and the waters not less blue. Perhaps it is this air and light, recalling the cities of the Mediterranean, that make one involuntarily look up to the top of these hills for the feudal castle, or the ruins of the Acropolis, which one thinks must crown them. I found myself so looking all the time I remained in the city. But on none of these heights is there anything more interesting, anything more vocal to the student of the past, than the sumptuous villas of the magnates of the Central Pacific Railway, who have chosen a hill-top to display their wealth to the city, but have erected houses like all other houses, only larger. San Francisco has had a good deal of history in her forty years of life; but this history does not, like that of Greece or Italy, write itself in stone, or even in wood.

Of the uniformity of political institutions over the whole

United States I have spoken already. Everywhere the same system of State governments, everywhere the same municipal governments, and almost uniformly bad or good in proportion to the greater or smaller population of the city ; the same party machinery organized on the same methods, " run " by the same wirepullers and " workers." In rural local government there are some diversities in the names, areas, and functions of the different bodies, yet differences slight in comparison with the points of likeness. The schools are practically identical in organization, in the subjects taught, in the methods of teaching, though the administration of them is as completely decentralized as can be imagined, even the State commissioner having no right to do more than suggest or report. So it is with the charitable institutions, with the libraries, the lecture-courses, the public amusements. All these are more abundant and better of their kind in the richer and more cultivated parts of the country, generally better in the North Atlantic than in the inland States, and in the West than in the South. But they are the same in type everywhere. It is the same with social habits and usages. There are still some differences between the South and the North ; and in the Eastern cities the upper class is more Europeanized in its code of etiquette and its ways of daily life. But even these variations tend to disappear. Eastern customs begin to permeate the West, beginning with the richer families ; the South is more like the North than it was before the war. Travel where you will, you feel that what you have found in one place, that you will find in another. The thing which hath been, will be , you can no more escape from it than you can quit the land to live in the sea.

Last of all, we come to man himself, — to man and to woman, not less important than man. The ideas of men and women, their fundamental beliefs and their superficial tastes, their methods of thinking and their fashions of talking, are what most concern their fellow-men ; and if there be variety and freshness in these, the uniformity of Nature and the monotony of cities signify but little. If I observe that in these respects also the similarity of type over the country is surprising, I shall be asked whether I am not making the old mistake of the man who fancied all Chinese were like one another because, noticing the dress and the pigtail, he did not notice minor differences of feature. A scholar is apt to think that all business men write the same hand, and a business man thinks the same of all scholars. Perhaps Americans think all Englishmen alike. And I may also be asked with whom I am comparing the Americans. With Europe as a whole? If so, is it not absurd to expect that the differences between different sections in one people should be as marked as those between different peoples? The United States are larger than Europe; but Europe has many races and many languages, among whom contrasts far broader must be expected than between one people, even if it stretches over a continent.

It is most clearly not with Europe, but with each of the leading European peoples, that we must compare the people of America. So comparing them with the people of Britain, France, Germany, Italy, Spain, one discovers more varieties between individuals in these European peoples than one finds in America. Scotchmen and Irishmen are more unlike Englishmen, the native of Normandy more unlike the native of Provence, the Pomeranian more unlike the Würtemberger, the Piedmontese more unlike the Neapolitan, the Basque more unlike the Andalusian, than the American from any part of the country is to the American from any other. Differences of course there are between the normal human being as developed in different regions of the country, — differences moral and intellectual as well as physical. You can generally tell a Southerner by his look as well as by his speech. In the mountain region of the South, — east Kentucky and east Tennessee, North Carolina and the southwestern corner of Virginia, — isolation coupled with poverty and a primitive rudeness of life have preserved a peculiar type, differing from that of the South generally. So Texas has a certain local character; so a native of Maine will probably differ from a native of Missouri, a Georgian from an Oregonian. But these differences strike even an American observer much as the difference between a Yorkshireman and a Lancastrian strikes the English, and is slighter than the contrast between a middle-class southern Englishman and a middle-class Scotchman, slighter than the differences between a peasant from Northumberland and a peasant from Dorsetshire. Or, to take another way of putting it: If at some great gathering of a political party from all parts of the United Kingdom you were to go round and talk to, say, one hundred, taken at random, of the persons present, you would be struck by more diversity between the notions and the tastes and mental habits of the individuals comprising that one hundred than if you tried the same experiment with a hundred Americans of the same education and position, similarly gathered in a convention from every State in the Union.

I do not in the least mean that people are more commonplace in America than in England, or that the Americans are less ideal than the English. Neither of these statements would be true. On the contrary, the average American is more alive to new ideas, more easily touched through his imagination or his emotions, than the average Englishman or Frenchman. I mean only that the native-born Americans appear to vary less, in fundamentals, from what may be called the dominant American type than Englishmen, Germans, Frenchmen, Spaniards, or Italians do from any type which could be taken as the dominant type in any of those nations. Or, to put the same thing differently, it is rather more difficult to take any assemblage of attributes in any of these European countries and call it the national type than it is to do the like in the United States.

These are not given as the impressions of a traveller. Such

impressions, being necessarily hasty, and founded on a comparatively narrow observation, would deserve little confidence. They sum up the conclusions of Europeans long resident in America, and familiar with different parts of the country. They are, I think, admitted by the most acute Americans themselves.   I have often heard the latter dilate on what seems to them the one crowning merit of life in Europe, — the variety it affords, the opportunities it gives of easy and complete changes of scene and environment.   The pleasure which an American finds in crossing the Atlantic, — a pleasure more intense than any which the European enjoys, — is that of passing from a land of happy monotony into regions where everything is redolent with memories of the past, and derives from the past no less than from the present a wealth and a subtle complexity of interest which no new country can possess.

Life in America is in most ways pleasanter, easier, simpler, than in Europe; it floats in a sense of happiness like that of a radiant summer morning.   But life in any of the great European centres is capable of an intensity, a richness blended of many elements, which has not yet been reached in America.   There are more problems in Europe calling for solution; there is more passion in the struggles that rage round them; the past more frequently kindles the present with a glow of imaginative light.   In whichever country of Europe one dwells, one feels that the other countries are near, that the fortunes of their peoples are bound up with the fortunes of one's own, that ideas are shooting to and fro between them.   The web of history woven day by day all over Europe is vast and of many colors; it is fateful to every European.   But in America it is only the philosopher who can feel that it will ultimately be fateful to Americans also; to the ordinary man the Old World seems far off, severed by a dissociating ocean, its mighty burden with little meaning for him.

Those who have observed the uniformity I have been attempting to describe have commonly set it down, as Europeans do most American phenomena, to what they call Democracy. Democratic government has in reality not much to do with it, except in so far as such a government helps to induce that deference of individuals to the mass which strengthens a dominant type, whether of ideas, of institutions, or of manners. More must be ascribed to the equality of material conditions, which, though it diminishes, is still more general than in Europe; to the fact that nearly every one is engaged either in agriculture, or in commerce, or in some handicraft; to the extraordinary mobility of the population, which in migrating from one part of the country to another, brings the characteristics of each part into the others; to the diffusion of education; to the cheapness of literature and universal habit of reading, which enable every one to know what every one else is thinking; but above all to the newness of the country, and the fact that four fifths of it have been made all at a stroke, and therefore all of a piece, as compared with the slow growth by which European countries have developed. Newness is the cause of uniformity, not merely in the external aspect of cities, villages, farm-houses, but in other things also; for the institutions and social habits which belonged a century ago to a group of small communities on the Atlantic coast have been suddenly extended over an immense area, each band of settlers naturally seeking to retain its customs and to plant in the new soil shoots from which trees like those of the old home might spring up. The variety of European countries is due not only to the fact that their race-elements have not yet become thoroughly commingled, but also that many old institutions have survived among the new ones; as in a city that grows but slowly, old buildings are not cleared away to make room for others more suited to modern commerce, but are allowed to stand, sometimes empty and unused, sometimes half adapted to new purposes. This scarcely happens in America. Doubtless many American institutions are old, and were old before they were carried across the Atlantic. But they have generally received a new dress, which, in adapting them to the needs of to-day, conceals their ancient character; and the form in which they have been diffused or reproduced in the different States of the Union is in all those States practically identical.

In each of the great European countries the diversity of primeval and mediæval times, when endless varieties of race, speech, and faith existed within the space of a few hundred miles, has been more or less preserved by segregative influences. In America a small race, of the same speech and faith, has spread itself out over an immense area, and has been strong enough to impose its own type, not only on the Dutch and other early settlers of the Middle States, but on the immigrant masses which the last forty years have brought.*

May one, then, expect that when novelty has worn off, and America counts her life by centuries instead of by decades, variety will develop itself, and complexities, or diversities, or incongruities (whichever one is to call them) such as European countries present, be deeper and more numerous?

As regards the outside of things this seems unlikely. Many of the small towns of to-day will grow into large towns, a few of the large towns into great cities; but as they grow they will not become less like one another. There will be larger theatres and hotels, more churches (in spite of secularist

---

* It may be thought that I have under-estimated the diversity already due to the presence of immigrants, and the greater diversity which the mingling of their blood with that of the native Americans will in time produce. However, in this chapter I am speaking of society as it now exists; and the recent immigrants have as yet affected it but little, save that the Germans have brought in a greater fondness for music, for the drama, and for out-of-door life in the cities. I greatly doubt whether the influence of the immigrants will be much more powerful in the future, so strong is the native type of thought and customs, and so quickly does it tell on the new-comers.

lecturers), and handsomer ones; but what is to make the
theatres and churches of one city differ from those of another?
Fashion and the immense facilities of intercourse tend to
wear down even such diversities in the style of building or
furnishing, or in modes of locomotion, or in amusements and
forms of social intercourse, as now exist.

As regards ideas and the inner life of men, the question is
a more difficult one.   At present there are only two parts of
the country where one looks to meet with the well-marked
individualities I refer to.   One of these is New England,
where the spirit of Puritanism, expressed in new literary
forms by Emerson and his associates, did produce a peculiar
type of thinking and discoursing, which has now, however,
almost died out, and where one still meets, especially among
the cultivated classes, a larger number than elsewhere of persons who have thought and studied for themselves, and are
unlike their fellows.   The other part of the country is the
Far West, where the wild life led by pioneers in exploration,
or ranching, or gold-mining has produced a number of striking
figures, men of extraordinary self-reliance, with a curious
mixture of geniality and reckless hardihood, no less indifferent
to their own lives than to the lives of others.   Of preserving
this latter type there is, alas! little hope; the swift march of
civilization will have expunged it in thirty years more.

When one sees millions of people thinking the same thoughts
and reading the same books, and perceives that as the multitude grows, its influence becomes always stronger, it is hard
to imagine how new points of repulsion and contrast are to
arise. new diversities of sentiment and doctrine to be developed.   Nevertheless I am inclined to believe that as the intellectual proficiency and speculative play of mind, which are now
confined to a comparatively small class, become more generally diffused; as the pressure of effort towards material success
is relaxed; as the number of men devoted to science, art, and
learning increases, — so will the dominance of what may be

called the business mind decline, and with a richer variety of knowledge, tastes, and pursuits, there will come also a larger crop of marked individualities and of divergent intellectual types.

Time will take away some of the monotony which comes from the absence of historical associations ; for even if, as is to be hoped, there comes no war to make battle-fields famous, like those of twenty-five years ago, yet literature and the lives of famous men cannot but attach to many spots associations to which the blue of distance will at last give a romantic interest. No people could be more ready than are the Americans to cherish such associations. Their country has a short past, but they willingly revere and preserve all the memories the past has bequeathed to them.

CHAPTER XVII.

THE TEMPER OF THE WEST.

WESTERN AMERICA is one of the most interesting subjects of study the modern world has seen. There has been nothing in the past resembling its growth, and probably there will be nothing in the future. A vast territory, wonderfully rich in natural resources of many kinds ; a temperate and healthy climate, fit for European labor ; a soil generally, and in many places marvellously, fertile ; in some regions mountains full of minerals, in others trackless forests where every tree is over two hundred feet high ; and the whole of this virtually unoccupied territory thrown open to an energetic race, with all the appliances and contrivances of modern science at its command, — these are phenomena absolutely without precedent in history, and which cannot recur elsewhere, because our planet contains no such other favored tract of country.

The Spaniards and Portuguese settled in tropical countries, which soon enervated them. They carried with them the poison of slavery ; their colonists were separated, some by long land journeys, and all by still longer voyages from the centres of civilization. But the railway and the telegraph follow the Western American. The Greeks of the sixth and seventh centuries before Christ, who planted themselves all round the coasts of the Mediterranean, had always enemies, and often powerful enemies, to overcome before they could found even their trading stations on the coast, much less occupy the lands of the interior. In Western America the presence of the Indians has done no more than give a touch of romance or a spice of danger to the exploration of some regions, such as Western Dakota and Arizona, while over the rest of the country the unhappy aborigines have slunk silently away, scarcely even complaining of the robbery of lands and the violation of plighted faith. Nature and Time seem to have conspired to make the development of the Mississippi basin and the Pacific slope the swiftest, easiest, completest achievement in the whole record of the civilizing progress of mankind since the founder of the Egyptian monarchy gathered the tribes of the Nile under one government.

The details of this development and the statistics that illustrate it have been too often set forth to need re-statement here. It is of the character and temper of the men who have conducted it that I wish to speak, — a matter which has received less attention, but is essential to a just conception of the Americans of to-day. For the West is the most American part of America ; that is to say, the part where those features which distinguish America from Europe come out in the strongest relief. What Europe is to Asia, what England is to the rest of Europe, what America is to England, that the Western States and Territories are to the Atlantic States, the heat and pressure and hurry of life always growing as we follow the path of the sun. In Eastern America there are still quiet spots, — in the valleys of the Alleghanies, for instance, in nooks of old New England, in university towns like Ithaca or Ann Arbor. In the West there are none. All is bustle, motion, and struggle, — most so, of course, among the native Americans ; yet even the immigrant from the secluded valleys of Thuringia, or the shores of some Norwegian fjord, learns the ways almost as readily as the tongue of the country, and is soon swept into the whirlpool.

It is the most enterprising and unsettled Americans that come West ; and when they have left their old haunts, broken their old ties, resigned the comforts and pleasures of their former homes, they are resolved to obtain the wealth and success for which they have come. They throw themselves into work with a feverish yet sustained intensity. They rise early, they work all day, they have few pleasures, few opportunities for relaxation.* I remember in the young city of Seattle, on Puget Sound, to have found business in full swing at seven o'clock A. M., — the shops open, the streets full of people. Everything is speculative, land (or, as it is usually called, " real estate ") most so ; the value of lots of ground rising or falling perhaps two or three hundred per cent in the year. No one has any fixed occupation ; he is a storekeeper to-day, a ranchman to-morrow, a miner next week. I found the waiters in the chief hotel at Denver, in Colorado, saving their autumn and winter wages to start off in the spring " prospecting" for silver " claims" in the mountains. Few men stay in one of the newer cities more than three or four weeks or months ; to have been there a whole year is to be an old inhabitant, — an oracle if you have succeeded, a by-word if you have not ; for to prosper in the West you must be able to turn your hand to anything, and seize to-day the chance which every one else will have seen to-morrow. This venturesome and shifting life strengthens the reckless and heedless habits of the people. Every one thinks so much of gaining that he thinks little of spending ; and in the general dearness of commodities, food (in the agricultural districts) excepted, it seems not worth while to care about small sums. In California for many years no coin lower than a ten-cent piece (5d.) was in circulation ; and even in 1881, though most articles of food were abundant, nothing was sold at a lower price than five cents. The most striking alternations of fortune, the great *coups* which fascinate men and make them play for all or

* In the newer towns — which are often nothing more than groups of shanties, with a large hotel, a bank, a church, and inn, some drinking-saloons and gambling-houses — there are few women and no homes. Everybody, except recent immigrants, Chinese, and the very poorest native Americans, lives in the hotel.

nothing, are of course commoner in mining regions than elsewhere.* But money is everywhere so valuable for the purposes of speculative investment, whether in land, live-stock, or trade, as to fetch very high interest. In Walla Walla (Washington Territory) I found in 1881 that the interest on debts secured on what were deemed good, safe mortgages was at the rate of fourteen per cent per annum, — of course payable monthly.

The carelessness is public as well as private. Tree-stumps are left standing in the streets of a large and flourishing town like Leadville because the municipal authorities cannot be at the trouble of cutting or burning them. Swamps are left undrained in the suburbs of a populous city like Portland, which every autumn breed malarious fevers; and the risk of accidents, to be followed by actions, does not prevent the railways from pushing on their lines along loosely heaped embankments, and over curved trestle bridges which seem as if they could not stand a high wind or the passage of a heavy train.

This mixture of science and rudeness is one of a series of singular contrasts which runs through the West, not less conspicuous in the minds of the people than in their surroundings. They value good government, and have a remarkable faculty for organizing some kind of government; but they are tolerant of lawlessness which does not directly attack their own interest. Horse-stealing and insults to women are the two unpardonable offences; all others are often suffered to go unpunished. I was in a considerable Western city, with a population of 70,000 people, some years ago, when the leading newspaper of the place, commenting on one of the train robberies that had been frequent in the State, observed that

* In California, in 1881, I was shown an estate of 600,000 acres which was said to have been lately bought for $225,000 (£45,000), by a man who had made his fortune in two years' mining, having come out without a penny.

so long as the brigands had confined themselves to robbing the railway companies and the express companies of property for whose loss the companies must answer, no one had greatly cared, seeing that these companies themselves robbed the public ; but now that private citizens seemed in danger of losing their personal baggage and money, the prosperity of the city might be compromised, and something ought to be done, — a sentiment delivered with all gravity, as the rest of the article showed.* Brigandage tends to disappear when the country becomes populous, though there are places in comparatively old States, like Illinois and Missouri, where the railways are still unsafe. But the same heedlessness suffers other evils to take root, — evils likely to prove permanent, including some refinements of political roguery which it is strange to find amid the simple life of forests and prairies.

Another such contrast is presented by the tendency of this shrewd and educated people to relapse into the oldest and most childish forms of superstition. Fortune-telling, clairvoyance, attempts to pry by the help of " mediums " into the book of Fate, are so common in parts of the West that the newspapers devote a special column, headed "astrologers," to the advertisements of these wizards and pythonesses.† I have counted in one issue of a San Francisco newspaper as many as eighteen such advertisements, six of which were of simple fortune-tellers, like those who used to beguile the peasant girls of Devonshire. In fact, the profession of a soothsayer or astrologer is a recognized one in California now, as it was in the Greece of Homer. Possibly the prevalence of mining speculation, possibly the existence of a large mass of ignorant immigrants from Europe, may help to account for the phe-

* This makes plausible the story of the Texas judge who allowed murderers to escape on points of law till he found the value of real estate declining, when he saw to it that the next few offenders were hanged.

† Ohio, in 1883, imposed a license tax of $300 a year on " astrologers, fortune-tellers, clairvoyants, palmisters, and seers."

nomenon, which, as California is deemed an exceptionally unreligious State, illustrates the famous saying that the less faith the more superstition.

All the passionate eagerness, all the strenuous effort, of the Westerns is directed towards the material development of the country. To open the greatest number of mines and extract the greatest quantity of ore ; to scatter cattle over a thousand hills ; to turn the flower-spangled prairies of the Northwest into wheat-fields ; to cover the sunny slopes of the Southwest with vines and olives, — this is the end and aim of their lives, this is their daily and nightly thought —

> "juvat Ismara Baccho
> Conserere atque olea magnum vestire Taburnum."

The passion is so absorbing, and so covers the horizon of public as well as private life, that it almost ceases to be selfish ; it takes from its very vastness a tinge of ideality. To have an immense production of exchangeable commodities, to force from Nature the most she can be made to yield, and send it east and west by the cheapest routes to the dearest markets, making one's city a centre of trade, and raising the price of its real estate, — this, which might not have seemed a glorious consummation to Isaiah or Plato, is preached by Western newspapers as a kind of religion. It is not really, or at least it is not wholly, sordid. These people are intoxicated by the majestic scale of the Nature in which their lot is cast, — enormous mineral deposits, boundless prairies, forests which, even squandered — wickedly squandered — as they now are, will supply timber to the United States for centuries ; a soil which, with the rudest cultivation, yields the most abundant crops ; a populous continent for their market. They see all round them railways being built, telegraph-wires laid, steamboat lines across the Pacific projected, cities springing up in the solitudes, and settlers making the wilderness to blossom like the rose. Their imagination revels in these sights and signs of progress, and they gild their own struggles for fortune with the belief that they are the missionaries of civilization and the instruments of Providence in the greatest work the world has seen. The following extract from a newspaper published at Tacoma, in the new State of Washington, expresses with frank simplicity the conception of greatness and happiness which is uppermost in the Far West; and what may seem a touch of conscious humor is, if humorous it be, none the less an expression of sincere conviction : —

WHY WE SHOULD BE HAPPY.

Because we are practically at the head of navigation on Puget Sound. Tacoma is the place where all the surplus products of the South and of the East, that are exported by way of the Sound, must be laden on board the vessels that are to carry them to the four corners of the world. We should be happy because, being at the head of navigation on Puget Sound, and the shipping point for the South and the East, the centre from which shall radiate lines of commerce to every point on the circumference of the earth, we are also nearer by many miles than any other town on Puget Sound to that pass in the Cascade mountains through which the Cascade division of the Northern Pacific Railroad will be built in the near future ; not only nearer to the Stampede pass, but easily accessible from there by a railroad line of gentle grade, — which is more than can be said of any town to the north of us.

We should be happy for these reasons, and because we are connected by rail with Portland on the Willamette, with St. Paul, Chicago, and New York ; because, being thus connected, we are in daily communication with the social, political, and financial centres of the western hemisphere ; because all the people of the South and of the East who visit these shores must first visit New Tacoma ; because from here will be distributed to the people of the Northwest all that shall be brought across the continent on the cars, and from here shall be distributed to merchants all over the United States the cargoes of ships returning here from every foreign port to load with wheat, coal, and lumber. We should be and we are happy because New Tacoma is the Pacific coast terminus of a transcontinental line of railroad ; because this is the only place on the whole Pacific coast north of San Francisco where through freight from New York can be loaded on ship directly from the cars in which it came from the Atlantic side.

Other reasons why we should be happy are, that New Tacoma is in the centre of a country where fruits and flowers, vegetables and grain, grow in almost endless variety; that we are surrounded with everything beautiful in Nature; that we have scenery suited to every mood; and that there are opportunities here for the fullest development of talents of every kind. We have youth, good health, and opportunity. What more could be asked?

If happiness is thus procurable, the Great West ought to be happy.* But there is often a malignant influence at work to destroy happiness, in the shape of a neighboring city which is making progress as swift or swifter, and threatens to eclipse its competitors. The rivalry between these Western towns is intense, and extends to everything. It is sometimes dignified by an unselfish devotion to the greatness of the city which a man has seen grow with his own growth from infancy to a vigorous manhood. I have known citizens of Chicago as proud of Chicago as a Londoner, in the days of Elizabeth, was proud of London. They show you the splendid parks and handsome avenues with as much pleasure as a European noble shows his castle and his pictures; they think little of offering hundreds of thousands of dollars to beautify the city or enrich it with a library or an art-gallery. In other men this laudable corporate pride is stimulated, not only by the love of competition which lies deep in the American as it does in the English breast, but also by personal interest; for the prosperity of the individual is inseparable from that of the town. As its fortunes rise or fall, so will his corner-lots or

* Tacoma has one glory which the inhabitants, it is to be feared, value less than those dwelt on in the article, — it commands the finest view of a mountain on the Pacific coast, perhaps in all North America, looking across its calm inlet to the magnificent snowy mass of Mount Tacoma (14,700 feet), rising out of deep dark forests thirty miles away.

the profits of his store.* It is not all towns that succeed. Some, after reaching a certain point, stand still, receiving few accessions; at other times, after a year or two of bloom, a town wilts and withers, trade declines, enterprising citizens depart, leaving only the shiftless and impecunious behind, the saloons are closed, the shanties fall to ruin; in a few years nothing but heaps of straw and broken wood, with a few brick houses awaiting the next blizzard to overthrow them, are left on the surface of the prairie. Thus Tacoma is harassed by the pretensions of the even more eager and enterprising Seattle; thus the greater cities of St. Paul and Minneapolis have striven for the last twenty years for the title of Capital of the Northwest. In 1870 St. Paul was already a substantial city, and Minneapolis just beginning to be known as the possessor of immense water advantages from its position on the Mississippi at the Falls of St. Anthony. Now, though St. Paul contains some 160,000 inhabitants, Minneapolis with 200,000 has distanced her in the race, and has become, having in the process destroyed the beauty of her Falls, the greatest flour-milling centre in America. The newspapers of each of such competing cities keep up a constant war upon the other; and everything is done by municipal bodies and individual citizens to make the world believe that their city is advancing, and all its neighbors standing still. Prosperity is largely a matter of advertising, for an afflux of settlers makes prosperity, and advertising, which can take many forms, attracts settlers. Many a place has lived upon its " boom " until it found some-

---

* In the West each town and district is specially vain of the size to which its vegetables grow, and the number of bushels of wheat to the acre its soil produces. After hearing repeated boasts from a succession of cities along a railroad line, I asked at one whether it was not the fact that their land got up to 100 bushels an acre? This was a little too much for them, — 73 bushels is the highest I have ever heard claimed, — and they answered, " Well, not perhaps quite that, but very nearly."

thing more solid to live on ; and to a stranger who asked in a small Far Western town how such a city could keep up four newspapers, it was well answered that it took four newspapers to keep up such a city.

Confidence goes a long way towards success, and the confidence of these Westerns is superb. I happened in 1883 to be at the city of Bismarck, in Dakota, when this young settlement was laying the corner-stone of its Capitol, intended to contain the halls of the legislature and other State offices of Dakota when that flourishing Territory should have become a State, or perhaps, for they talked of dividing it, two States. The town was then only some five years old, and may have had six or seven thousand inhabitants. It was gayly decorated for the occasion, and had collected many distinguished guests, — General U. S. Grant, several governors of neighboring States and Territories, railroad potentates, and others. By far the most remarkable figure was that of Sitting Bull, the famous Sioux chief who had surprised and slain a detachment of the American army some years before. Among the speeches made, — in one of which it was proved that as Bismarck was the centre of Dakota, Dakota the centre of the United States, and the United States the centre of the world, Bismarck was destined to " be the metroplitan hearth of the world's civilization," — there came a short but pithy discourse from this grim old warrior, in which he told us, through an interpreter, that the Great Spirit moved him to shake hands with everybody. However, the feature of the ceremonial which struck us Europeans most was the spot chosen for the Capitol. It was not in the city, nor even on the skirts of the city ; it was nearly a mile off, on the top of a hill in the brown and dusty prairie. " Why here ? " we asked. " Is it because you mean to enclose the building in a public park ? " " By no means ; the Capitol is intended to be in the centre of the city : it is in this direction that the city is to grow." It is the same everywhere, from the Mississippi to the Pacific. Men seem to live in the future rather than in the present: not that they fail to work while it is called to-day, but that they see the country, not merely as it is, but as it will be twenty, fifty, a hundred years hence, when the seedlings shall have grown to forest-trees.

This constant reaching forward to and grasping at the future does not so much express itself in words, for they are not a loquacious people, as in the air of ceaseless haste and stress which pervades the West.* They remind you of the crowd which Vathek found in the hall of Eblis, each darting hither and thither with swift steps and unquiet mien, driven to and fro by a fire in the heart. Time seems too brief for what they have to do, and result always to come short of their desire. One feels as if caught and whirled along in a foaming stream chafing against its banks, such is the passion of these men to accomplish in their own life-times what in the past it took centuries to effect. Sometimes in a moment of pause — for even the visitor finds himself infected by the all-pervading eagerness — one is inclined to ask them : " Gentlemen, why, in Heaven's name, this haste? You have time enough. No enemy threatens you. No volcano will rise from beneath you. Ages and ages lie before you. Why sacrifice the present to the future, fancying that you will be happier when your fields teem with wealth, and your cities with people? In Europe we have cities wealthier and more populous than yours, and we are not happy. You dream of your posterity; but your posterity will look back to yours as the golden age, and envy those who first burst into this silent, splendid Nature, who first lifted up their axes upon these tall trees, and lined these waters with busy wharves. Why, then, seek to complete in a few decades what the other nations of the world took thousands of years over in the older continents? Why do rudely

* In the West men usually drop off the cars before they have stopped, and do not enter them again till they are already in motion, hanging on like bees to the end of the tail-car as it quits the depot.

and ill things which need to be done well, seeing that the welfare of your descendants may turn upon them? Why, in your hurry to subdue and utilize Nature, squander her splendid gifts? Why allow the noxious weeds of Eastern politics to take root in your new soil, when by a little effort you might keep it pure? Why hasten the advent of that threatening day when the vacant spaces of the continent shall all have been filled, and the poverty or discontent of the older States shall find no outlet? You have opportunities such as mankind has never had before, and may never have again. Your work is great and noble ; it is done for a future longer and vaster than our conceptions can embrace. Why not make its outlines and beginnings worthy of these destinies, the thought of which gilds your hopes and elevates your purposes?"

Being once suddenly called upon to " offer a few remarks " to a Western legislature, and having on the spur of the moment nothing better to offer, I tendered some such observations as these, seasoned, of course, with the compliments to the soil, climate, and " location " reasonably expected from a visitor. They were received in good part, as indeed no people can be more kindly than the Western Americans ; but it was surprising to hear several members who afterwards conversed with me remark that the political point of view — the fact that they were the founders of new commonwealths, and responsible to posterity for the foundations they laid, a point of view so trite and obvious to a European visitor that he pauses before expressing it — had not crossed their minds. If they spoke truly, — and subsequent observation led me to think they did, — there was in their words further evidence of the predominance of material efforts and interests over all others, even over those political instincts which are deemed so essential a part of the American character. The arrangements of his government lie in the dim background of the picture which rejoices the Western eye. The foreground is filled by ploughs and saw-mills, ore-crushers and railway locomotives. These so absorb his thoughts as to leave little time for constitutions and legislation; and when constitutions and legislation are thought of, it is as means for better securing the benefits of the earth and of trade to the producer, and preventing the greedy corporation from intercepting their fruits.

Politically, and perhaps socially also, this haste and excitement, this absorption in the development of the material resources of the country, are unfortunate. As a town built in a hurry is seldom well built, so a society will be the sounder in health for not having grown too swiftly. Doubtless much of the scum will be cleared away from the surface when the liquid settles and cools down. Lawlessness and lynch law will disappear; saloons and gambling-houses will not prosper in a well-conducted population; schools will improve, and universities grow out of the raw colleges which one already finds even in the newer Territories. Nevertheless, the bad habits of professional politics, as one sees them on the Atlantic coast, are not unknown in these communities; and the unrestfulness, the passion for speculation, the feverish eagerness for quick and showy results, may so soak into the texture of the popular mind as to color it for centuries to come. These are the shadows which to the eye of the traveller seem to fall across the glowing landscape of the Great West.

CHAPTER XVIII.

THE FUTURE OF POLITICAL INSTITUTIONS.

THE task of forecasting the future is one from which a writer does well to turn away, for the coasts of history are strewn with the wrecks of predictions launched by historians and philosophers. No such ambitious task shall be essayed by me. But as I have described the institutions of the American commonwealth as they stand at this moment, seldom expressing an opinion as to their vitality or the influences which are at work to modify them, I may reasonably be asked to state, before bringing this book to close, what processes of change these institutions seem to be at this moment undergoing. Changes move faster in our age than they ever moved before, and America is a land of change. No one doubts that fifty years hence it will differ at least as much from what it is now as it differs now from the America which Tocqueville described. The causes whose action will mould it are far too numerous, too complex, too subtly interwoven, for any one to be able to guess what their joint result will be. All we can ever say of the future is that it will be unlike the present. I will therefore attempt, not to predict future changes, but only to indicate some of the processes of change now in progress which have gone far enough to let us see that they are due to causes of unmistakable potency, causes likely to continue in activity for some time to come.

I begin with a glance at the Federal system, whose equilibrium it has been the main object of the Federal Constitution

to preserve. That equilibrium has been little disturbed. So
far as law goes, it has suffered no change since the amendments to the Constitution which recorded and formulated the
results of the Civil War. Before the war many Americans
and most Europeans expected a dissolution of the Union,
either by such a loosening of the Federal tie as would reduce
the Union to a mere league, or by the formation of several
State groups wholly independent of one another. At this
moment, however, nothing seems less likely than another secession. The States' Rights spirit has declined. The material interests of every part of the country are bound up with
those of every other. The capital of the Eastern cities has
been invested in mines in the West, in iron-works and manu-
factories in the South, in mortgages and railroads everywhere.
The South and the West need this capital for their development, and are daily in closer business relations with the East.
The produce of the West finds its way to the Atlantic through
the ports of the East. Every produce market, every share
market, vibrates in response to the Produce Exchange and
Stock Exchange of New York. Each part of the country
has come to know the other parts far better than was possible
in earlier times ; and the habit of taking journeys hither and
thither grows with the always-growing facilities of travel.
Many families have sons or brothers in remote States ; many
students come from the West and the South to Eastern universities, and form ties of close friendship there. Railways
and telegraphs are daily narrowing and compressing the vast
area between ocean and ocean. As the civilized world was a
larger world in the days of Herodotus than it is now, — for it
took twice as many months to travel from the Caspian Sea to
the Pillars of Hercules as it takes now to circumnavigate the
globe; one was obliged to use a greater number of languages, and the journey was incomparably more dangerous,
— so now the United States, with their sixty-two millions of
people, extending from the Bay of Fundy to the Gulf of Cali-

fornia, are a smaller country for all the purposes of government and social intercourse than they were before the cession of Louisiana in 1803, for it took longer then to go from Boston to Charleston than it takes now to go from Portland in Maine to Portland in Oregon, and the journey was far more costly and difficult.

Even the Pacific States, which might have seemed likely to form a community by themselves, are being drawn closer to those of the Mississippi basin. Population will in time become almost continuous along the lines of the Northern and Southern Pacific Railways; and though the deserts of Nevada may remain unreclaimed, prosperous communities round the Great Salt Lake will form a link between California and the Rocky Mountain States. With more frequent communication, local peculiarities and local habits of thought diminish; the South grows every day less distinctively Southern, and country folk are more influenced by city ideas. There is now not a single State with any material interest that would be benefited, probably none with any sentiment that would be gratified, by separation from the body of the Union. No great question has arisen tending to bind States into groups and stimulating them to joint action. The chief problems which lie before the country wear an aspect substantially the same in its various sections, and public opinion is divided on them in those sections upon lines generally similar. In a word, the fact that the government is a Federal one does not at this moment seem to make any difference to the cohesion of the body politic. The United States are no more likely to dissolve than if they were a unified republic like France, or a unified monarchy like Italy.

As secession is improbable, so also is the extinction of the several States by absorption into the central government. It was generally believed in Europe when the North triumphed over secession in 1865 that the Federal system was virtually at an end. The legal authority of Congress and the President had been immensely developed during the struggle; a powerful army, flushed with victory, stood ready to enforce that authority; and there seemed reason to think that the South, which had fought so stubbornly, would have to be kept down during many years by military force. However, none of these apprehended results followed. The authority of the central government presently sank back within its former limits, some of the legislation, based on Constitutional amendments, which had extended it for certain purposes, being cut down by judicial decision. The army was disbanded; self-government was soon restored in the lately insurgent States; and the upshot of the years of civil war and reconstruction has been, while extinguishing the claim of State sovereignty, to replace the formerly admitted State rights upon a legal basis as firm as they ever occupied before. At this moment State rights are but slightly in question, nor has either party an interest in advocating the supersession of State action in any department of government. The conservatism of habit and well-settled legal doctrine which would resist any such proposal is very strong. State autonomy, as well as local government within each State, is prized by every class in the community, and bound up with the personal interest of those who feel that these comparatively limited spheres offer a scope to their ambition which a wider theatre might deny.

It is nevertheless impossible to ignore the growing strength of the centripetal and unifying forces. I have already referred to the influence of easier and cheaper communications, of commerce and finance, of the telegraph, of the filling up of the intermediate vacant spaces in the West. There is an increasing tendency to invoke congressional legislation to deal with matters, such as railroads, which cannot be adequately handled by State laws, or to remove divergencies, such as those in bankrupt laws and the law of marriage and divorce, which give rise to practical inconveniences. The advocates of such proposals as liquor-prohibition and the restriction of the hours of labor are more and more apt to carry their action into the Federal sphere, while admitting that the Federal Constitution would need amendment in order to enable Congress to effect what they desire. State patriotism, State rivalry, State vanity, are no doubt still conspicuous ; yet the political interest felt in State governments is slighter than it was forty years ago, while national patriotism has become warmer and more pervasive. The *rôle* of the State is socially and morally, if not legally, smaller now than it then was, and ambitious men look on a State legislature as little more than a stepping-stone to Congress. It would be rash to assert that disjunctive forces will never again reveal themselves, setting the States against the National government, and making State rights once more a matter of practical controversy. But any such force is likely, so far as we can now see, to prove transitory ; whereas the centripetal forces are permanent and secular forces, working from age to age. Wherever in the modern world there has been a centrifugal movement tending to break up a state united under one government, or to loosen the cohesion of its parts, the movement has sprung from a sentiment of nationality, and has been reinforced, in almost every case, by a sense of some substantial grievance, or by a belief that material advantages were to be secured by separation. The cases of Holland and Belgium, of Hungary and Germanic Austria, of the Greeks and Bulgarians in their struggle with the Turks, of Iceland in her struggle with Denmark, all illustrate this proposition. When such disjunctive forces are absent, the more normal tendency to aggregation and centralization prevails. In the United States all the elements of a national feeling are present, — race,* language, literature, pride in past achievements, unifor-

---

* The immense influx of immigrants has not greatly affected the sense of race unity, for the immigrant's child is almost always eager to become to all intents and purposes an American. Moreover, the immigrants are

mity of political habits and ideas; and this national feeling, which unifies the people, is reinforced by an immensely strong material interest in the maintenance of a single government over the breadth of the continent. It may therefore be concluded that while there is no present likelihood of change from a federal to a consolidated republic, and while the existing legal rights and functions of the several States may remain undiminished for many years to come, the importance of the States will decline as the majesty and authority of the National government increase.

The next question to be asked relates to the component parts of the National government itself. Its equilibrium stands now as stable as at any former epoch. Yet it has twice experienced violent oscillations. In the days of Jackson, and again in those of Lincoln, the Executive seemed to outweigh Congress. In the days of Tyler, Congress threatened the Executive; while in those of Andrew Johnson it reduced the Executive to impotence. That no permanent disturbance of the balance followed the latter of these oscillations shows how well the balance had been adjusted at starting. At this moment there is nothing to show that any one department is gaining on any other. The Judiciary — if indeed the judges can be called a political department — would seem to have less discretionary power than seventy years ago; for by their own decisions they have narrowed the scope of their discretion, determining points in which, had they remained open, the personal impulses and views of the Bench might have had room to play. Congress has been the branch of government with the largest facilities for usurping the powers of the other branches, and probably with the most

so dispersed over the country that no single section of them is in any State nearly equal to the native population. Here and there in the West Germans have tried to appropriate townships or villages, and keep English-speaking folk at a distance; but this happens on so small a scale as to cause no disquiet.

disposition to do so. Congress has constantly tried to encroach both on the Executive and on the States, — sometimes, like a wild bull driven into a corral, dashing itself against the imprisoning walls of the Constitution. But although Congress has succeeded in occupying nearly all of the area which the Constitution left vacant and unallotted between the several authorities it established, Congress has not become any more distinctly than in earlier days the dominant power in the State, the organ of national sovereignty, the irresistible exponent of the national will. In a country ruled by public opinion, it could hold this position only in virtue of its capacity for leading opinion ; that is to say, of its courage, promptitude, and wisdom. Since it grows in no one of these qualities, it wins no greater ascendency, — indeed, its power, as compared with that of public opinion, seems rather to decline. Its division into two co-ordinate Houses is no doubt a source of weakness as well as of safety. Yet what is true of Congress as a whole is true of each House taken separately. The Senate, to which the eminence of many individual senators formerly gave a moral ascendency, has lost as much in the intellectual authority of its members as it has gained in their wealth. The House, with its far greater numbers and its far greater proportion of inexperienced members, suffers from the want of internal organization, and seems unable to keep pace with the increasing demands made on it for constructive legislation. One is sometimes inclined to think that Congress might lose its hold on the respect and confidence of the nation, and sink into a subordinate position, were there any other authority which could be substituted for it. There is, however, no such authority ; for law-making cannot be given to a person or to a court, while the State legislatures have the same faults as Congress in a greater degree. We may accordingly surmise that Congress will retain its present place ; but so far as can be gathered from present phenomena, it will retain this place in respect, not of the satisfaction of the people with its services, but of their inability to provide a better servant.

The weakness of Congress is the strength of the President. Though it cannot be said that his office has risen in power or dignity since 1789, there are reasons for believing that it may reach a higher point than it has occupied at any time since the Civil War. The tendency everywhere in America to concentrate power and responsibility in one man is unmistakable. There is no danger that the President should become a despot; that is, should attempt to make his will prevail against the will of the majority. But he may have a great part to play as the leader of the majority and the exponent of its will. He is in some respects better fitted both to represent and to influence public opinion than Congress is. No doubt he suffers from being the nominee of a party, because this draws on every act he does the hostility of zealots of the opposite party. But the number of voters who are not party zealots increases, — increases from bad causes as well as from good causes; for as a capable President sways the dispassionately patriotic, so a crafty President can find means of playing upon those who have their own ends to serve. A vigorous personality attracts the multitude, and attracts it the more the huger it grows; while a chief magistrate's influence excites little alarm when exerted in leading a majority which acts through the constitutional organs of government. There may therefore be still undeveloped possibilities of greatness in store for the Presidents of the future. But as these possibilities depend, like the possibilities of the British and German Crowns, — perhaps, one may add, of the Papacy, — on the wholly unpredictable element of personal capacity in the men who may fill the office, we need speculate on them no further.

From the organs of government I pass to the party system, its machinery and its methods. Nothing in recent history suggests that the statesmen who claim to be party leaders, or the politicians who act as party managers, are disposed either to loosen the grip with which their organization has clasped the country, or to improve the methods it employs. Changes in party measures there will of course be in the future, as there have been in the past; but the professionals are not the men to make them changes for the better. The Machine will not be reformed from within; it must be assailed from without. Two heavy blows have been lately struck at it. The first was the Civil Service Reform Act of 1883. If this Act is honestly administered, and its principle extended to other federal offices, — if States and cities follow, as a few have done, in the wake of the National government, — the Spoils system may before long be rooted out; and with that system the power of the Machine will crumble. The Spoils system has stood for fifty years, and the bad habits it has formed cannot at once be unlearned. But its extinction will deprive professionals of their chief present motive for following politics. The tares which now infest the wheat will presently wither away, and the old enemy will have to sow a fresh crop of some other kind. The second blow is the frequent appearance, not merely in federal elections, but in State and municipal elections, of a body of independent men pledged to vote for honest candidates, irrespective of party. The absence for a number of years past of genuine political issues dividing the two parties, which has worked ill in taking moral and intellectual life out of the parties, and making their contests mere scrambles for office, has at last worked well in disposing intelligent citizens to sit more loose to party ties, and to consider, since it is really on men rather than on measures that they are required to vote, what the personal merits of candidates are. Thirty years ago, just at the time when the fruits of Jacksonism — that is to say, of wild democratic theory, coupled with sordid and quite undemocratic practice — had begun to be felt by thoughtful persons, the urgency of the slavery question compelled the postponement of reforms in political methods, and made patriotic men fling themselves into party warfare with unquestioning zeal. When the winning of elections, no less than the winning of battles, meant the salvation of the Union, no one could stop to examine the machinery of party. For ten years after the war, the party which was usually in the majority in the North was the party which had saved the Union, and on that score commanded the devotion of its old adherents; while the opposite party was so much absorbed in struggling back to power that it did not think of mending its ways. During the last ten or fifteen years, the war issues being practically settled, public-spirited citizens have addressed themselves to the task, which ought to have been undertaken in 1850, of purifying politics. Their efforts began with city government, where the evils were greatest, but have now become scarcely less assiduous in State and national politics.

Will these efforts continue, and be crowned by a growing measure of success?

To a stranger revisiting America at intervals, the progress seems to be steadily, though not swiftly, upward. This is also the belief of those Americans who, having most exerted themselves in the struggle against Bosses and spoilsmen, have had most misrepresentation to overcome and most disappointments to endure. The Presidents of this generation are abler men than those of forty years ago, and less apt to be the mere creatures of a knot of party managers. The poisonous influence of slavery is no longer felt. There is every day less of sentimentalism, but not less of earnestness in political discussions. There is less blind obedience to party, less disposition to palliate sins committed from party motives. The number of able men who occupy themselves with scientific economics and politics is larger, their books and articles are more widely read. The Press more frequently helps in the work of reform; the pulpit deals more largely with questions of practical philanthropy and public morals. That it should be taken as a good sign when the young men of a city throw them-

selves into politics, shows that the new generation is believed
to have either a higher sense of public duty, or a less slavish
attachment to party ties than that whose votes have prevailed
for the last twenty years. Above all, the nation is less self-
sufficient and self-satisfied than it was in days when it had
less to be proud of. Fifty years ago the Americans walked
in a vain conceit of their own greatness and freedom, and
scorned instruction from the effete monarchies of the Old
World, which repaid them with contemptuous indifference.
No despot ever exacted more flattery from his courtiers than
they from their statesmen. Now, when Europe admires their
power, envies their prosperity, looks to them for instruction
in not a few subjects, they have become more modest, and
listen willingly to speakers and writers who descant upon their
failings. They feel themselves strong enough to acknowledge
their weaknesses, and are anxious that the moral life of the
nation should be worthy of its expanding fortunes. As these
happy omens have become more visible from year to year,
there is a reasonable presumption that they represent a steady
current which will continue to work for good. To judge of
America rightly, the observer must not fix his eye simply upon
her present condition, seeking to strike a balance between the
evil and the good that now appear. He must look back at
what the best citizens and the most judicious strangers perceived and recorded fifty, thirty, twenty years ago, and ask
whether the shadows these men saw were not darker than
those of to-day, whether the forecasts of evil they were
forced to form have not in many cases been belied by the
event. Tocqueville was a sympathetic as well as penetrat-
ing observer. Many of the evils he saw, and which he thought
inherent and incurable, have now all but vanished. Other
evils have indeed revealed themselves which he did not dis-
cern ; but these may prove as transient as those with which he
affrighted European readers in 1834. The men I have met in
America, whose recollections went back to the fourth decade

of this century, agreed in saying that there was in those days a more violent and unscrupulous party spirit, a smaller respect for law, a greater disposition to violence, less respect for the opinion of the wise, a completer submission to the prejudices of the masses, than there is to-day. Neither the Irish nor the Germans had arrived upon the scene, but New York was already given over to spoilsmen. Great corporations had scarcely arisen, yet corruption was neither uncommon nor fatal to a politician's reputation. A retrospect which shows us that some evils have declined or vanished, while the regenerative forces are more numerous and more active in combating new mischiefs than they ever were before, encourages the belief that the general stream of tendency is towards improvement, and will in time bring the public life of the country nearer to the ideal which democracy is bound to set before itself.

When the Americans say, as they often do, that they trust to time, they mean that they trust to reason, to the generally sound moral tone of the multitude, to a shrewdness which after failures and through experiments learns what is the true interest of the majority, and finds that this interest coincides with the teachings of morality. They can afford to wait, because they have three great advantages over Europe, — an absence of class distinctions and class hatreds, a diffusion of wealth among an immense number of small proprietors all interested in the defence of property, an exemption from chronic pauperism and economical distress, work being generally abundant, many careers open, the still unoccupied or undeveloped West providing a safety-valve available in times of depression. With these advantages the Americans conceive that were their country now left entirely to itself, so that full and free scope could be secured to the ameliorative forces, political progress would be sure and steady, the best elements would come to the top, and when the dregs had settled, the liquor would run clear.

In a previous chapter I have observed that this sanguine view of the situation omits two considerations. One is that the country will not be left to itself. European immigration continues; and though about two thirds of the immigrants make valuable citizens, the remainder — many by their political ignorance and instability, some few by their proneness to embrace anti-social doctrines — are a source of danger to the community, lowering its tone, providing material for demagogues to work on, threatening outbreaks like those of Pennsylvania in 1877, of Cincinnati in 1884, of Chicago in 1886.

The other fact to be borne in mind is of still graver import. There is a part of the Atlantic where the westward-speeding steam-vessel always expects to encounter fogs. On the fourth or fifth day of the voyage, while still in bright sunlight, one sees at a distance a long, low, dark-gray line across the bows, and is told this is the first of the fog-banks which have to be traversed. Presently the vessel is upon the cloud, and rushes into its chilling embrace, not knowing what perils of icebergs may be shrouded within the encompassing gloom. So America, in her swift onward progress, sees, looming on the horizon and now no longer distant, a time of mists and shadows, wherein dangers may lie concealed whose form and magnitude she can scarcely yet conjecture. As she fills up her western regions with inhabitants, she sees the time approach when all the best land will have been occupied, and when the land now under cultivation will have been so far exhausted as to yield scantier crops even to more expensive culture. Although transportation may also have then become cheaper, the price of food will rise; farms will be less easily obtained, and will need more capital to work them with profit: the struggle for existence will become more severe. And while the outlet which the West now provides for the overflow of the great cities will have become less available, the cities will have grown immensely more populous; pauperism, now confined to some six or seven of the greatest, will be more widely spread; wages will probably sink, and work be less abundant. In fact, the chronic evils and problems of old societies and crowded countries, such as we see them to-day in Europe, will have reappeared on this new soil.

High economic authorities pronounce that the beginnings of this time of pressure lie not more than thirty years ahead. Nearly all of the best arable land in the West is already occupied, so that the second and third best will soon begin to be cultivated; while the exhaustion already complained of in farms which have been under the plough for three or four decades will be increasingly felt. It will be a time of trial for democratic institutions. The future of the United States during the next half century sometimes presents itself to the mind as a struggle between two forces, — the one beneficent, the other malign; the one striving to speed the nation on to a port of safety before this time of trial arrives; the other to retard its progress, so that the tempest may be upon it before the port is reached. And the question to which one reverts in musing on the phenomena of American politics is this: Will the progress now discernible towards a wiser public opinion and a higher standard of public life succeed in bringing the mass of the people up to the level of what are now the best districts in the country before the days of pressure are at hand? Or will existing evils prove so obstinate, and European immigration so continue to depress the average of intelligence and patriotism among the voters, that when the struggle for life grows far harder than it now is, the masses will yield to the temptation to abuse their power, and will seek violent, and because violent probably vain and useless, remedies for the evils which will afflict them?

If the crisis should arrive while a large part of the population still lacks the prudence and self-control which a democracy ought to possess, what result may be looked for? This is a question which no experience from similar crises in the past helps us to answer, for the phenomena will be new in the history of the world. There may be pernicious experiments tried in legislation. There may be occasional outbreaks of violence. There may even be — though nothing at present portends it — a dislocation of the present frame of government. One thing, however, need not be apprehended, the thing with which alarmists most frequently terrify us : there will not be anarchy. The forces which restore order and maintain it when restored are as strong in America as anywhere else in the world.

While admitting the possibility of such a time of strife and danger, he who has studied America will not fail to note that she will have elements of strength for meeting it which are lacking in some European countries. The struggles of labor and capital do not seem likely to take the form of a widely prevailing hatred between classes. The distribution of landed property among a great many small owners is likely to continue. The habits of freedom, together with the moderation and self-control which they foster, are likely to stand unimpaired, or to be even confirmed and mellowed by longer use. The restraining and conciliating influence of religion is stronger than in France or Germany, and more enlightened than in those Continental countries where religion now seems strongest. I admit that no one can say how far the United States of fifty years hence will in these respects resemble the United States of to-day. But if we are to base our anticipations on the facts of to-day, we may look forward to the future, not indeed without anxiety, when we mark the clouds that hang on the horizon, yet with a hope that is stronger than anxiety.

CHAPTER XIX.

SOCIAL AND ECONOMIC FUTURE.

IF it be hard to forecast the development of political institutions and habits, how much harder to form a conception of what the economic and social life of the United States will have become when another half century of marvellously swift material progress has more than quintupled its wealth and more than tripled its population, and when the number of persons pursuing arts and letters, and educated to enjoy the most refined pleasures of life, will have become proportionately greater than it is now. The changes of the last fifty years, great as they have been, may then prove to have been no greater than those which the next fifty will have brought. Prediction is even more difficult in this sphere than in the sphere of government, because the forces at work to modify society are more numerous, as well as far more subtle and complex, and because not only the commercial prosperity of the country, but its thought and culture, are more likely than its politics to be affected by the course of events in the Old World. All I can attempt is, as in the last preceding chapter, to call attention to some of the changes which are now in progress, and to conjecture whether the phenomena we now observe are due to permanent or to transitory causes. I shall speak first of economic changes and their influence on certain current problems ; next, of the movements of population and possible alterations in its character ; lastly, of the tendencies which seem likely to continue to affect the social and intellectual life of the nation.

The most remarkable economic feature of the years that have elapsed since the war has been the growth of great fortunes. There is a passage in the " Federalist," written in 1788, which says, " The private fortunes of the President and senators, as they must all be American citizens, cannot possibly be sources of danger." Even in 1833, Tocqueville was struck by the equal distribution of wealth in the United States and the absence of capitalists. To-day, however, there are more great millionnaires, as well as more men with a capital of from $250,000 to $1,000,000 (£50,000 to £200,000) in America than in any other country; and fifty years hence it will probably contain as many large fortunes as will exist in all the countries of Europe put together. Nor are these huge accumulations due to custom and the policy of the law, which in England keep property, and especially landed property, in the hands of a few by the so-called custom of primogeniture. An American testator usually distributes his wealth among his children equally. However rich he may be, he does not expect his daughters to marry rich men, but is just as willing to see them mated to persons supporting themselves by their own efforts. And he is far more inclined than Europeans are to bestow large part of his wealth upon objects of public utility, instead of using it to found a family. In spite of these dispersing forces, great fortunes grow with the growing prosperity of the country, and the opportunities it offers of amassing enormous piles by bold operations. Even an unspeculative business may, if skilfully conducted, bring in greater gains than can often be hoped for in Europe, because the scale of operations is in America so large that a comparatively small percentage of profit may mean a very large income. These causes are likely to be permanent; nor can any legislation that is compatible with the rights of property as now understood, do much to restrict them. We may therefore expect that the class of very rich men — men so rich as to find it difficult to spend their income in enjoying life, though they may go on employing it in business — will continue to increase.

It may be suggested that the great fortunes of to-day are due to the swift development of the West, so that after a time they will cease to arise in such numbers, while those we now see will have been scattered. The development of the West must, however, continue for forty or fifty years to come ; and though the wealthy do not seek to keep their wealth together after their death by artificial means, many are the sons of the rich who start with capital enough to give them a great advantage for further accumulation. There are as yet comparatively few careers to compete with business ; nor is it as easy as in Europe to spend a fortune on pleasure. The idle rich of America, who, though relatively few, are numerous enough to form a class in the greatest Atlantic cities, seem by no means the most contented class in the country.

The growth of vast fortunes has helped to create a political problem, for they become a mark for the invective of the more extreme sections of the Labor party. But should its propaganda so far prosper as to produce legislative attacks upon accumulated wealth, such attacks will be directed (at least in the first instance), not against individual rich men, but against incorporated companies, since it is through corporations that wealth has made itself obnoxious. Why the power of these bodies should have grown so much greater in the United States than in Europe, and why they should be more often controlled by a small knot of men, are questions too intricate to be here discussed. Companies are in many ways so useful that any general diminution of the legal facilities for forming them seems improbable ; but I conceive that they will be even more generally than hitherto subjected to special taxation, and that their power of taking and using public franchises will be further restricted. He who considers the irresponsible nature of the power which three or four men, or perhaps one man, can exercise through a great corporation, such as a railroad or telegraph company ; the injury they can inflict on the public as well as on their competitors ; the cynical audacity with which they have often used their wealth to seduce officials and legislators from the path of virtue, — will find nothing unreasonable in the desire of the American masses to regulate the management of corporations and narrow the range of their action. The same remark applies with even more force to combinations of men not incorporated, but acting together, — the so-called Trusts; *i. e.*, commercial rings, or syndicates. The next few years or even decades may be largely occupied with the effort to deal with these phenomena of a commercial system far more highly developed than the world has yet seen elsewhere. The economic advantages of the amalgamation of railroads, and the tendency in all departments of trade for large concerns to absorb or supplant small ones, are both so marked that problems of this order seem likely to grow even larger and more urgent than they now are. Their solution will demand not only great legal skill, but great economic wisdom.

Of the tendency to aggregation there are happily no signs, so far as relates to agriculture. The only great landed estates are in the Far West, particularly in California, together with some properties held by land companies or individual speculators in the Upper Mississippi States, — properties which are being generally sold in small farms to incoming settlers. In the South, large plantations are more rare than before the war, and much of the cotton crop is raised by peasant farmers. It is of course possible that cultivation on a large scale may in some regions turn out to be more profitable than that of small freeholders ; agriculture as an art may be still in its infancy, and science may alter the conditions of production in this highly inventive country. But at present nothing seems to threaten that system of small proprietors tilling the soil they live on which so greatly contributes to the happiness and stability of the commonwealth. The motives which in

Europe induce rich men to buy large estates are here wholly wanting, for no one gains either political power or social status by becoming a landlord.

Changes in economic conditions have begun to bring about changes in population which will work powerfully on the future of society and politics. One such change has been passing on New England during the last twenty years. Its comparatively thin and ungenial soil, which has generally hard rock at no great depth below the surface, and has been cultivated in many places for nigh two hundred years, is now unable to sustain the competition of the rich and virgin lands of the West. The old race of New England yeomen have accordingly begun to sell or abandon their farms and to migrate to the upper valley of the Mississippi, where they make the prosperity of the Northwestern States. The lands which they have left vacant are frequently occupied by immigrants, — sometimes French Canadians, but chiefly Irish, for the Germans come but little to New England; and thus that which was the most purely English part of America is now becoming one of the most Celtic, since the cities also are full of Irish and Canadians. It is impossible not to regret the disappearance of a picturesquely primitive society which novelists and essayists have made familiar to us, with its delightful mixture of homely simplicity and keen intelligence. Of all the types of rustic life which imagination has since the days of Theocritus embellished for the envy or refreshment of the dwellers in cities, this latest type has been to modern Europe the most real, and not the least attractive. It will soon have passed away; nor will the life of the robust sons of the Puritans in the Northwestern prairies, vast and bare and new, reproduce the idyllic quality of their old surroundings. But the Irish squatters on the forsaken farms rear their children under better conditions than those either of the American cities or of the island of their birth, and they are replenishing New England with a vigorous stock.

Another change may possibly be seen when in the course of a few years or decades immigration begins to turn towards a Southern region, the far greater part of which has remained until now undeveloped. Western North Carolina, northern Georgia and Alabama, and eastern Tennessee possess enormous mineral deposits, only a few of which have yet begun to be worked. There are splendid forests; there is in many places a soil believed to be fertile, little of which has been brought under cultivation; while the climate is in general not too hot for white labor. It seems probable that when the vacant spaces of the Northwest are no longer wide enough to receive the continued influx of settlers, these regions will become the seat of industries attracting and employing a vast population; and this population may in large measure come from the more crowded parts of the Northern States, carrying with it Northern habits and ideas which will quicken the progress of a backward part of the South, and bring her into a more perfect harmony with the rest of the country.

The mention of the South raises a group of questions bearing on the future of the negro and the relations he will sustain to the whites. To set forth even the main data needed for discussing these questions would need several chapters; so I must content myself with remarking that the best authorities now hold that the increase in the black population, even in the Gulf States, is less rapid than the census returns of 1880 had been thought to show,* and does not constitute a present source of danger. The negroes have not so far, like those in some of the West India Islands, relapsed into sloth and barbarism. Neither climate nor soil makes it so easy as in those islands to raise by a few weeks' labor food enough to support a family through the year; while the promixity of trading and manufacturing towns draws a number of the negroes into closer

---

* The enumeration of the negroes in 1870 was defective in many parts of the South, and the increase shown by the figures of 1880 was therefore greater than the reality.

relations with the whites, and gives an impulse towards progress to the whole mass. Although the line of separation between whites and blacks is more sharply drawn than before the Civil War, and is in some matters drawn by law as well as by custom, and although there is no mixture of blood by intermarriage, there seems to be but slight ill feeling between the races, slight disposition on the part of the whites to oppress, or on that of the negroes to combine against their former masters. The gift of the suffrage, though rendered of little direct effect by the wiles of the whites, who in one way or another continue to suppress the negro vote in all important elections, has had the effect of raising to some extent both the white's view of the negro and the negro's view of himself. The South has changed, is changing, and must continue to change, in so many regards that it would be rash to conjecture the attitude of the colored population forty years hence, when a generation accustomed to freedom and more generally instructed — for at present more than half the colored population of school age are not in school, and only about one tenth of the adults can read a newspaper with ease — has come to maturity. All that can be said is that at present thoughtful observers in the South seem to feel little anxiety, and expect that for many years to come the negroes, naturally a good-natured and easy-going race, will be content with the position of an inferior caste, doing the hard work, and especially the field work, of the country, but becoming gradually permeated by American habits and ideas, and sending up into the higher walks of life a slowly increasing number of their ablest members. It might be thought that this elevating process would be accelerated by the sympathy of the colored people at the North, who enjoy greater educational opportunities. But statistics show that the negro race increases comparatively slowly to the north of latitude 40°, and it does not even there blend with the whites. A very high authority estimates the probable colored population in

1900 at ten millions out of a total population of eighty millions, and adds the remark that, "considering the limited area
of land in which negroes have an advantage over whites by
physiological adaptation to climate, and the industrial advantage of the whites where climatic conditions are equal, it is
doubtful whether there is room in the South for so large a
population."*

Two other questions relating to changes in population must
be adverted to before we leave this part of the subject. There
are Europeans who hold — and in this physiologically-minded
age it is natural that men should hold — that the evolution
of a distinctively American type of character and manners
must be still distant, because the heterogeneous elements of
the population (in which the proportion of English blood is
smaller now than it was fifty years ago) must take a long time
to become mixed and assimilated. This is a plausible view ;
yet I doubt whether differences of blood have the importance
which it assumes. What strikes the traveller, and what the
Americans themselves delight to point out to him, is the amazing solvent power which American institutions, habits, and
ideas exercise upon new-comers of all races. The children
of Irishmen, Germans, and Scandinavians are far more like
native Americans than prevalent views of heredity would
have led us to expect. Nor is it without interest to observe
that Nature has here repeated on the western continent that
process of mixing Celtic with Germanic and Norse blood
which she began in Britain more than a thousand years ago.†

* General Francis A. Walker, in the *Encyclopædia Britannica*, article
"United States." He observes that in 1790 the colored people were 19.3
per cent of the population of the United States, whereas in 1880 they were
only 13.1.

† The ratio borne by the Celtic elements in the population of Britain
(*i. e.*, the Picts and Gaels of northern Britain and the Cymry of middle and
western Britain who survived the onslaught of the Angles and Saxons in
the fifth and sixth centuries) to the Teutonic elements in that population
as it has stood during the last three centuries, may probably be a ratio

This parallel may seem fanciful; yet those who lay stress on race characteristics and expect the American people of the future to be sensibly changed by immigration, may be asked to remember that in that immigration neither the Celtic nor the Teutonic element has so far been able to preponderate. I venture, however, to believe that the intellectual and moral atmosphere into which the settlers from Europe come has more power to assimilate them than their race qualities have power to change it, and that the future of America will be less affected by this influx of new blood than any one who has not studied the American democracy of to-day can realize. The influence of European immigration is so far to be sought, not so much in any tinging of the national character, as in the unfortunate results it has had upon the public life of cities, and the unexpectedly severe strain it has put on universal suffrage. Nor must another source of evil pass unnoticed. The most conspicuous evidence of American prosperity has been hitherto seen in the high standard of living to which the native working classes of the North have risen, in the abundance of their food and the quality of their clothing, in the neatness and comfort of their homes, in the decent orderliness of their lives, and the fondness for reading of their women. The settlers of the last half century, though at first far behind the native Americans in all these respects, have tended to rise to their level, and, except in a few of the larger cities, have after fifteen or twenty years practically adopted American

not very different from that which the Irish immigrants to America bear to the German immigrants; so that the relative proportions of Celtic and Teutonic blood, as these proportions existed in the Americans of fifty years ago, have not been greatly altered by the Irish and the German immigration of the last five decades. The analogy may be carried one step farther by observing that the Scandinavians who now settle in the Northwestern States, as they have come later than Celts or Germans, so also have come in a proportion to Celts and Germans corresponding to that borne to the previous inhabitants of Britain by the Danes and Norwegians who poured their vigorous blood into the veins of the English race from the ninth century onwards.

standards of comfort. But within the last decade new swarms of European immigrants have invaded America, drawn from their homes in the eastern parts of Central Europe by the constant cheapening of ocean transit and by that more thorough drainage, so to speak, of the inland regions of Europe which is due to the extension of railways. These immigrants, largely of Slavonic race, come from a lower stratum of civilization than the German immigrants of the past, and since they speak foreign tongues, are less quickly amenable to American influences, and probably altogether less improvable than are the Irish. There seems to be a danger that if they continue to come in large numbers they may retain their own low standard of decency and comfort, and menace the continuance among the working class generally of that far higher standard which has hitherto prevailed in all but a few spots in the country. Already the United States, which twenty years ago rejoiced in the increase of immigration, begins to regard it with disquiet; and laws are passed to prevent the entrance, not only of laborers brought under contract, but of criminals and of persons who seem likely to become a burden upon the community.*

The intrusion of these inauspicious elements is not the only change in the population which may cause anxiety. For many years past there has been an indraught of people from the rural districts to the cities. More than one fourth of the whole sixty millions are now, it is estimated, to be found in cities with a population exceeding 8,000, and the transfer of people from a rural to an urban life goes on all the faster

* Such laws are of course difficult of enforcement, because when the immigrants arrive it is seldom possible to say which ought to be refused ingress as paupers or criminals; and it has accordingly been proposed to throw upon United States consuls at European ports of departure the duty of sifting those who seek to embark for America, and granting certificates to those who are approved. I am told that at present only about 500 are annually sent back to Europe out of an average of more than 500,000 who annually arrive.

because it is due, not merely to economic causes, such as operate all the world over, and to the spirit of enterprise which is strong in the American youth, but also to the distaste which the average native American — a more sociable and amusement-loving being than the English or German peasant — feels for the isolation of farm life and the monotony of farm labor. Even in 1844 R. W. Emerson wrote: " The cities drain the country of the best part of its population, the flower of the youth of both sexes goes into the towns, and the country is cultivated by a much inferior class." Since then the Western forests have been felled and the Western prairies brought under the plough by the stalwart sons of New England and New York. But now again, and in the West hardly less than in the East, the complaint goes up that native American men and women long for a city life, and gladly leave tillage to the new-comers from Germany and Scandinavia. Whether a city-bred population will have the physical vigor which the native rural population displays, — a population which in some of the Western States strikes one as perhaps more vigorous than any Europe can show, — is at least doubtful ; for though American cities have sanitary advantages greater than those of most towns in Europe, the stress and strain of their city life is more exhausting. And it need scarcely be added that in the oldest and most highly civilized districts of the country, and among the more refined sections of the people, the natural increase of population is much smaller than it is among the poorer and the ruder. In highly developed communities, the principle of natural selection is apt to be reversed ; marriages are later and families smaller among the best nurtured and most cultivated class than they are among the uneducated and improvident ; more children are born to the physically weak and morally untrained than to those among the rich whose natural gifts would in ages of force have enabled them to prevail in the struggle for existence. In New England and the Eastern States generally, though there are many families, historic by the number of eminent names they have produced, which still flourish and count their consinhood by hundreds, it is nevertheless true that the original English race grows less swiftly than the Irish or the German, and far less swiftly than it did some sixty years ago.* Yet here also that assimilative power of which I have spoken comes to the help of the nation. Those who rise from the less cultivated class, who do not belong to what Dr. Holmes calls the Brahmin caste, still surviving in New England and once strong in Virginia, are breathed upon by the spirit of the country ; they quickly absorb its culture and carry on its traditions ; and they do so all the more readily because the pervading sense of equality makes a man's entrance into a class higher than that wherein he was born depend solely on his personal qualities.

European readers may ask whether the swift growth, not only of wealth, but of great fortunes in the United States will not end in creating an aristocracy of rich families, and therewith a new structure of society. I see no ground for expecting this, not merely because the wealthiest class passes down by imperceptible gradations of fortune to a working-class far better off than the working-classes of Europe, but also because the faith in equality and the love of equality are too deeply implanted in every American breast to be rooted out by any economic changes. They are the strongest beliefs and passions of the people. They make no small part of the people's daily happiness ; and I can more easily imagine the United States turned into a monarchy on the one hand, or a group of petty republics on the other, than the aristocratic ideas and habits of Germany, or even of England, established on American soil. Social exclusiveness there may be, — signs of it are

---

* General F. A. Walker gives the rate of increase of the native whites in the United States at 31.25 per cent in the decade 1870–80, but that of native whites born of native parents at 28 per cent. The average size of the native white family decreased in the same decade from 5.09 to 5.04.

already discernible; but visible and overt recognitions of
rank differences, whether in the use of hereditary titles, or in
the possession by one class of special privileges, or in the
habit of deference by one class to another, would imply a
revolution in national ideas and a change in what may be
called the chemical composition of the national mind, which
is of all things the least likely to arrive.

I have left to the last the most difficult problem which a
meditation on the future of American society raises. From
those first days of the Republic in which its people realized
that they were Americans and no longer merely English
colonists, it has been a question of the keenest interest for
them, as it is now for the world, when and how and in what
form they would develop a distinctively new and truly national type of character and genius. In 1844 Emerson said,
addressing those who had lately seen the coincidence of two
fateful phenomena, — the extension of railways into the West,
and the establishment of lines of swift ocean steamers to
Europe : —

" We in the Atlantic States by position have been commercial, and
have imbibed easily a European culture. Luckily for us, now that
steam has narrowed the Atlantic to a strait, the nervous, rocky West
is intruding a new and continental element into the national mind,
and we shall yet have an American genius. We cannot look on the
freedom of this country in connection with its youth without a pre-
sentiment that here shall laws and institutions exist on some scale of
proportion to the majesty of Nature. To men legislating for the area
between the two oceans, betwixt the snows and the tropics, somewhat
of the gravity of Nature will infuse itself into the code."

Nearly half a century has passed since these words were
spoken ; but many events have intervened to delay that full
expression of the national gifts in letters and arts, as well as
in institutions, by which a modern people must reveal the
peculiar nature of its genius. Emerson would doubtless have
admitted in 1874 that the West had contributed less of a

"new and continental element" than he expected, and that the "majesty of Nature" had not yet filled Congress with its inspiration.   Probably another generation must arise, less preoccupied with the task of material development than the two last have been, before this expression can be looked for. Europe, which used to assume in its contemptuous way that neither arts nor letters could be expected from commercial America, — as Charles Lamb said that the whole Atlantic coast figured itself to him as one long counter spread with wares, — Europe has now fallen into the opposite error of expecting the development of arts and letters to keep pace with and be immediately worthy of the material greatness of the country.   And the Americans themselves have perhaps, if a stranger may be pardoned the remark, erred in supposing that they made, either in the days of the first settlements or in those when they won their independence, an entirely new departure, and that their new environment and their democratic institutions rendered them more completely a new people than the children of England, continuing to speak the English tongue and be influenced by European literature, could in truth have been expected to become.   As Protestants have been too apt to forget the traditions of the mediæval Church, and to renounce the glories of Saint Anselm and Saint Bernard and Dante, so the Americans of forty years ago — for this is a mistake which they are beginning to outgrow — sought to think of themselves as superior in all regards to the aristocratic society from which they had severed themselves, and looked for an elevation in their character and an originality in their literature which neither the amplitude of their freedom nor the new conditions of their life could at once produce in the members of an ancient people.

What will be either the form or the spirit of transatlantic literature and thought when they have fully ripened, is a question on which I do not attempt to speculate, for the forces that shape literature and thought are the subtlest the historian

has to deal with.   I return to the humbler task of pointing to
causes whose already apparent power is producing a society
such as has never yet been seen in Europe.   Nowhere in the
world is there growing up such a vast multitude of intelligent,
cultivated, and curious readers.   It is true that of the whole
population a majority of the men read little but newspapers,
and many of the women little but novels.   Yet there remains
a number to be counted by millions who enjoy and are moved
by the higher products of thought and imagination ; and it
must be that as this number continues to grow, each generation
rising somewhat above the level of its predecessors, history
and science, and even poetry, will exert a power such as they
have never yet exerted over the masses of any country.   And
the masses of America seem likely to constitute one half of
civilized mankind.   There are those now living who may see
before they die two hundred and fifty millions of men dwelling between the Atlantic and the Pacific, obeying the same
government, speaking the same tongue, reading the same
books.   A civilized society like this is so much vaster than
any which history knows of, that we can scarcely figure to
ourselves what its character will be, nor how the sense of its
immensity will tell upon those who address it.   The range of
a writer's power will be such as no writers have ever yet
possessed, and the responsibility which goes hand in hand
with the privilege of moving so great a multitude will devolve
no less upon the thinkers and poets of England than upon
those of America.

   The same progress which may be expected in the enjoyment
of literature and in its influence may be no less expected in
the other elements of what we call civilization.   Manners are
becoming in America more generally polished, life more
orderly, equality between the sexes more complete, the refined pleasures more easily accessible than they have ever yet
been among the masses of any people.   And this civilization
attains a unity and harmony which makes each part of the

nation understand the other parts more perfectly, and enables an intellectual impulse to be propagated in swifter waves of light than has been the case among the far smaller and more ancient states of Europe.

While this unity and harmony strengthen the cohesion of the Republic, while this diffused cultivation may be expected to overcome the economic dangers that threaten it, they are not wholly favorable to intellectual creation, or to the variety and interest of life. I will try to explain my meaning by describing the impression which stamps itself on the mind of the stranger who travels westward by railway from New York to Oregon. In Ohio he sees communities which eighty years ago were clusters of log-huts among forests, and which are now cities better supplied with all the appliances of refined and even luxurious life than were Philadelphia and New York in those days. In Illinois he sees communities which were in 1848 what Ohio was in 1808. In the new States of Dakota and Washington he sees settlements just emerging from a rudeness like that of primitive Ohio or Illinois, and reflects that such as Ohio is now, such as Illinois is fast becoming, such in some twenty years more will Dakota and Washington have become, the process of development moving, by the help of science, with an always accelerated speed. "If I return this way thirty years hence," he thinks, " I shall see, except in some few tracts which Nature has condemned to sterility, nothing but civilization — a highly developed form of civilization — stretching from the one ocean to the other ; the busy, eager, well-ordered life of the Hudson will be the life of those who dwell on the banks of the Yellowstone, or who look up to the snows of Mount Shasta from the valleys of California." The Far West has hitherto been to Americans of the Atlantic States the land of freedom and adventure and mystery, the land whose forests and prairies, with trappers pursuing the wild creatures, and Indians threading in their canoes the maze of lakes, have touched their imagination and supplied a back-

ground of romance to the prosaic conditions which surround
their own lives.   All this will have vanished ; and as the world
has by slow steps lost all its mystery since the voyage of
Columbus, so America will from end to end be to the Americans even as England is to the English.   What new background of romance will be discovered ?   Where will the
American imagination of the future seek its materials when
it desires to escape from dramas of domestic life ?   Where
will bold spirits find a field in which to relieve their energies
when the Western World of adventure is no more ?   As in
our globe, so in the North American continent, there will be
something to regret when all is known, and the waters of
civilization have covered the tops of the highest mountains.

He who turns away from a survey of the government and
society of the United States and tries to estimate the place
they hold in the history of the world's progress cannot repress
a slight sense of disappointment when he compares what he
has observed and studied with that which idealists have hoped
for, and which Americans have desired to create.   " I have
seen," he says, " the latest experiment which mankind have
tried, and the last which they can ever hope to try under
equally favoring conditions.   A race of unequalled energy
and unsurpassed variety of gifts, a race apt for conquest and
for the arts of peace, which has covered the world with the
triumphs of its sword and planted its laws in a hundred
islands of the sea, sent the choicest of its children to a new
land rich with the bounties of nature, bidding them increase
and multiply, with no European enemies to fear and few of
those evils to eradicate which Europe inherits from its feudal
past.   They have multiplied till the sapling of two centuries
ago overtops the parent trunk ; they have drawn from their
continent a wealth which no one dreamed of, they have kept
themselves aloof from Old World strife, and have no foe in
the world to menace them ; they have destroyed, after a
tremendous struggle, the one root of evil which the mother

country in an unhappy hour planted among them. And yet the government and institutions, as well as the industrial civilization, of America, are far removed from that ideal commonwealth which European philosophers imagined, and Americans expected to create." The feeling expressed in these words, so often heard from European travellers, is natural to a European, who is struck by the absence from America of many of those springs of trouble to which he has been wont to ascribe the ills of Europe. But it is only the utterance of the ever-fresh surprise of mankind at the discovery of their own weaknesses and shortcomings. Why should either philosophers in Europe or practical men in America have expected human nature to change when it crossed the ocean, when history could have told them of many ideals not less high, and hopes not less confident than those that were formed for America which have been swallowed up in night? The vision of a golden age has often shimmered far off before the mind of men when they have passed through some great crisis or climbed to some specular mount of faith, as before the traveller when he has reached the highest pastures of the Jura, the line of Alpine snows stands up and glitters with celestial light. Such a vision seen by heathen antiquity still charms us in that famous poem of Virgil's which was long believed to embody an inspired prophecy; such another rejoiced the souls of pious men in the days of Constantine when the Christian Church, triumphant over her enemies, seemed about to realize the kingdom of heaven upon earth. Such a one reappeared to the religious reformers of the sixteenth century, who conceived that when they had purged Christianity of its corrupt accretions, the world would be again filled with the glory of God, and men order their lives according to his law. And such a vision transported men just a century ago, when it was not unnaturally believed that in breaking the fetters by which religious and secular tyranny had bound the souls and bodies of men, and in proclaiming the principle that government sprang from the consent of all, and must be directed to their good, enough had been done to enable the natural virtues of mankind to secure the peace and happiness of nations. Since 1789 many things have happened, and men have become less inclined to set their hopes upon political reforms. Those who still expect a general ameliora- tion of the world from sudden changes look to an industrial and not a political revolution, or seek in their impatience to destroy all that now exists, fancying that from chaos some- thing better may emerge. In Europe, whose thinkers have seldom been in a less cheerful mood than they are to-day. there are many who seem to have lost the old faith in progress ; many who feel, when they recall the experiences of the long pilgrimage of mankind, that the mountains which stand so beautiful in the blue of distance, touched here by flashes of sunlight, and there by shadows of the clouds, will, when one comes to traverse them, be no Delectable Mountains, but scarred by storms and seamed by torrents, with wastes of stone above, and marshes stagnating in the valleys. Yet there are others whose review of that pilgrimage convinces them that though the ascent of man may be slow, it is also sure ; that if we compare each age with those which preceded it, we find that the ground which seems for a time to have been lost is ultimately recovered, we see human nature growing gradually more refined, institutions better fitted to secure justice, the opportunities and capacities for happiness larger and more varied, so that the error of those who formed ideals never yet attained lay only in their forgetting how much time and effort and patience under repeated disappointment must go to that attainment.

This less sombre type of thought is more common in the United States than in Europe, for the people not only feel in their veins the pulse of youthful strength, but remember the magnitude of the evils they have vanquished, and see that they have already achieved many things which the Old World has longed for in vain. And by so much as the people of the United States are more hopeful, by that much are they more healthy. They do not, like their forefathers, expect to attain their ideals either easily or soon; but they say that they will continue to strive towards them, and they say it with a note of confidence in the voice which rings in the ear of the European visitor and fills him with something of their own sanguine spirit. America has still a long vista of years stretching before her in which she will enjoy conditions far more auspicious than any European country can count upon. And that America marks the highest level, not only of material well-being, but of intelligence and happiness, which the race has yet attained, will be the judgment of those who look, not at the favored few for whose benefit the world seems hitherto to have framed its institutions, but at the whole body of the people.

INDEX.